Business and Industry in Nazi Germany

BUSINESS AND INDUSTRY
IN NAZI GERMANY

Edited by
Francis R. Nicosia
and
Jonathan Huener

Berghahn Books
NEW YORK • OXFORD

Published in 2004 by
Berghahn Books

www.berghahnbooks.com

© 2004 The Center for Holocaust Studies at
the University of Vermont

Library of Congress Cataloging-in-Publication Data
Business and industry in Nazi Germany / edited by Francis R. Nicosia and
Jonathan Huener.
    p. cm.
Based on lectures presented at a symposium organized by the Center
for Holocaust Studies at the University of Vermont in 2002.
Includes bibliographical references and index.
ISBN 1-57181-653-4 (alk. paper) – ISBN 1-57181-654-2 (pbk.:
alk. paper)
    1. Industrial policy—Germany—History. 2. Big business—Ger-
many—History. 3. Germany—Politics and government—1933–
1945. 4. Nationalsozialistische Deutsche Arbeiter-Partei—History.
5. National socialism—History. I. Nicosia, Francis R., 1944–
II. Huener, Jonathan. III. University of Vermont, Center for Holocaust Studies.

HD3616.G42B87 2004
338.0943'09'043–dc22

2003062961

British Library Cataloguing in Publication Data
A catalogue record for this book is available from
the British Library.

Printed in the United States on acid-free paper.

CONTENTS

PREFACE

THE FIRST FIVE ESSAYS in this book are based on lectures delivered at the Miller Symposium on "Business and Industry under the Nazi Regime," held at the University of Vermont in April 2002. Organized by the Center for Holocaust Studies at the University of Vermont, this was the second symposium bearing the name of Leonard and Carolyn Miller, generous supporters of the Center's work and great friends of the university.

Established to honor the work of Professor Raul Hilberg, who served on the faculty of the University of Vermont for more than three decades, the Center for Holocaust Studies is committed to furthering the cause of Holocaust education and to serving as a forum for the presentation and discussion of new perspectives on the history of Nazi Germany and its crimes. Professor Hilberg's pioneering and ongoing research is a model and a standard for scholars, and it is his work in the field that remains an inspiration for the Center's programming and for publications such as this. The Miller Symposia have made an important contribution to the Center's efforts to explore insufficiently charted areas in the history of the Third Reich. Our goal in organizing them has been to address topical, even controversial themes in the history of Nazi Germany and the Holocaust, relying on the expertise of some of the most accomplished authorities in the field.

The first Miller Symposium, held in April 2000, resulted in the anthology *Medicine and Medical Ethics in Nazi Germany: Origins, Practices, Legacies* (Berghahn Books, 2002), which the reader may regard as a companion to the present volume. The second Miller Symposium brought together scholars who are among the most respected and innovative analysts of business, industry, and finance in the years of the Third Reich. Their contributions to this volume address the complicity and collaboration of corporations and financial institutions in the crimes of the regime and, in the process, address some of the salient themes and issues in the field. These include, for example, the broader theme of business-state relations under the Nazi dictatorship, the reorganization of the banking and insurance industries and their participation in the regime's aryanization policies, the complicity of Germany's enormous chemical industry in the Holocaust, the motives and profits associated with the forced and slave labor practices of German industry and the SS, and the role of American corporations in the Nazi wartime economy.

The essays assembled here, based on the authors' original scholarship, will serve as an introduction to some of the most current research and controversies in the business history of the Third Reich. This volume, then, will be of interest to students and scholars of twentieth-century German history and the Nazi era; to students of business, business ethics, and labor and industrial relations; and to general readers in the history of the Third Reich and the Holocaust.

Both the Miller Symposium and this volume owe a tremendous debt to Leonard and Carolyn Miller, whose continuing support for the Center for Holocaust Studies has helped to sustain and expand its programming over the years. The editors also recognize and thank Edwin Colodny, the School of Business Administration at the University of Vermont, Wolfgang Mieder, and the symposium's organizing committee, which included Kathy Johnson, Arthur Kunin, David Scrase, and the editors of this volume. Kathy Johnson in particular deserves a special note of thanks for her tireless efforts, in both organizing the symposium itself and assembling materials for this publication. We also wish to thank Kelly McDonald of Saint Michael's College for her invaluable computer assistance in the preparation of this book. A final word of thanks is due to Volker Berghahn of Columbia University for his contribution to this anthology. Recognized around the world as a leading authority on Germany's history, economy, industry, and commerce in the nineteenth and twentieth centuries, Professor Berghahn has provided us with a thoughtful synthesis and conclusion. Not only does his analysis provide an appropriate context for these essays, but it also suggests some avenues for further investigation of the issues raised in this volume.

INTRODUCTION

Business and Industry in Nazi Germany in Historiographical Context

———— ⊗⊗⊗ ————

Francis R. Nicosia and Jonathan Huener

IN 1946, as the world began to confront the enormity of Nazi Germany's crimes, the International Military Tribunal in Nuremberg was in the process of conducting trials of some of the leading figures of Hitler's regime as the perpetrators of those crimes. That same year, Max Weinreich published an important and prescient book, *Hitler's Professors: The Part of Scholarship in Germany's Crimes Against the Jewish People,* in which he posed a question that few could have had on their minds so soon after World War II had ended: "[A]re Germany's intellectual leaders guilty of complicity in the crimes against humanity for which Germany's top politicians and generals have been brought to trial?"[1] Weinreich quickly answered his own question in the following way:

> It seems to me that only one answer is possible. With the political and military leaders, the intellectual leaders first declared Germany the final judge of her own acts and then renounced accepted morality. With the political and military leaders, they arrogated to themselves the right to dispose of millions of people for their own and their fatherland's greater glory. With the political and military leaders, they prepared, instituted, and blessed the program of vilification, disfranchisement, dispossession, expatriation, imprisonment, deportation, enslavement, torture, and murder.[2]

Notwithstanding Weinreich's misgivings, the Allied powers did put some representatives of the professions in the Third Reich on trial at subsequent military tribunals in the Allied occupation zones beginning in 1946. Among them were twenty-three Nazi physicians and members of the German medical establishment, sixteen judges as representatives of the legal profession, representatives of German industries such as Alfried Krupp AG and IG Farben, and others, all tried by the American Military Tribunal at Nuremberg between 1946 and 1949. They were not exactly the scholars (philosophers, historians, scientists) that Weinreich had in mind when he published his book, but they were members of the educated elites that the military and political leadership of the Nazi state had to co-opt for the successful implementation of their murderous policies.

More than thirty years elapsed before a few scholars of Nazi Germany and the Holocaust began to consider seriously the role of the German professions in the planning and implementation of Nazi crimes against humanity, principally the extermination of the Jews and Gypsies throughout Europe, and the mentally and physically disabled in Germany. Perhaps, as Harold James asserts, this delay was a natural consequence of the evolution of scholarly research that came to place "victims at the center of historical writing about National Socialism."[3] In the late 1970s, however, scholars began to confront the role of thousands of perpetrators in the professions, from lawyers and judges to scientists and physicians, from bankers and industrialists to scholars, teachers, and artists. Among the earliest studies of the professions in Nazi Germany, Alan Beyerchen's *Scientists Under Hitler: Politics and the Physics Community in the Third Reich* (1977), and Joseph Borkin's *The Crime and Punishment of IG Farben: The Unholy Alliance of Adolf Hitler and Germany's Great Chemical Combine* (1978) scrutinized scientists and members of the chemical industry, and their roles in the policies of the Third Reich.[4] But it was really not until the mid-1980s, about forty years after the publication of Max Weinreich's book, that historians began to consider in earnest the role of the professions and the inclusion of professionals in the category of perpetrators of Nazi crimes against humanity. Even the 1990 appearance of Konrad Jarausch's *The Unfree Professions: German Lawyers, Teachers, and Engineers, 1900–1950*, which seeks to answer the question of how educated professionals could have supported the Nazi movement and Hitler's policies, was viewed as an examination of a largely unexplored subject.[5]

Among those works on the professions in Nazi Germany are studies of German business and its role in the crimes of the Third Reich. Two of the contributors to this volume, Gerald Feldman and Volker Berghahn, are among the scholars who have written extensively on

German economic and business history both before 1933 and after 1945, during the Wilhelminian and Weimar periods, as well as in the post–World War II Federal Republic.[6] Earlier treatments of the relationship of big business to National Socialism, even dating back to the 1930s, tended to focus on the extent to which the financial support of German corporations might have facilitated the rise of the Nazis to power during the Weimar years. For example, Henry Ashby Turner's groundbreaking book, *German Big Business and the Rise of Hitler*, published in 1985, comes to the unexpected conclusion that big business generally did not support Hitler and his program prior to the Nazi *Machtübernahme* in 1933.[7] With a focus on large industrial concerns such as Flick, Krupp, IG Farben, Siemens, and others, Turner argues that German business leaders were generally not receptive to Nazi overtures, at least not until after the party's first electoral breakthrough in 1930 that was achieved largely without the financial support of big business. Turner's analysis comes close to a comprehensive analysis of German business and its relationship to National Socialism, albeit for the period before Hitler's assumption of power in 1933. But, even as recently as 1991, Peter Hayes pointed to the "lack of a systematic and comprehensive study of the role of German big business" in the "Nazi assault on the European Jews."[8]

It has only been since the late 1980s that a growing body of scholarship on German business and industry during the Nazi years has appeared. A few earlier studies had considered the economic policies of the Nazi regime directed against the Jews in Germany, especially the process of aryanization of Jewish businesses, but they did not really illuminate the role of German corporations in this process.[9] Against the backdrop of a growing willingness on the part of German institutions of all kinds to confront the Nazi past and their roles in it, some German corporations belatedly allowed access to their records for the years 1933 to 1945, after years of claiming that most everything from the Nazi period had been destroyed in air raids.[10] The increasing attention being paid to the victims of Nazi policy, and the restitution and compensation proceedings carried out by survivors and their families, stimulated scholarly examination of subjects such as aryanization of Jewish businesses, forced and slave labor, and the economics, technology, and business of mass murder. Probably none of these studies represents the kind of comprehensive history that Hayes calls for above, but taken together they do provide us with a large and ever-growing historiography on the subject of business and industry in Nazi Germany.

Among the outstanding studies of German corporations in the Nazi era that have appeared over the past fifteen years in the United States and Germany are those by some of the contributors to this volume. Coming on the heels of his earlier work on the Deutsche Bank during the Third Reich, Harold James's *The Deutsche Bank and the Nazi Economic War Against the Jews*, published in 2001, considers the bank's role in the expropriation of Jewish-owned enterprises during the Nazi years.[11] Gerald Feldman's *Allianz and the German Insurance Business, 1933–1945*, also published in 2001, presents a conflicting picture of collaboration and conflict between Germany's most prominent insurance corporation, Allianz AG, and the Nazi regime.[12] It considers issues such as damages in the *Kristallnacht* pogrom of 1938, the insuring of forced labor facilities, and the problems of denazification and restitution, to name but a few. Peter Hayes's *Industry and Ideology: IG Farben in the Nazi Era,* which appeared in 1987, examines the relationship of the German chemical giant to Hitler's regime, in particular its exploitation of thousands of slave laborers, many of them prisoners from Auschwitz, and its general involvement in the extermination of the Jews.[13] Simon Reich has undertaken extensive research on the activities of the German subsidiary of Ford Motor Company, specifically regarding the issue of forced and slave labor at the Ford-Werke during the Third Reich. He was instrumental in Ford's own account of the activities of its German subsidiary during World War II.[14]

Various other studies of individual German businesses have appeared over the past fifteen years. Besides Harold James, several other scholars have examined the activities of German banks in the Nazi era. Among these studies are Jonathan Steinberg's *The Deutsche Bank and Its Gold Transactions during the Second World War* (1999), Johannes Bähr's *Der Goldhandel der Dresdner Bank im Zweiten Weltkrieg* (1999), Michael Hepp's *Deutsche Bank und Dresdner Bank: Gewinn aus Raub, Enteignung und Zwangsarbeit 1933–1944* (1999), and *A History of the Deutsche Bank, 1870–1995* (1995), coedited by Lothar Gall, Gerald Feldman, Harold James, Carl-Ludwig Holtfrerich, and Hans Büschgen.[15] Scholars have also written about large and powerful German corporations such as Daimler Benz, Volkswagen, Siemens, and BMW during the Third Reich. They include Hans Pohl, *Die Daimler-Benz AG in den Jahren 1933–1945* (1986) and Neil Gregor, *Star and Swastika: Daimler Benz in the Third Reich* (1998), Hans Mommsen, *Das Volkswagenwerk und seiner Arbeiter im Dritten Reich* (1996), Wilfried Feldenkirchen,

Siemens 1918–1945 (1999), and Horst Mönnich, *BMW: Eine Deutsche Geschichte* (1989).[16] For German subsidiaries of American corporations in Nazi Germany, one can, along with Simon Reich's work on the German subsidiary of Ford Motor Company, consult Edwin Black's account of the German subsidiary of IBM in his *IBM and the Holocaust: The Strategic Alliance between Nazi Germany and America's Most Powerful Corporation* (2001).[17]

Finally, the exploitation of forced and slave labor by German and SS industries is a key element of the history of German business and industry during the Third Reich. One of the contributors to this volume, Michael Thad Allen, has made the most recent contribution to the literature on the topic of both slave labor and SS industrial enterprises with his book *The Business of Genocide: The SS, Slave Labor, and the Concentration Camps* (2002).[18] Other recent works on forced and slave labor include: Wolf Gruner's *Der geschlossene Arbeitseinsatz deutscher Juden. Zur Zwangsarbeit als Element der Verfolgung 1938–1943* (1997); Ulrich Herbert's *Hitler's Foreign Workers: Enforced Labor in Germany under the Third Reich* (1997); Paul Jaskot's *The Architecture of Oppression: The SS, Forced Labor and the Nazi Monumental Building Economy* (2000); and Bernd C. Wagner's *IG Auschwitz: Zwangsarbeit und Vernichtung von Häftlingen des Lagers Monowitz 1941–1945* (2000), to name but a few.[19] Moreover, there is also a growing body of literature on forced labor in specific cities or regions of Germany during the Third Reich.[20]

The various works discussed above reveal that the picture of German business and industry in the Third Reich is a complex one that includes, as Gerald Feldman notes in the first essay in this volume, both willing and reluctant collaboration with the Nazi state. Omer Bartov has argued that in the Nazi war against the Soviet Union there was "a widespread zeal for economic expansion which made the idea of a *Raubkrieg* (predatory war) in the East particularly popular among Germany's industrialists and business community."[21] Others, like Peter Hayes below, assert that the business decisions of the corporate elite in Germany during the Nazi period were normally dictated not so much by profits as by "political duties and economic necessities that left little room for maneuver or choice." It seems, then, that a complex mix of greed and survival in a rigid and highly controlled economic environment characterized corporate policy. Whatever their motives, it is clear that many German business leaders were unwilling to avoid complicity in the crimes of the Third Reich.

Gerald Feldman's analysis of financial institutions in the Third Reich is based on extensive experience on the historical commissions of the Dresdner Bank and BankAustria, and on his recent history of the Allianz insurance corporation. Feldman is quick to emphasize the importance of placing banks, insurance companies, and the personalities involved "in the context of the political, economic, social, and personal networks in which they are embedded." Only then, he argues, can the analyst cast a broader view and offer a more nuanced interpretation of the German financial sector in this period.

It would seem that the logic and goals of their industries would have led representatives of banks and insurance companies to oppose the Nazi Party and its economic programs, but their "powers of resistance and political judgment," according to Feldman, "... had never been seriously fortified by a commitment to democratic ideas and practices." Feldman then proceeds to explain how the depression and the political crises accompanying it influenced the "vulnerability of the business community in its dealings with the Nazis and the rapid adaptation to Nazi rule." Such adaptability did not, however, mean that leaders of the financial sector always enjoyed a harmonious relationship with the party and state. Indeed, the insurance and banking industries were frequently objects of the party's suspicion, and after 1945, many leaders of these sectors were quick to portray themselves as victims of Nazism who worked to protect their firms and the free market from party radicals. Feldman urges his readers to take economic radicals in the Nazi party seriously, for they existed as an "ever-ready source of leverage that the regime leadership could use to bind the financial sector and produce that anticipatory obedience and corrupting opportunism on which the regime depended." Obedience and opportunism could take many forms, and were frequently characteristic of what historian Ian Kershaw has described as "working toward the Führer."

There are abundant examples of the financial sector's complicity in the crimes and corruption of the Nazi state. According to Feldman, these actions on the part of representatives of the banking and insurance industries challenge the historian to "examine what the consequences of their policies of appeasement and collaboration in defense of their business interests meant under the actual conditions of the Third Reich." This is the focus of the remainder of his analysis, as he outlines the financial sector's complicity, corruption, and eager participation in the aryanization initiatives of the regime, leading him to conclude that "the practice of seeking opportunity and trying to keep on doing business as usual, however unusual the business, brought the banks and insurance companies so close to the Holocaust itself."

Harold James suggests at the outset of his essay that historians have not sufficiently investigated the important changes in the organization of corporate bureaucracies in the 1930s and beyond. By specifically addressing German banks during the years of the Third Reich, James accounts for the ways in which organizational shifts in this sector led to increased collaboration with the Nazi regime and, no less, a transformation in business values.

James's focus is on four men whose diverse experiences during the Nazi era illustrated transformations in the banking industry: Georg Solmssen, a conservative German nationalist of Jewish background who had converted to Christianity, and who, prior to the Nazi rise to power, had been far more concerned about the party's economic and political agendas than its anti-Semitism; Karl Ritter von Halt, the first member of the Nazi Party appointed to the Managing Board of the Deutsche Bank; Walter Pohle, a main force behind the Germanization of Czech banking and the seizure of Czech assets; and Hermann Abs, the period's most well-known and most controversial German banker who, on the one hand, was instrumental in the aryanization practices of the regime and who, on the other, had connections to Helmut James von Moltke and resistance figures of the Kreisau Circle.

In the face of the regime's new economic climate, many bankers became increasingly passive and marginalized. It is, then, hardly surprising that these men frequently "retreated into that environment with which they were most familiar: the comfortable certainties of a rational economic world." Guilty of a certain "moral shortsightedness," many bankers, in James's words, "tried ever harder not to look beyond the ends of their own noses," with the result that they also revealed themselves as complicit in National Socialist crimes.

Shifting the reader's focus from the financial sector to the chemical industry, Peter Hayes, in the third essay in this volume, addresses the symbiosis between big business and the state in the years of the Nazi regime. The chemical industry, and specifically the IG Farben and Degussa corporations, is a particularly telling example of an enterprise that effectively responded to the economic pressures exerted by the regime, as well as to the incentives and profits that cooperation with the state would offer. "[T]he combination," according to Hayes, "proved irresistible in the aftermath of a depression and in the context of a dictatorship."

Although the Nazi-directed business climate imposed limitations on the firms' freedom of choice, both were able to adapt to the state's economic and industrial goals of the 1930s, and both had much to gain from the Nazi rise to power: government contracts, participation in the aryanization of Jewish-owned businesses, increased demand for products in the military sector of the economy and, finally, the profits and status gained through participation in the destruction of Europe's Jews. "Both enterprises," as Hayes explains, "became implicated in pillaging and exploiting the Jews largely as part of efforts to preserve vital monopoly positions against possible encroachment." Such positioning was a motive force in, for example, these firms' efforts to gain control of Jewish firms, in Degussa's processing of precious metals plundered from Jews, in the sale of the fumigation agent Zyklon B, and in both firms' exploitation of forced and slave labor.

The use of forced and slave labor at their production facilities reveals a particularly interesting aspect of corporate behavior under the Nazis. It was not the perceived profitability of exploiting cheap labor that motivated these firms to participate in this murderous practice. Rather, Hayes argues, "[e]ngaging forced labor functioned as proof that each firm was doing its utmost to achieve the production goals laid down by the regime, and thus that each was worthy of retaining its unchallenged hold on manufacturing a commodity essential to both the 'people's community' and each corporation's future." Indeed, such efforts on the part of Degussa and IG Farben appear to illustrate what the reader might regard as a "corporate" form of "working toward the Führer." Pressures and incentives, obedience and opportunism, ideology and economic interest, all of these functioned to encourage and ensure the adaptation and compliance not only of individuals in the financial sector, but also of corporations, large and small.

Although the majority of forced and slave labor in Nazi Germany took place under the supervision of German corporations, the SS, as Michael Thad Allen explains, also played an important role in the organization, provision, and distribution of labor. Challenging the common assumption that the SS was motivated solely by greed and profit, Allen emphasizes the role of that organization's ideological mission and bureaucratic numbness in its exploitation of labor. This developed, in Allen's own words, into "a bizarre trade in broken and exhausted prisoners in a network of slavery that spread across the breadth of Europe."

Allen then proceeds to outline the development of SS slave labor practices in the early years of the regime, most prominently in concentration camps, where labor served as an instrument of terror, control, and punishment. It was not until the latter part of the 1930s that slave labor began to serve the emerging SS industrial empire effectively, when it was aggressively deployed in, among other sectors, the building-supply industry. World War II saw new efforts to expand the SS slave labor project. "Far from responding to pragmatic calculations of the war economy," Allen argues, the SS leadership worked to expand the use of slave labor as part of a "racial-supremacist social engineering project." It was in the context of this growing "New Order" envisaged by the SS that camps in occupied Polish territory such as Maidanek, Auschwitz, and Stutthof were expanded to accommodate slave laborers and the industrial enterprises they were to serve. During the last years of the Third Reich, in the age of "total war," SS industry experienced yet another reorganization as it responded to the demands of military production with new contracts and further deployment of slave labor. Not least, the SS expanded its role as a "labor lord" for private industry and the armaments ministry. In the final analysis, Allen concludes, the SS administration of slave labor was intrinsically linked to the Holocaust, functioning as a "business of genocide" that simultaneously deployed and destroyed workers in the service of the state, its war, and its racist plans for European domination.

Many are aware of the active participation of SS enterprises or firms such as IG Farben in the crimes of the Nazi regime. In recent years, however, scholars have begun to direct their attention to the behavior of foreign and foreign-based corporations during the years of the Third Reich. This is the focus of political scientist Simon Reich's essay, as he uses the case of the Ford Motor Company and its German subsidiary to address the issue of corporate social responsibility. As Reich notes, in the current era of globalization and increasing availability of information, there appears to be a growing sense of corporate accountability and a growing trend toward judging the behavior of corporations in the Nazi era. Moreover, the scrutiny of scholars has extended beyond the "obvious collaborators" to assess the accountability and complicity of "less obvious" firms such as, for example, the German subsidiary Ford-Werke.

Reich's expertise in this area is based on years of research and, more recently, on his participation in an investigation into Ford-Werke's business in the 1930s and 1940s. This investigation set out to evaluate: (1) Ford-Werke's relationship to the Nazi state and the extent to which it was put under Nazi control after 1941; (2) whether the American parent company of Ford-Werke was able to influence or control its subsidiary; and (3) whether Ford-Werke used forced or slave labor and benefited from it. In the course of his essay, Reich goes on to discuss these three issues and, in conclusion, addresses as well the broader problem of how a given firm might choose to confront its past, or not. In the case of Ford, the accusations of collaborative behavior that were leveled against it resulted not in reflex denials and defensive postures, but in a thorough and credible investigation. Ford's open and transparent response to accusations of wrongdoing has not necessarily been the norm among large corporations, but it does suggest a responsible path for firms to follow in the future.

In the concluding chapter, Volker Berghahn seeks to integrate the five preceding essays. As these authors and their readers grapple with the extent to which business and industry bore political responsibility for the rise and stability of the Nazi regime, and the extent of their complicity in its crimes, Berghahn provides a context for these issues. Through an insightful historiographical discussion, he provides a "post-1945" history of business and industry under the Nazi regime and, no less, suggests a number of paths for future research in this area.

Early in his essay, Berghahn addresses the problem of collective guilt, an issue central to the basic problems of political responsibility and culpability, and accounts for shifts in the validity and political utility of this concept. As the emerging Federal Republic of Germany became increasingly integrated into the Western defense and economic spheres, it became more important to gain West German support in the resuscitation of a free-market German economy and the establishment of a democratic and parliamentary political structure. The notion of collective guilt, therefore, began to fade in significance, and the emerging West German business elite was particularly adept at benefiting from this change in sentiment. Not only did West German business leaders show themselves to be remarkably adaptable to a new political climate, but they also proved effective in undermining, deflecting, and defending themselves against charges of the business community's collective responsibility for Nazi crimes.

In West Germany, early postwar analyses of the Third Reich tended to regard it as an aberration in the course of Germany's history, while in the broader structural analyses of National Socialism that were emerging in the 1950s and 1960s, business leaders tended to emerge "not so much as individuals, but as members of collectives and power cartels." The neo-Marxist and Weberian historiography of the 1960s and 1970s built upon these postwar structuralist interpretations to indict further the German business community, but it was the work of Henry A. Turner and others that rose to challenge the Marxist argument that German big business had underwritten Hitler, his movement, and his rise to power. Meanwhile, other developments in the historical profession in the areas of social history and cultural history were slow to take root in the field of business history, and it was not until the 1980s that business historians in the Federal Republic of Germany began to confront the vague but increasingly important notions of experience, perception, and *mentalité*, notions that had gained currency in Western European and North American historiography many years earlier.

In suggesting an agenda for the future, Volker Berghahn cites two phases in the relationship between business and industry in the Nazi era: the years 1936–1939, and the years 1940–1942. The former was a period in which the regime was "launched on a course of violent expansionism to implement its Social Darwinist and racist aims," while the latter was a period marked for many businessmen by "boundless optimism and far-reaching self-nazification." Berghahn also encourages the reader to hypothesize about the future structure and organization of a Nazi economic order had the regime not been defeated so quickly. To what extent would business leaders have been able to see profit in the regime's aims of economic domination? To what extent would the business community have been guided by the racist imperatives the regime had gone to such lengths to establish in the 1930s?

Such questions can never be answered with total accuracy, but they do lead us to consider many of the issues that we face today in a culture increasingly dominated by large corporations. Indeed, many of the questions raised in this volume are of immediate relevance to contemporary controversies over globalization, the relationship of corporations to the state, corporate labor practices, corporate corruption, and the notion of corporate social responsibility. Some argue that corporations and governments threaten democracy and economic freedom in their common pursuit of power and profit, and that the self-interest of corporate culture cultivates indifference in popular culture and exacerbates social and economic inequities. Others contend that economic growth and globalization are forces for advancing the goals of freedom and democracy in the long term. The most compelling issue emerging from this volume is, of course, the extent to which the experience of business and industry under National Socialism is instructive for the dilemmas we face today. Do the pursuit of profit today, and the social effects of such pursuits, in any way mirror the complicity of some German firms in the expropriation of Jewish-owned businesses, the exploitation of labor, or other assaults on the liberty and dignity of Hitler's victims? In what ways do the problems of state control over corporate life in the Third Reich inform our understanding of growing corporate control over the state today? As we confront the multiple problems of an evolving business-state relationship today, we are compelled to consider the lessons of the past.

Notes

1. Max Weinreich, *Hitler's Professors: The Part of Scholarship in Germany's Crimes Against the Jewish People* (New Haven: Yale University Press, 1999), 242.
2. Ibid.
3. Harold James, *The Deutsche Bank and the Nazi Economic War Against the Jews* (New York: Cambridge University Press, 2001), 3.
4. Alan Beyerchen, *Scientists Under Hitler: Politics and the Physics Community in the Third Reich* (New Haven: Yale University Press, 1977); Joseph Borkin, *The Crime and Punishment of IG Farben: The Unholy Alliance of Adolf Hitler and Germany's Great Chemical Combine* (New York: Free Press, 1978).
5. Konrad Jarausch, *The Unfree Professions: German Lawyers, Teachers, and Engineers, 1900–1950* (New York: Oxford University Press, 1990).
6. See, for example, Gerald D. Feldman, *Army, Industry and Labor in Germany, 1914–1918* (Princeton: Princeton University Press, 1966); idem, *Iron and Steel in the German Inflation, 1916–1923* (Princeton: Princeton University Press, 1977); and idem, *The Great Disorder: Politics, Economics, and Society in the German Inflation, 1914–1924* (New York: Oxford University Press, 1993). See also Volker Berghahn, *The Americanization of West German Industry, 1945–1973* (Cambridge: Cambridge University Press, 1985); Volker Berghahn and Detlev Karsten, *Industrial Relations in West Germany* (Oxford: Berg Publishers, 1987); and Volker Berghahn, ed., *Quest for Empire: European Strategies of German Big Business in the Twentieth Century* (New York: Berghahn Books, 1996).
7. Henry A. Turner, *German Big Business and the Rise of Hitler* (New York: Oxford University Press, 1985).
8. Peter Hayes, "Profits and Persecution: Corporate Involvement in the Holocaust," in *Perspectives on the Holocaust: Essays in Honor of Raul Hilberg,* ed. James S. Pacy and Alan P. Wertheimer (Boulder: Westview Press, 1995), 51.
9. See, for example, Helmut Genschel, *Die Verdrängung der Juden aus der Wirtschaft im Dritten Reich* (Göttingen: Musterschmidt-Verlag, 1966).
10. See Gerald D. Feldman, "The German Insurance Business in National Socialist Germany," *Bulletin of the German Historical Institute, Washington, D.C.* 31 (2002): 21.

11. James, *The Deutsche Bank*.
12. Gerald D. Feldman, *Allianz and the German Insurance Business, 1933–1945* (New York: Cambridge University Press, 2001).
13. Peter Hayes, *Industry and Ideology: IG Farben in the Nazi Era* (Cambridge: Cambridge University Press, 1987).
14. Ford Motor Company, *Research Findings About Ford-Werke Under the Nazi Regime* (Dearborn, MI: Ford Motor Company, 2001).
15. Jonathan Steinberg, *The Deutsche Bank and Its Gold Transactions during the Second World War* (Munich: Beck, 1999); Johannes Bähr, *Der Goldhandel der Dresdner Bank im Zweiten Weltkrieg. Ein Bericht des Hannah-Arendt-Instituts* (Leipzig: Kiepenheuer und Witsch, 1999); Michael Hepp, *Deutsche Bank und Dresdner Bank: Gewinn aus Raub, Enteignung und Zwangsarbeit 1933–1944* (Bremen: Stiftung für Sozialgeschichte des 20. Jahrhunderts, 1999); Lothar Gall et al., eds., *A History of the Deutsche Bank, 1870–1995* (London: Weidenfeld & Nicolson, 1995).
16. Hans Pohl, *Die Daimler-Benz AG in den Jahren 1933–1945* (Wiesbaden: Steiner Verlag, 1986); Neil Gregor, *Star and Swastika: Daimler Benz in the Third Reich* (New Haven: Yale University Press, 1998); Hans Mommsen, *Das Volkswagenwerk und seiner Arbeiter im Dritten Reich* (Düsseldorf: Econ, 1996); Wilfried Feldenkirchen, *Siemens 1918–1945* (Columbus: Ohio State University Press, 1999); Horst Mönnich, *BMW: Eine Deutsche Geschichte* (Vienna: Paul Zsolnay Verlag, 1989).
17. Edwin Black, *IBM and the Holocaust: The Strategic Alliance Between Nazi Germany and America's Most Powerful Corporation* (New York: Crown Publishers, 2001).
18. Michael Thad Allen, *The Business of Genocide: The SS, Slave Labor, and the Concentration Camps* (Chapel Hill: University of North Carolina Press, 2002).
19. Wolf Gruner, *Der geschlossene Arbeitseinsatz deutscher Juden. Zur Zwangsarbeit als Element der Verfolgung 1938–1943* (Berlin: Metropol, 1997); Ulrich Herbert, *Hitler's Foreign Workers: Enforced Labor in Germany under the Third Reich* (Cambridge: Cambridge University Press, 1997); Paul Jaskot, *The Architecture of Oppression: The SS, Forced Labor and the Nazi Monumental Building Economy* (London: Routledge, 2000); Bernd C. Wagner, *IG Auschwitz: Zwangsarbeit und Vernichtung von Häftlingen des Lagers Monowitz 1941–1945* (Munich: K.G. Saur, 2000).
20. See, for example, Wolf Gruner, *Zwangsarbeit und Verfolgung: Österreichische Juden im NS-Staat 1938–1945* (Innsbruck: Studienverlag, 2000); Andreas Heusler, *Ausländereinsatz: Zwangsarbeit für die Münchner Kriegswirtschaft 1939–1945* (Munich: Hugendubel, 1996); Katharina Hoffmann, ed., *Nationalsozialismus und Zwangsarbeit in der Region Oldenburg* (Oldenburg: Bibliotheks- und Informationssystem der Universität Oldenburg, 1999); Ernst Kaiser and Michael Knorn, *"Wir lebten und schliefen zwischen den Toten": Rüstungsproduktion, Zwangsarbeit und Vernichtung in den Frankfurter Adlerwerken* (Frankfurt am Main: Campus, 1996).
21. Omer Bartov, *Hitler's Army: Soldiers, Nazis, and War in the Third Reich* (New York: Oxford University Press, 1991), 181.

Chapter One

FINANCIAL INSTITUTIONS IN NAZI GERMANY
Reluctant or Willing Collaborators?

———∞∞∞———

Gerald D. Feldman

I WOULD LIKE to begin this essay by answering the question posed in the title. Banks and insurance companies, the two types of enterprises to be discussed here, were at times reluctant and at times willing collaborators with the National Socialist regime. How reluctant or willing they were varied with time, place, and the relevant interests and issues, and since corporations are not monoliths, with the individuals involved as well. This does not mean that generalizations cannot be made and conclusions drawn if they are placed in a well-grounded historical context. On the surface, this should seem reasonable and obvious to persons engaged in historical studies. The reality is, however, that this is a field in which commentary has not been limited to historians, and that has long been a playground for ideologists, journalists, and others for whom sound historical practice and method have often been of minor importance or no importance at all. Financial institutions seem to have an especially magnetic attraction to such persons.

Thus, most recently a professor of communications, Christopher Simpson, has republished the well-known OMGUS (Office of the Military Government of the United States) reports of 1946 on the Deutsche and Dresdner Banks. In his inadequate introduction, Simpson speaks of the kind of contextualization practiced by the historians working on the histories of the various banks as "spin-doctoring" for the banks that commissioned them to do this work.[1] On the one hand, Simpson treats the OMGUS reports, written slightly over a year after the war ended and for prosecutorial purposes by persons who were also trustbusters interested in the breaking up of the big banks and who had a deficient understanding of the German banking system and its history, as some kind of holy writ, and he never properly places them into context. He asserts that "[N]o scholarship on Nazi-era banking produced in any language for almost forty years matched the OMGUS work in its scope, overall accuracy, or depth of documentary evidence."[2] The forty years in question conveniently include the first publication of the OMGUS reports in German in 1986, but preclude all the work done since 1986.[3]

On the other hand, the extraordinary amount of new material discovered in the recently opened archives of the former Communist bloc states is trivialized in Simpson's introduction, and the work that has been published on the basis of this new material is belittled as "spin-doctoring" even where this work is demonstrably more critical and damaging to the historical reputations of some bankers than are the old OMGUS reports.[4] What is most disturbing, however, is the apparent expectation that historians today can and should write in the tone and style of the persons who wrote those reports, or of journalists and publicists out to tell an appealing story of high crimes and misdemeanors.

Historians, however, are not and cannot be state prosecutors. While they certainly can and do enjoy the luxury of condemning human actions and behavior, they are in no position to do much more than that. In this respect, they are not of much help to their readers, who are quite capable of forming their own judgments. What they can do for the reader is, in fact, to provide some kind of context that makes the behavior of historical actors intelligible and differentiated. It is important that readers can understand, for example, what separated Kurt Schmitt, the General Director of Allianz AG from 1921 to 1933, Reich Economics Minister under Hitler in 1933–1934, and then General Director of the Munich Reinsurance Company from 1935 to 1945, from his murderous enemy and proponent of the publicly chartered insurance companies, the Gauleiter of Pomerania, Franz Schwede-Coburg. Schmitt's engagement with National Socialism was very different from that of Schwede-Coburg, and it is not misguided "politeness" or "spin-doctoring" for Allianz that demands a nuanced discussion of Schmitt, but rather the fact that understanding the role of business in National Socialism and of the functioning of the National Socialist regime itself will inevitably be sacrificed if one succumbs to muckraking for its own sake and self-satisfying but tiresome moral outrage.[5] Enterprises, however, do not exist in outer space. They must also be understood as institutions embedded in their societies, and the functioning of enterprises is not to be understood in terms of a priori theoretical constructs and imaginary structures, but rather in terms of the political and economic conditions to which enterprises must respond and which they sometimes help to mold. They need to be understood in the context of the political, economic, social, and personal networks in which they are embedded.[6]

I

This said, and in this spirit, let me turn to a discussion of the subject at hand, which is based on my work on the historical commissions of the Deutsche Bank and BankAustria, my membership on the Advisory Council of the Dresdner Bank, and my recently published history of the Allianz AG. Thanks to this involvement in both banking and insurance, I have been compelled to take a somewhat broader and comparative view of the financial sector as a whole, while my recent research on the Austrian banks and insurance companies should add certain dimensions that are often neglected. I realize that the financial sector is often one of the most mysterious areas of the economy both to "normal" historians and to the educated public, and I shall try to present the problems and issues involved in a nontechnical manner.

In considering the role of banks and insurance companies in the Third Reich, it is useful to begin with some understanding of the atmosphere surrounding these enterprises arising from the specific nature of their activities. While insurance companies like to speak of "production" in connection with the sale of new policies and the acquisition of new customers, and banks today talk about offering new "products" to their customers, important segments of the general public often think they produce nothing at all and that their chief activities are charging interest and collecting fees and premiums. The peculiar mixture of enthusiasm and opprobrium with which the public and the media respond to scandals and bankruptcies associated with financial institutions is indicative of the deep suspicion to which they are subject. This has especially been the case in Germany. These suspicions and attitudes go back a long way, and their association with anti-Semitism is well known.

If one is to understand the performance of banks and insurance companies in the National Socialist period, then it is essential to bear in mind the suspicion and hostility under which they labored. Important elements in the National Socialist Party saw them as instruments for grasping rather than producing capital, and these socialist-minded Nazis had very specific alternatives in mind to the existing private banking and insurance organizations. They were hostile to the German universal banking system, that is, to the combination of investment and commercial banking, and wanted to break up the great banks in favor of regional banks that would better serve small and medium sized industry and local and regional interests, with credit at lower rates than those charged by the big banks. Ironically, Nazi solutions to the banking question were not so different from those advocated by Roosevelt-era New Dealers charged with the reorganization of the German banking system after the war.[7] In the case of insurance, the more ideological wing of the Party favored the publicly chartered insurance companies over private insurance, and it was no trivial matter that Hans Goebbels, the brother of the Propaganda Minister, and Franz Schwede-Coburg, the Gauleiter of Pomerania, were very active in fighting private insurance. The insurance companies were accused of charging excessive premiums, favoring high interest rates, and paying excessively high executive salaries. As usual, these charges were accompanied by complaints that they were heavily infiltrated with Jews.[8]

Logically, the bankers and insurance industry leaders should have detested the Nazis, and some of them did. At the same time, however, their powers of resistance and political judgment that, as was true of most businessmen, had never been seriously fortified by a commitment to democratic ideas and practices, had been very much weakened by the Great Depression, the crisis of capitalism, and the political crisis that accompanied it. This has nothing to do with the old question of alleged financial support of the Nazis by big business and other legends, but rather with the vulnerability of the business community in its dealings with the Nazis and the rapid adaptation to Nazi rule. It is easy to forget that the Great Depression dealt a profound blow to the German business community's commitments to liberal economic practice, such as they were. In contrast to business attitudes after the Great War, from which German business emerged with an extraordinary sense of superiority to the bureaucracy and even to the military, and to the rashness with which industry used its economic and financial advantages to attempt to dictate policy during the inflation and then, after the currency reform, joined with the banks to maintain an air of knowing what was best for the nation during the brief period of shaky recovery, German business was anything but its old arrogant self by 1931. It accepted and even welcomed state interventionism in the form of exchange controls, state oversight of financial institutions, bank closures and state management, and subsidization. This was the case, among other things, because its moral authority had been shaken by a succession of serious business scandals since the late 1920s, a factor whose importance has yet to receive its full due from historians of the Weimar Republic.

In the case of the banks, the collapse of the Darmstädter und Nationalbank (Danat Bank) in July 1931, followed by the Dresdner Bank, reinforced the arguments of some that the banks favored big and corrupt customers, like the Nordwolle firm, whose bankruptcy had ruined the Danat and paved the way for the collapse of the Dresdner as well. Infighting among the banks also did not help, and the banking crisis, which severely deepened the Great Depression, not only led to demands for tougher regulation of the banks, but also led to the passage of an important new banking act shortly after the Nazis came to power.[9]

In the insurance business, the great trauma was provided by the collapse of the Frankfurter Allgemeine Versicherungs Gesellschaft, the FAVAG, in 1929–1930, which was the result of improper investment of insurance resources by the company's management. As in the case of the Danat collapse, some Jewish leadership was involved, and this was something on which the anti-Semites could play. Ultimately, the FAVAG portfolio was taken over by Allianz. While FAVAG's shareholders were left out in the cold, its policyholders did not suffer from the event. It was, nonetheless, a bad blow to the reputation of the private insurance sector and also led to increased regulation by the Reich Supervisory Board for Insurance. Indeed, the private insurance business was to suffer yet another severe blow in 1936, when the Austrian Phoenix Company, a company with a large Jewish component, collapsed, and a veritable international rescue operation was required to maintain the worth of its policies. After the March 1938 Anschluss, the forced union of Austria with Nazi Germany, Allianz also was able to pick up some of the more profitable pieces of this enterprise.[10]

In any case, the banking and insurance businesses in Germany and later in Austria (the banking crisis of 1931 had, after all, begun with the collapse of the Creditanstalt) entered the Third Reich politically vulnerable and, of course, financially weakened by the Great Depression. They were subject to increased regulation, and now faced the hostility of leading figures in a one-party dictatorship as well. Nevertheless, it is important not to confuse vulnerability with total passivity. Some of the leaders of the financial sector had begun to cultivate National Socialist leaders already after the September 1930 elections. Very prominent in this respect was Emil Georg von Stauss of the Deutsche Bank, who had good contacts with Hermann Göring, and was generally viewed in business circles as a "moderate" and sensible Nazi. Stauss organized dinner parties at which Göring could pursue contacts with other business leaders. It was through such events that Göring came into contact with General Director Kurt Schmitt of Allianz, and one of Schmitt's most important directors, Eduard Hilgard. Another important contact with some members of the financial community was Walther Funk, an economic journalist who had thrown his lot with the Nazis and who arranged meetings with Hitler for Schmitt, Allianz's supervisory board chairman, the banker August von Finck, and others.[11]

The leaders of the financial community survived the initial assaults of the Party quite well because they had strong and skillful support from leading personalities close to the regime. One of these was Hjalmar Schacht, the President of the Reichsbank. Schacht had supported Hitler's appointment as Chancellor, orchestrated an investigation of the banking crisis, and steered a new banking law into existence that left the banking structure more or less as it was.[12] Another was Kurt Schmitt, who took a positive posture toward the new regime, joined the party once the Nazis had taken power, and accepted Göring's invitation to become Economics Minister in June 1933. Schmitt, who was similar to Stauss in his attitudes, was as indifferent to ideology as he was fed up with parliamentary government, and convinced himself that only the Nazis had the energy and will to deal with the unemployment question free of party-political hindrances. When he took the job of Economics Minister, he fantasized that he was becoming General Director of the German economy, and that he would be able to suppress the radicals. He was to learn otherwise, and a heart attack enabled him to leave office after a thoroughly miserable year.[13]

Indeed, the great banks and private insurance industry remained objects of suspicion, and they were to find themselves periodically in conflict with the radicals in the Party until 1945. What, however, does this mean for the historian today studying banks and insurance companies in the Third Reich? After 1945, many of the leaders of both sectors considered themselves victims of National Socialism and viewed their wartime engagement as a heroic struggle to save their enterprises and private enterprise in general from the National Socialist economic radicals. This was certainly the line taken by Kurt Schmitt, who recounted in 1946: "the business community itself could not defend

itself through its free liberal and capitalistic associations; it had therefore to be brought into an organization that was recognized by the
Reich Government."[14] This was also the position of Dr. Eduard Hilgard, the Allianz Director who served as the head of the Reich Group
Insurance, the peak organization of the insurance industry. In a postwar unpublished report on Allianz during the National Socialist period,
Hilgard praised Schmitt for reorganizing the industrial and commercial
branches of the economy into "Economic Groups" with the object of
blocking the efforts of the German Labor Front to take over the economy. Hilgard also credited Schmitt for summoning him and others like
him to lead these "Economic Groups" and defend the interests of the
various branches of the economy against Nazi incursions. He went on:

> In this way I also became one of the leading men in the aforementioned
> organizations and thereby entered into an office which in the following
> period provided me with a mass of very responsible work but along with it
> enmities and persecutions of the most hateful kind and finally severe eco-
> nomic harm in the wake of a so-called denazification that lacked any under-
> standing of the real happenings in the Third Reich. When I today look back
> on our activity in public offices at that time, then I believe I can say that it
> was basically because of our engagement that the German private insurance
> industry survived the Third Reich with its basic structure intact. This also
> justified our decision at that time not to remain on the sidelines and let
> things take their course but to try with all means at our disposal to attain
> influence over the way things went and to protect the branch of the econ-
> omy entrusted to our care from being ruled by the Party and its organs.[15]

This raises the question of how seriously to take the "socialism" of
the National Socialists. A standard answer often is that it should not be
taken seriously at all since the Nazis were highly eclectic, pragmatic,
and opportunistic in their economic policies and thinking. The question might have been a more significant one if, heaven forbid, National
Socialism had lasted more than twelve years and survived into a postwar period. Under such circumstances it is quite conceivable that the
radicals in the Party and SS might well have moved against the private
financial sector, which they hated, and might also have built up large-
scale public or semipublic industrial empires in competition with the
private sector. In the short term and especially under wartime conditions, such economic adventurism, like plans to revamp the legal code
and create a new National Socialist civil as well as criminal legal system,
was not feasible. The radicals certainly did try in the cases of both

banking and insurance. The war seemed to provide a welcome opportunity for the advocates of regional banking and the savings banks to press for the "rationalization" of the banking industry by sharply cutting down the number of the branches of the big universal banks to satisfy the manpower shortage and prepare the way for a postwar reform of the entire banking system. Thus, a decree was issued on 5 December 1939 empowering the Reich Economics Minister to make whatever changes or reforms he deemed appropriate, even if they might "deviate from existing law."[16] Not only was much of the "rationalization" to save manpower carried out at the expense of the private banks, but the Party radicals and leaders of public sector banking used their influence with the radical Reich Party Leader Martin Bormann to set up a "Bormann Committee" in the spring of 1942 to "reform" the banking business.

While the banking sector was able to respond to these pressures by using its influence with the Reich Economics Ministry officials who were friendly to private business and by putting more Nazis on the supervisory boards and even on their boards of management, the entire experience produced a great deal of unease in the private banking sector.[17] In the case of the insurance business, the legal basis for total control over the industry had been developed as early as 1934, when §81 of the Reich Insurance Ordinance was modified to allow the Reich Supervisory Board for Insurance, which was under the Reich Economics Ministry, to set aside existing clauses in the general insurance conditions if it deemed such action "in the public interest."[18] Hilgard, Schmitt, and the other private insurance leaders seemed to have won out in their battle with Schwede-Coburg and the radicals in 1938–1939 by using their influence with Göring and the Reich Economics Ministry, and even procuring a Führer order that the nationalization of the insurance industry was not to be debated for at least a decade. However, the radicals, with the support of Bormann and SS ideologues, launched a new campaign in 1942 and then used the efforts to comb out the economy for manpower purposes to act prejudicially against the private insurers. Here, too, the private insurers felt that their position was anything but secure.[19] From the perspective of these developments, therefore, the radical elements in the Nazi regime should be taken very seriously, not simply because they were ever-present irritations and presented a serious danger for the future, but also because they were an ever-ready source of leverage that the regime leadership could use to bind the financial sector and produce that anticipatory obedience and corrupting opportunism on which the regime depended.

Thus, the coordination of the economy was more often than not a process of self-coordination that began surprisingly early in the case of banking and insurance, and is especially evident at the higher levels of the company and in connection with the crises and scandals mentioned above. In making such generalizations, however, it is important to recognize that the great enterprises in banking and insurance did have their own individual histories and paths in coming to terms with the goals of the regime. At the Deutsche Bank, its Managing Board Speaker, Oscar Wassermann, agreed to leave the board by the end of 1933, but his colleagues announced his departure on June 1, and two other Jewish directors were removed at the same time. At the Dresdner Bank, the cleansing of Jewish managing board members began even before 1933 because of the takeover of the bank by the government in the crisis of 1931, and the removal of the leading directors, who happened to be Jewish. Because the Dresdner Bank was effectively an organization under state control, the "Law for the Restoration of the Professional Civil Service" of April 1933 could be employed to purge the remaining Jewish directors in 1933–1934.[20]

Removal of Jews was far less a priority at Allianz since there were few Jews in the top echelons of the company. But it must also be said, to the credit of the leadership, that Jewish personnel continued to be employed as late as 1938, and that pension questions were handled with an eye toward fairness to old and valued employees. Moreover, there was a certain amount of self-interest involved, since as long as there was a desire to hold on to Jewish customers, there was a need to continue employing Jewish agents. One of the most prominent Jewish directors, Maximilian Eichbaum of the Magdeburg branch, was kept on until 1935 and then sent abroad to work for a company associated with Allianz in South Africa, where he survived the war. The other prominent Jewish director, James Freudenburg of the Neue Frankfurter, which was the successor to the FAVAG, was less fortunate. He resigned in 1934 and died in Auschwitz in 1942. It is essential to note that the leaders of Allianz very much regretted Freudenburg's retirement and made a point of stating that they were accepting his resignation only because of the "prevailing circumstances," and that they valued him personally as well as professionally.[21]

It was one thing to eliminate Jews from the boards, and quite another to replace them with Nazis. While it was advantageous to have persons in leadership positions with good party connections such as Stauss and Schmitt, this did not mean that one wanted die-hard Nazis on managing boards or directing business organizations if one could help it. In the case of Allianz and then of the Munich Reinsurance Company, for example, Kurt Schmitt's Honorary SS Brigadeführer uniform and his Reich Minister title may have helped in obviating the need for bringing the more fanatical type of party member into the board. Also, Schmitt's successor as General Director and close associate, Hans Hess, hated the Nazis and seems to have been uniquely successful in keeping the Nazis at arms-length from the direction of the company. Here, he was undoubtedly helped by Hilgard, who was placed in what Schmitt frankly described as the *Dreckzone,* that is, the area of dirty work in the Reich Group, by keeping Schwede-Coburg and Hans Goebbels at bay. Matters were undoubtedly also helped by the fact that the chairman of the Allianz Supervisory Board, Wilhelm von Finck, was one of the biggest supporters of the House of German Art in Munich, a matter of which Hitler, ever the supporter of the arts, took positive note.[22]

The Deutsche Bank tried to resist pure political appointments to its Managing Board. When it appeared necessary, it then tried to get away cheaply by appointing a noted sportsman and Olympics organizer with a reasonable amount of banking knowledge and no major political importance, Karl Ritter von Halt. Their second Nazi appointment in 1943, Robert Frowein, was also not a party member of any significance, and only the third, Heinrich Hunke, was a Nazi with real ideological commitments and considerable ambition.[23] The upper reaches of the Dresdner Bank were much more nazified by comparison, the managing board being "graced" with Carl Lüer, who was also Supervisory Board Chair of the chemical firm Degussa, and a Nazi since 1927. Particularly notorious was Karl Rasche, who had close SS connections and never saw a weapon he did not love, and Emil Meyer, another man with close SS connections. Rasche and Meyer were linked with Wilhelm Keppler and Fritz Kranefuß, two notorious Nazis in the Dresdner Bank who were members of the Himmler circle.[24]

Having or not having Nazi managing and supervisory board members were not the acid tests of engagement with the policies and crimes of the regime. It was precisely because they were on the defensive that bankers and insurance executives felt compelled to legitimize their existence to the regime by proving that they could serve it better than their critics, and this meant taking initiatives that would enable them to hold their own and successfully compete against Nazi alternatives. This is not simply a matter of anticipatory obedience, but rather of the integration of political considerations into their business decision-making in such a way as to preempt opportunities and anticipate the goals of the regime. Working "toward the Führer," to use the phrase Ian Kershaw has taken to be the essence of the internal dynamic driving the National Socialist regime toward greater radicalization, was something that businessmen did or found themselves doing, whether they wished so or not.[25]

What I would call their "linguistic turn," that is, their appropriation of National Socialist rhetoric, was itself symptomatic of this development. A splendid illustration was a speech by Hilgard before the Conference of the Reich Labor Community of Banks and Insurance Companies of the German Labor Front on 15 October 1936. It was not a particularly happy occasion for Hilgard, who disliked the Labor Front and its interference in the business of the banks and insurance companies, and who wanted to prevent further interference. What better way, however, than to give a verbal demonstration of his enthusiasm for the ideology of the new order:

> Whether we now advertise to bring the individual national comrade to enter into the risk community of the insured, whether we have to regulate damage payments, or whether we have to consider certain social or demographic perspectives in the setting up of premium schedules, whether we follow the lead of the state in the investment of the capital resources in our trust, or whether we promote great plans and factories in the making by taking over the risks, we always have the duty to consider each individual decision from the perspective of its effect on the totality. I believe that we fulfill our National Socialist duty best when we strive again and again to find a fruitful connection between our economic responsibility for the profitability of the insurance business and the readiness to sacrifice for the entire people. Opinions may differ many times over the individual paths chosen but in the will so to act there ought to be one single community in all the plants of the insurance industry.[26]

It is easy to dismiss such rhetoric as so much self-serving blather, but when Hilgard spoke to bankers and insurance people about following the leadership of the state in the investment of capital, he was talking about something very concrete and expensive indeed.

Even before the announcement of the Four Year Plan for German rearmament in late 1936, the industry had already been making "voluntary" investments at the government's request, agreeing to subscribe to two hundred million marks worth of the 1935 government loan issue, Allianz alone taking 25 percent of the subscription. Once the Four

Year Plan was announced, Allianz made a special show of enthusiasm, with Hilgard leading the way. Thus, Hilgard personally intervened to have the company renounce all profits on its fire insurance contracts for new factories for raw and other materials for the Four Year Plan. With the implementation of the plan, however, the government became less and less interested in voluntarism, and Hilgard informed his colleagues in January 1939 that the life insurance companies were expected to provide a minimum of 30 percent of their premium income to the bond drive. The Reichsbank reported in April that the insurance industry had purchased 620,231,600 RM in Reich securities issued by the Reich in 1938. It anticipated, however, that the industry would provide eight hundred million RM in 1939. By 1940, the sums reached 1.4 billion marks for the year.[27] The banks, of course, were even more involved in the Reich loans since they marketed them, but the ceaseless efforts of the Reich to raise money for its rearmament meant that the banks were compelled to hold increasing amounts of government debt as the market for government paper narrowed. Not surprisingly, the banks and insurance companies felt very uncomfortable holding so much in government loans and sought every opportunity available to invest their money in industry as the housing construction and mortgage market became more and more constricted. What this meant, however, was not only increasing involvement in financing the armaments and the war economy as well, but also becoming mortgaged to the success of the regime.[28]

II

The strategies of self-defense and damage control inevitably implicated the leaders of the financial sector in the corruption and crimes of the regime. Hilgard certainly did do everything possible to protect the interests of his industry, his company, and himself in dealing with the leaders of the Third Reich. He owed some of his success in meeting the challenge to his leadership of the Reich Group Insurance to favors he had done for Göring and Göring's friends in providing them with insurance on favorable terms. He protected the insurers from having to pay twenty million marks insurance to the Reich Finance Ministry for the damages done to Jewish businesses and buildings during the Kristallnacht pogrom of November 1938. Jews were denied the right to collect insurance for the damage, and all payments to them were going to be confiscated in any case, but Göring had the clever idea of collecting from the insurance companies as well as the Jews. Hilgard and his colleagues succeeded in reducing the payment to 1.3 million Reichsmark. They did not argue that the pogrom was a civic disturbance and was therefore not covered by insurance, which was, in fact, the case. Instead, they used connections in the Reich Economics Ministry and the Reich Justice Ministry to fight the Reich Finance Ministry and Göring's powerful Four Year Plan authority. In doing so they used the arguments of Goebbels and other Nazi leaders that the murder of Councilor of Legation vom Rath by a Jew in Paris (the murder was used as a pretext to spark the pogrom) was really the work of world Jewry. Thus, Jews had provoked the righteous wrath of the German people, which led to the destruction of 9–11 November and the decrees of 12 November 1938 that deprived the Jews of all insurance claims, made them responsible for the payment of the damages, and levied an "Atonement Tax" of one billion marks. Thus, Hilgard argued:

> Through the decree of November 12, 1938, the entirety of Jewry has been proclaimed guilty of the Paris murder and thereby of a provocation against the German people. When the provocateur brings about the provocative event, then he must accept being treated as the perpetrator himself. It will not do that the politically condemned Jews be treated as legally guiltless with respect to insurance. As a consequence, the charge of deliberate or at least gross negligence in bringing about the insurance situation can be justifiably made against German and stateless Jews. Thereby the insurance claims become null and void.[29]

Indeed, Hilgard was a master when it came to employing National Socialist logic, and insisted, "The Aryan policy holder will not be able to understand that the end result would be that the Aryan community of the insured should in the end bear the burden." He also managed to reduce the total potential liability of the companies by declaring that the synagogues were "not worthy of reconstruction." After the war, Hilgard and Schmitt claimed to have deplored National Socialist anti-Semitism, and there is good reason to believe that Schmitt at least genuinely did abhor the regime's policies, and that Hilgard did not really share Nazi views either. Nevertheless, they, above all Hilgard, were prepared to use anti-Semitic language and justifications when it served their interests, and they became participants in the cover of the pogrom's true nature and origins.

Business ethics were increasingly sacrificed in such exercises in damage control, and there certainly was some consciousness that international reputation and legal norms were at stake.[30] This especially and grotesquely illustrated by the cases of Jewish assets surrendered by banks and insurance companies under the 11th Implementation Decree of the Reich Citizenship Law of 25 November 1941.[31] Under this notorious decree, which was closely associated with the transport of the German Jews to the East, every German Jew who had taken up regular residence abroad as of 27 November 1941, was automatically deprived of citizenship and his property was considered forfeit to the Reich. Thus, German Jews sent to Auschwitz or other camps were considered as "living abroad," and were normally compelled to sign away their assets to the Reich before being deported. This decree, however, also covered a large class of persons who had left Germany between 1933 and 1941 and resided elsewhere. Previously, the Nazis had taken away the citizenship of some of these persons and ordered the confiscation of their property if they had engaged in anti-German activities, or had managed to flee without paying taxes. The Gestapo regularly informed the banks and insurance companies of the names of such persons and ordered their accounts confiscated or the repurchase value of their insurance companies turned over to the Revenue Office in Berlin-Moabit. Under the November 1941 decree, however, the responsibility for locating and identifying the accounts and policies of Jews who fell under the decree lay with the banks and insurance companies themselves. They were given six months to accomplish this task and were threatened with fines and even imprisonment for failure to comply.

This created an extraordinarily difficult situation for the companies in question. On the one hand, under wartime conditions they simply did not have the necessary labor force to go through all their accounts or life insurance companies and determine who did and who did not potentially fall under the decree. While it was probably easier to identify Jewish bank accounts because most of the accounts of Jews who had left Germany were blocked accounts that could be used only within Germany or be used only with permission, this was not true in all cases where taxes had been fully paid and accounts simply left in Germany. The situation with insurance policies was even more difficult, since one could not be certain of "Jewishness" with respect to most names. Nearly all of the policies had been taken out before 1933, many of them contained no telltale correspondence, and so-called premium-free policies were extremely uninformative.

The banks and financial institutions were also concerned about another matter, namely, whether the Jews they did identify fell under the decree. If, for example, a Jew had emigrated to the United States in 1933 and taken up American citizenship in 1935, then he was no longer a German citizen residing abroad on 27 November 1941, but a former German citizen who had become an American citizen, who could not lose his German citizenship again, and whose property was the private property of a non-German citizen. The banks thus feared that if they reported and surrendered the money, securities, and other deposited assets of such persons, they could be subject to legal action abroad. The matter was made worse by the insistence of the Gestapo that the persons involved not be informed of the forfeiting of their assets. As the Reich Group for Private Banking pointed out in January 1942: "Such mistakes must be avoided if at all possible since they not only lead to a damaging of the confidence in the German banking business abroad, but also make the banks liable to legal action. If in addition the banks refrain from any informing of their customers, then their behavior is a violation of general business principles under paragraph 362 of the commercial code, which can only be set aside by a change of the law."[32] The banks apparently thought they could maintain their reputations and confidence abroad if they could get confirmation from the Gestapo in each case that the property in question was forfeit or if they could write to the customers. Whatever the case, the banks and insurance companies regularly sought extensions on the deadline for providing the necessary information, while the Gestapo itself found it did not have the manpower needed to answer the inquiries addressed to it.

The thought naturally comes to mind that this might have been a form of sly resistance on the part of the institutions in question, but there really is no evidence to this effect, and there is no record of any bank or insurance company being fined for failure to do its best in turning over Jewish assets. On the contrary, the record shows that many accounts and insurance policies were turned over, but that most of these assets had been taken before 1941. Certainly there was a lack of enthusiasm for the decree, which was time-consuming, expensive, and unprofitable. It is very likely that some bank and insurance company employees found the entire business unpleasant and perhaps unethical. One should not overdo the sense of business ethics or legal qualms, however. Wherever it was possible to make a profit, the attempt was made. Thus, insurance companies offered the Reich the possibility of continuing to pay the premiums on Jewish policies that were nearing their term so as to maximize the return on them both for the German Reich, as the new policyholder so to speak, and for the insurance company, which had most to gain when policies were allowed to reach their term rather than be repurchased at existing face value.[33] An odd exercise in equity and good faith indeed!

This suggests, however, that there is a good deal more involved than simply anticipatory obedience and damage control out of fear of what the radical Nazis might otherwise do. The point here is not to argue that Hilgard, or Schmitt, or Hermann Josef Abs of the Deutsche Bank, or Carl Goetz of the Dresdner Bank, or a host of other bankers and insurance company executives were lying when they said that they felt embattled throughout the National Socialist period, and that they believed they were doing the right thing by taking responsibility and thereby preventing the worst. This would be far too simple. It is also not only a problem of selective memory, although there was plenty of that, and some people, like Hilgard and Abs, had a great deal more selecting to do than others. Rather, it is the meaning that they attached to their total experience in the Third Reich, their self-legitimation, and the way in which this dominated and overwhelmed their actual understanding of the day-to-day activities in which they engaged that constitutes the challenge for the historian. The research problem, as I see it, is not only to challenge the claims made by these businessmen against the facts where there are real contradictions, for example, between what they told denazification authorities and what they really did, but even more to examine what the consequences of their policies of appeasement and collaboration in defense of their business interests meant under the actual conditions of the Third Reich. I would like to argue here that these strategies of self-defense almost invariably drove the banks and insurance companies into further servitude to the regime and complicity in its crimes, and drove them increasingly to adapt to the opportunity structure created by the regime, and to treat the abnormal business opportunities offered by the regime as normal and acceptable business.

From the very outset, the regime offered opportunities as well as dangers. There were rewards for getting rid of Jews and promoting Nazis in a company like Allianz. The aforementioned director Freudenburg of Allianz became a liability in 1933, while the Nazi director Busch in Düsseldorf became an asset. As one director wrote to a colleague in April 1933 in connection with their fire insurance business:

> As a consequence of the political transformation, we have repeatedly had to defend ourselves against the reproach of being pro-Jewish. The loss of the juvenile home contract is, along with a substantially lower premium bid on

the part of the Düsseldorf Lloyd, to be attributed to the claim by the interested party that we were under Jewish influence. Unfortunately, I could not counter this in time because I did not know about it. We almost lost the insurance of the higher schools and public schools in Hesse, but this could be prevented through timely clarification of the situation. In this connection, it will interest you to know that Dr. Freudenburg has announced his departure from the managing board of our corporation. On the other side, we have done business with the National Socialist Party and it is to be expected that Herr Busch in Düsseldorf will make a contract of truly substantial dimensions.[34]

Schmitt's early support of the regime paid off handsomely. Allianz became a major insurer of Nazi organizations such as the National Socialist Teachers League, the Reich Lawyers League and, thanks to the connection with the Reich Master of the Hunt Göring, a major supplier of hunting insurance.[35]

Insurance companies like Allianz participated in the aryanization of Jewish assets. Aryanization was a means of getting new policyholders, and insurers and bankers could work hand-in-hand in the taking over of Jewish businesses. Thus, in July 1939, in the wake of Allianz's licensing to sell insurance in the recently acquired Sudetenland, Hilgard paid a visit to Director Carl Kimmich of the Deutsche Bank to introduce his son, Dr. jur. Hanns Hilgard, who was being sent to build up the insurance business for Allianz in the Sudeten area. Eduard Hilgard wanted his son introduced to the branch directors of banks associated with Allianz in the area so as to assist in this effort. As Kimmich reported to Director Paul Vernickel of the Reichenberg branch of the Deutsche Bank, "Hilgard among other things is thinking of the many aryanizations and the insurance questions connected with them as well as industry in general."[36]

Similarly, Schmitt, who became a very active supervisory board chairman for the German General Electric Company (AEG) and worked closely with its General Director, Hermann Bücher, a person known to be critical of anti-Semitism, nevertheless participated very actively in the aryanization of the Loewe firm in 1936 when it proved the only way of gaining permission for the recapitalization of the AEG and the acquisition of the Loewe company. They agreed to place Loewe on the supervisory board rather than the managing board of the AEG, as had originally been promised, and to remove Loewe's banker, Arthur Solmssen of the Deutsche Bank, from the supervisory board, and then to eliminate the remaining Jews on the Board. Loewe himself finally went in 1938. The pressure to get rid of the Jews came from the Reich

Labor Front, but Schmitt and Bücher succumbed to it because their interests were at stake.[37]

This points to yet another aspect of the increasing involvement with the regime. This was that businessmen, especially in the financial sector, continued to believe that they could carry on normal business free of politics. The problem was that the longer the Third Reich lasted, the more it became impossible to distinguish between normal business and criminal business in a wide variety of areas. That is, business opportunities were increasingly defined by the conditions created by the regime, namely, conditions of war, conquest, systematic theft and transfer of assets along racial lines, and mass murder. For the historical investigation of the exploitation of these business activities, three aspects are of particular interest. First, there is the degree and manner of involvement. Second, there is the issue of knowledge, that is, how aware were those involved of the tainted nature of the activities in question, and how high did this knowledge go? Third, what were the mechanisms used to deal with the unpleasant realities connected with this business? Let me take a number of examples that have attracted considerable attention of late.

As the example of Hilgard, his son, and the Deutsche Bank director, Karl Kimmich shows, both banking and insurance were involved in aryanization, and I would note here that the insurance companies were not simply acting as insurers seeking to offer their services to the new owners of aryanized properties. One of the most important forms of coverage for insurance policies was real estate, and Allianz and other insurance companies were implicated in the purchase of Jewish-owned properties. There can be no question about the top leadership knowing about aryanization and making money or improving their assets in the purchase of such properties, or mediating the sales connected with aryanizations. A more interesting question is how they treated the victims insofar as it was in their power to determine what they would pay for aryanized property, and here research has suggested a mixed answer, although more still needs to be done. On the one hand, banks and insurers seem to have offered fair prices for assets sold by Jews in the earlier phase of the regime and especially when they were dealing with former customers or business associates of long standing within Germany. The role played by Hermann Josef Abs in the cases of the Bankhaus Mendelssohn and the Petschek interests appears to have been as decent as the circumstances permitted, and was so judged after the war. The same cannot be said of lesser known individuals or firms, however, and certainly not of Jewish properties and assets taken after 1937. Aryanization had simply become a business for most of those involved.[38]

Indeed, when one digs deeply enough, one discovers that financial institutions were part of the network of governmental and private institutions engaged in Germany's long-term imperial and racial goals, and that aryanization was part and parcel of these efforts. In the case of Holland, the Dresdner Bank and Allianz provide an especially interesting example of the tying of business networks and political authorities for short-term and long-term goals. What is initially interesting in this case is the connection between Dresdner Bank and Allianz and the operations of the former Jewish banking house of Lippmann Rosenthal, which was used by the German occupation regime to acquire the assets of Dutch Jews.

Allianz had an interest in acquiring control of a Dutch insurance company, and the most important source of the shares of this company was the Dresdner Bank. On 17 March 1942, the Dresdner's Securities Section wrote to Allianz that it was very pleased by the interest expressed by Hilgard in the Dutch Company, and that, as agreed, it had consulted with the Reich Commissar for the Occupied Dutch Territories to arrange that Allianz have first call on all shares of the company, above all those that had been in Jewish possession and were now available through Lippmann Rosenthal. Thus:

> it can be expected that very shortly the Jewish securities, under which shares of the aforementioned company can be found, will be up for sale. In view of the desired amalgamation between the German and Dutch economies, the relevant German agencies naturally have an interest in seeing that the delivery of the blocks of shares gathered among the Jewish assets, wherever possible as complete blocks, be directed over to the German hands most appropriate for such amalgamation.... Beyond this, the interested German party will as a rule have the sole permission to buy up all the wares offered on the Dutch exchange.[39]

Thus, in late April, Allianz bought 300,000 guilders worth of shares in the Dutch company previously in Jewish and enemy hands, and the Dresdner Bank offered another 61,000 guilders from former Jewish holdings a month later, another 45,000 guilders worth in June, and 10,000 guilders worth in August. Finally, it is worth noting that Allianz not only bought Jewish securities of Dutch insurance companies from Lippmann Rosenthal via the Dresdner Bank, but it also provided transportation insurance in 1943–1944 for the shipment of securities and other valuables from Lippmann Rosenthal to Germany.

As bankers caught on to the linkages between aryanization and National Socialist resettlement policies in the East, they exercised their imaginations about ways to benefit from the new situations created by the regime. Thus, in October 1939, the Böhmische Escompte Bank, which was allied to the Dresdner Bank, contacted the latter about the solution to problems that encompassed Latvia and the Protectorate of Bohemia and Moravia. In the former, now under Russian occupation and as part of the Nazi-Soviet agreement, ethnic Germans were to be resettled, and the Dresdner was busy helping the German government to calculate the value of their assets for compensation. In the latter, the authorities were having difficulty finding ethnic Germans *(Volksdeutsche)* to purchase Jewish retail enterprises because of the unwillingness of Germans living in Germany to settle down in the Protectorate. The Latvian ethnic Germans, argued the Böhmische Escompte Bank, might be willing to come to the Protectorate, and they would have both the money and the skills to take over these businesses. This would, at the same time, give the two allied banks an opportunity to act as intermediaries in the resettlement and aryanization business and, in the process, gain long-term customers for the Böhmische Escompte Bank.[40]

At the same time, they responded with alacrity to government prodding with respect to the policies to be pursued in occupied and satellite areas. Thus, when SA Group Leader and special envoy to Slovakia Manfred von Killinger asked the German banks in Bratislava to develop a plan to use government-guaranteed funds for aryanization and settlement to help small- and medium-sized business, the Böhmische Union-Bank enthusiastically responded: "Until now, among all the German banks, we have carried through the most transfers of Jewish enterprises into Aryan, German hands and are further engaged in this respect in the interest of the *Volkstum* (racial community). We will certainly not lack in business enthusiasm and we want to do everything possible to ease the work of construction for the ethnic German population here."[41]

Similarly, financial institutions were anything but cold to the prospects lying in the "wild East" following the invasion of the Soviet Union. Allianz leadership was frustrated by the denial of licenses to do business in the newly occupied territories, but they certainly cannot be accused of not having tried.[42] At the same time, close attention was paid to the prospects for the future by banks and companies associated with them, as was demonstrated in chilling reports on Russia and the Ukraine from Friedrich Görnandt of the South East European Grain

Trading Corporation to Director Hans Friedl of the Creditanstalt in late 1941 and early 1942. Görnandt's company was part of a group of grain trading firms that had been aryanized by the Creditanstalt after the Anschluss with Austria. They were now being asked to supply experienced personnel for the management of the grain harvest in the Ukraine by the Reich food agencies and occupation authorities. Hermann Göring was promising, however, that the grain business would be privatized at the beginning of 1943, and this held out the prospect that those firms that supplied such personnel would be given a priority when privatization came, and would also be well rewarded with hardship pay for working "under unspeakably primitive conditions." They were being called upon to demonstrate the spirit of the royal merchant and Hanseatics, who had once gone overseas, but were now being called upon to seize this "unprecedented chance for their economic future. Here much more is involved, namely, that the utilization and exploitation of the products of Russia's soil for Germany and the rest of Europe in our great struggle for existence after our unrivalled military successes and with the concentration on our final goal."[43]

For the time being, the occupation regime was relying on the old collective farms and the methods of accounting and distribution previously employed by the Soviets, but there was a desperate need for a bank accounting and control system to monitor the collection and shipment of foodstuffs collected from Ukrainian peasants. Therefore, banking personnel were also needed, and Görnandt urged Friedl to insure that the Creditanstalt and the traders connected with it be placed "in the vanguard for the future."[44] This future, as Görnandt told Friedl a year later, was to be one in which "the mobilization of the Russian grain harvests is intended not only for the supplying of Germany … but it is rather the supplying of all of Europe from the Russian space which our Führer has in mind, so that the needy peoples—the Italians, Belgians, Scandinavians, Dutch, Spaniards, and Greeks—who must have grains independently of overseas supplies, can get as much as they need." He had in mind particularly the Ukrainian bread basket, and once this was controlled by Germany, the Russian forces would be finished off quickly since, without this food supply, Görnandt argued, "a mass starvation of previously unknown dimensions among the Russian population would be the certain outcome of an extended war." Thus, Germany and a German-dominated Europe would enjoy autarky in its food supply at Russian expense and, as Görnandt reported to the banker of his company, Vigor: "The great future development of Vigor, as I see it, will without question take place in Russia at the moment when, as is anticipated, a free economy is in place."[45]

The history was to turn out differently from what was anticipated here, but financial institutions had no intention of being passive bystanders for as long as such visions seemed practicable. It was in this way that the practice of seeking opportunity and trying to keep on doing business as usual, however unusual the business, brought the banks and insurance companies so close to the Holocaust itself. This is what one learns from the recent gold reports by the Deutsche Bank and the Dresdner Bank following the rather sensational discovery that both banks had dealt not only in stolen gold, and here not only gold collected as booty and confiscated gold from the occupied territories, but in actual victim gold, that is, gold taken from Jewish victims in the killing fields and camps in the East. Such gold was normally shipped to the Reichsbank, processed into gold bars at Degussa, and then bought by the Deutsche Bank and Dresdner Bank. The banks paid the Reichsbank in much-needed Swiss francs, for resale by their Istanbul branches on the free Turkish gold market, where they received a price that was much higher than would have been received in Switzerland. I should note in passing that the gold in question, at least from the Dresdner Bank, was insured by Allianz.

This is not the place to go into the details of these operations, but there are certain aspects of the reports that are worth emphasizing. First, the gold in question was not used to finance vital raw materials purchases in Turkey, which were in fact paid for in weapons. Rather, it was purchased by German diplomats and secret agents in Turkey who were interested in building up their own private resources and in protecting themselves from the Turkish inflation. It was a private, lucrative business in which all involved made money. Second, SS or Nazi connections had nothing to do with either the amount of victim gold involved or the persons responsible for these operations. The Deutsche Bank had more victim gold than the Dresdner, despite the latter's SS connections. The officials at the Dresdner Bank who were responsible for the operation were not the directors with SS connections, but rather nonparty persons in the Foreign Business Bureau who had very bad relations with the more nazified members of the bank. Similarly, the person in charge of all gold operations at the Deutsche Bank was Hermann Josef Abs, a Catholic and not a member of the party. He worked very closely with Director Alfred Kurzmeyer, a former Mendelssohn Bank director and Swiss citizen, who had close SS connections, above all with the notorious Oswald Pohl. Here again, however, one was dealing with a business operation of very little or no military importance or interest. From this it follows that this was not a necessary operation forced upon the banks, but rather a lucrative business they sought. Third, both reports come to the conclusion that the leaders of the two banks, Carl Goetz and Hermann Josef Abs, must have known that the gold had dubious origins, which is not to say that they knew it came from the teeth of Jewish victims. They had close relations with Emil Puhl, the head of the Reichsbank, associations with Degussa, and a considerable amount of travel in eastern and southeastern Europe behind them. They knew the Reich had long ago used up its own gold. They were simply morally indifferent to the question of the gold's origins.

Finally, both reports suggest that this moral indifference extended into the postwar period, when the Dresdner Bank, in collaboration with the German government, conducted a rather dramatic operation to get the gold back in 1964–1965 using German diplomatic personnel and taking advantage of NATO privileges. In the case of the Deutsche Bank, Kurzmeyer and Abs managed to have the gold from the Deutsche Bank's Turkish branch transferred to a depot in Switzerland, and Abs was careful to keep the gold in Switzerland as long as he was in office. In 1997 the gold, now suspect, was sold and the proceeds turned over to Jewish organizations. It has thus taken a long time for the criminal nature of these operations to be recognized.[46]

These were by no means the only and most serious banking and insurance operations that were close to the economic programs of mass starvation in the East and to the Holocaust. Allianz and a consortium of insurance companies were involved in insuring the factories in nearly all the external camps of the concentration camps, including Auschwitz. Allianz also insured the clothes and materials produced by the Jews of the Łódź Ghetto for the German army.[47] The Deutsche Bank in Kattowitz provided credits to construction firms building the IG Farben Bunawerke in Auschwitz and the Waffen SS barracks there as well, and also gave credits to the firm of Topf, which manufactured the crematoria.[48] Here again, one comes upon the questions of who was responsible and who knew what, and how high up decisions and knowledge went. In the case of the Allianz insurance of the factories, much was owed to a sub-inspector, Max Baier, who was an "Old Fighter" in the National Socialist movement with good connections in the party and SS. Baier, however, operated out of the central office in Berlin and was known to some of the leading directors. Also, insurance of factories requires inspection, and the job of inspectors is to see what is going on. The trouble is that the reports are not very informative, although one of them does note that the danger of theft was minimal because of the high level of security. In the case of Łódź, the Jewish Council had to report directly to the German ghetto authorities with respect to the quantities and value of the items involved. The company thus had no direct contact with the Jewish leaders of the Ghetto themselves. Still, this was a very large contract, and the contracts were negotiated by the branch in Posen. It is difficult to believe that those involved did not know the kind of conditions that existed in Łódź, but it is not at all clear how much was reported and how much information was passed on to the headquarters of Allianz and the other insurance companies involved in Berlin.

Finally, the credits given for Auschwitz construction projects were handled by the Deutsche Bank branch in Kattowitz and Bielitz. Here again, it is inconceivable that the bank directors did not know at least something about the number of forced laborers involved and the conditions at the construction sites, especially since they reported in detail on the progress of the construction and the firms involved. What one would like to know is how well informed the Berlin central office in charge of the branches was, since it ultimately had to approve the credits. It probably knew a great deal more than it wanted to know.

It should be clear from this discussion that financial institutions assumed a very important place in the economy of the Third Reich. From this perspective, the real miracle is how rapidly the German financial community in the West recovered from its engagement with the Third Reich. It is, of course, easily explained by the coming of the Cold War, the end of denazification efforts, and the unanticipated boom that began in 1950 in which the skills of the business community appeared indispensable. What is missing is much investigation of the five years in between, when large numbers of businessmen were subjected to internment, denazification proceedings, and restitution claims as they sought to suppress and repress the real history of the previous years and to vindicate themselves by claiming they were never Nazis at all, or even were "victims" of the Third Reich. Denazification and restitution records are difficult to work with, but they tell a great deal about what happened between 1933 and 1945.[49] While the view of business as victim was spread through well-organized public relations efforts and the development of the uncritical self-history that was the stock and trade of German business until fairly recently, recent studies suggest that they had convinced themselves.[50] I would go even further and suggest that the denazification process was a good training ground for their self-defense, but that the way had been prepared by the business politics of the Third Reich, which had promoted self-deception and a shortsighted but highly opportunistic and self-serving approach when faced with political risk.

It has taken a long time to rethink the role of financial institutions in particular, and business more generally, in the Third Reich, and to begin to recognize the dynamic relationship between business efforts to defend its interests and to conduct business as usual, and the relationship of all this to the goals of the regime. These goals were not determined by financial institutions or big business. Sometimes they were shared, but often they were quite beyond the imaginations of the businessmen. What the history suggests is, as the British Marxist historian Tim Mason found himself arguing some time ago, that politics always had priority over economics.[51] This also meant, however, that what began as appeasement from the side of financial institutions inevitably ended up as collaboration and taking of profits such as they were, for as long as they lasted, and from wherever they came.

Notes

1. Christopher Simpson, ed., *War Crimes of the Deutsche Bank and the Dresdner Bank: Office of Military Government (U.S.) Reports* (New York: Holmes and Meier, 2001). For a fuller exposition of my views on this production, see Gerald D. Feldman, "Wer Spinnt?" *German Politics and Society* 20 (2002): 40–55.

2. Ibid., 13.

3. *OMGUS – Finance Division, Financial Investigation Section: Ermittelungen Gegen die Deutsche Bank 1946/1947,* bearbeitet von der Hamburger Stiftung für Sozialgeschichte des 20. Jahrhunderts (Nördlingen: Greno Verlagsgesellschaft, 1985), and *OMGUS – Finance Division, Financial Investigation Section: Ermittelungen Gegen die Dresdner Bank, 1946,* bearbeitet von der Hamburger Stiftung für Sozialgeschichte des 20. Jahrhunderts (Nördlingen: Greno Verlagsgesellschaft, 1986). The German editions are more up-to-date than Simpson's, and have useful annotations.

4. Harold James, *The Deutsche Bank and the Nazi Economic War Against the Jews* (New York: Cambridge University Press, 2001), is especially critical with respect to Hermann Josef Abs, for example.

5. Hence the approach taken in Gerald D. Feldman, *Allianz and the German Insurance Business, 1933–1945* (New York: Cambridge University Press, 2001), 315–319, 331–344. For the charge of excessive "politeness," see Franziska Augstein's review of the book in the *Süddeutsche Zeitung* 233 (10 October 2001): 35.

6. Much work has recently been done on the role of networks in the Holocaust, as is demonstrated in a collection edited by Gerald D. Feldman and Wolfgang Seibel, *Networks of Persecution: Division of Labor in the Holocaust* (New York: Berghahn Books, 2003).

7. See the discussions in Christopher Kopper, *Zwischen Markwirtschaft und Dirigismus. Bankenpolitik im "Dritten Reich" 1933–1939* (Bonn: Bouvier, 1995), chaps. 2–3; Gerald D. Feldman, "Responses to Banking Concentration in Germany, 1900–33," in *A Century of Banking Consolidation in Europe: The History and Archives of Mergers and Acquisitions,* ed. Manfred Pohl, Teresa Tortella, and Hermann van der Wee (Aldershot and Burlington: Ashgate Publishing Ltd., 2001), 195–212; Simon Niklas Hellmich, "Großbanken und Sparkassen aus der Sicht der nationalsozialistischen Wirtschafts- und Soziallehren," in *Finanzinstitutionen in Mitteleuropa während des Nationalsozialismus. Geld und Kapital. Jahrbuch der Gesellschaft für mitteleuropäische Banken- und Sparkassengeschichte,* ed. Harold Wixforth (Stuttgart: Franz Steiner Verlag, 2000), 17–42. For the similarity between National Socialist and American perceptions of the banks and their roles, see Carl-Ludwig Holtfrerich, "The Deutsche Bank 1945–1957: War, Military Rule and Reconstruction," in *A History of the Deutsche Bank, 1870–1995,* ed. Lothar Gall et al. (London: Weidenfeld and Nicholson, 1995), 402–414, especially 408. Needless to say, the political background of the American attitudes was Jeffersonian, not fascist.

8. Feldman, *Allianz,* 42–44, 95–96, 99.

9. Kopper, *Bankenpolitik,* 93–125; Gerald D. Feldman, "The Economic Origins and Dimension of European Fascism," in *Enterprise in the Period of Fascism in Europe,* ed. Harold James and Jakob Tanner (Aldershot and Burlington: Ashgate Publishing Ltd., 2002), 3–13; Gerald D. Feldman, "The Deutsche Bank from World War to World Economic Crisis," in *A History of the Deutsche Bank,* ed. Gall et al., 240–276; Gerald D. Feldman, "Jakob Goldschmidt, the History of the Banking Crisis of 1931, and the Problem of Freedom of Manoeuvre in the Weimar Economy," in *Zerissene Zwischenkriegszeit: Wirtschaftshistorische Beiträge. Knut Borchardt zum 65. Geburtstag,* ed. Christoph Buchheim, Michael Hutter, and Harold James (Baden-Baden: Nomos, 1994), 307–328.

10. Feldman, *Allianz,* 17–26; Gerald D. Feldman, "Insurance Company Collapses in the World Economic Crisis: The Frankfurter Allgemeine Versicherungs-AG (FAVAG) and the Austrian Phönix," in *The Interwar Depression in an International Context,* ed. Harold James [Schriften des Historischen Kollegs. Kolloquien 51] (Munich: Oldenbourg Verlag, 2002), 57–76.

11. On Stauss, see Harold James, "The Deutsche Bank and the Dictatorship 1933–1945," in *A History of the Deutsche Bank,* ed. Gall et al., especially 308–317; on Allianz leader contacts with Göring and other Nazis, see Feldman, *Allianz,* 50–59.

12. Kopper, *Bankenpolitik,* 67–155.

13. Feldman, *Allianz,* chap. 2.

14. Kurt Schmitt to Franz Hayler, 31 October 1946, Firmenhistorisches Archiv, Allianz AG (hereafter FHA), NL 1/17.

15. Eduard Hilgard, "Die Allianz im 2. Weltkrieg" (unpublished manuscript, 1950), in FHA, AZ 1.3/2, 53–54.

16. Johannes Bähr, "'Bankenrationalisierung' und Großbankenfrage. Der Konflikt um die Ordnung des deutschen Kreditgewerbes während des Zweiten Weltkrieges," in *Finanzinstitutionen,* ed. Wixforth, 71–93, especially 75.

17. Ibid., and Kopper, *Bankenpolitik,* 349–353.

18. André Botur, *Privatversicherung im Dritten Reich. Zur Schadensabwicklung nach der Reichskristallnacht unter dem Einfluß nationalsozialistischer Rassen- und Versicherungspolitik* [Berliner Juristische Universitätsschriften, Zivilrecht, Bd. 6] (Berlin: Verlag A. Spitz, 1995), 71–73.

19. Feldman, *Allianz,* chap. 4, and 304–344, and 415–427. It is interesting to note that Allianz hired the economics professor Jens Jessen during the war to represent their case against the Nazi economic quack, Professor Klaus-Wilhelm Rath of Göttingen, who was used by Schwede-Coburg to attack the private insurance industry. Jessen was executed for his role in the July 1944 plot against Hitler.

20. For the Deutsche Bank, see James, "The Deutsche Bank and the Dictatorship," 291–301; and idem, *Deutsche Bank and Nazi Economic War Against the Jews,* 21–36. For the Dresdner Bank, see Dieter Ziegler, "Die Verdrängung der Juden aus der Dresdner Bank 1933–1938," *Vierteljahrshefte für Zeitgeschichte* 47 (1999): 187–216. For the Commerzbank and more generally, see Bernhard Lorentz, "Die Commerzbank und die 'Arisierung' im Altreich," *Vierteljahrshefte für Zeitgeschichte* 50 (2002): 238–268.

21. Feldman, *Allianz,* 125–149.

22. Ibid., 79–84, 109–110.

23. James, "The Deutsche Bank and the Dictatorship," 298–301; Kopper, *Bankenpolitik,* 288–291.

24. Kopper, *Bankenpolitik,* 282–287.

25. Ian Kershaw, *Hitler: 1889–1936 Hubris* (New York: Norton, 1999), 529–531.

26. The speech is to be found in FHA, S 17.6/8.

27. Feldman, *Allianz,* 157–158, 162–163.

28. Kopper, *Bankenpolitik,* chap. 5; James, "The Deutsche Bank and the Dictatorship," 285–291.

29. Feldman, *Allianz,* 209–210.

30. For a full discussion and the quotations, see ibid., chap. 5.

31. For the insurance side, see ibid., 262–274; for the banks, see the excellent discussion in Harold James, *Verbandspolitik im Nationalsozialismus. Von der Interessenvertretung zur Wirtschaftsgruppe. Der Centralverband des Deutschen Bank- und Bankiergewerbes 1932–1945* (Munich and Zurich: Piper Verlag, 2001), chap. 6. See also his important introduction on the role of the Wirtschaftsgruppe in *Privatbanken in der NS-Zeit. Rundschreiben der Wirtschaftsgruppe Privates Bankgewerbe 1934–1945. Erschließungsbank zur Mikrofiche-Edition.*

32. Wirtschaftsgruppe Privates Bankgewerbe an den Reichsminister der Finanzen, 10. Jan. 1942, Bundesarchiv Berlin (hereafter BAB), R 2/9172b, Bl. 62–63.

33. Feldman, *Allianz,* 272.

34. Director Robert Röse to Director Carl Gehrke, 21 April 1933, FHA, B 2.4.5/145.

35. Feldman, *Allianz,* 120–124.

36. Director Carl Kimmich to Paul Vernickel, 10 July 1939, BAB, 80 Ba 2/P779, Bl. 18.

37. See Peter Hayes, "State Policy and Corporate Involvement in the Holocaust," in *The Holocaust and History: The Known, the Unknown, the Disputed, and the Reexamined,* ed. Michael Berenbaum and Abraham J. Peck (Bloomington: Indiana University Press, 1998), 197–218, especially 201.

38. Dealing with financial institutions and aryanization in Germany, but also with Austria, Czechoslovakia, and elsewhere are: Feldman, *Allianz,* 125–149; James,

Nazi Economic War Against the Jews; and idem, *Verbandspolitik,* chap. 4. Banks thus played a substantial role in aryanization in Germany but also in both Austria and Czechoslovakia. See Dieter Ziegler, "Die deutschen Großbanken im 'Altreich' 1933–1939"; Gerhard Botz, "Arisierungen in Österreich"; and Oliver Rathkolb, "Vermögenswerte jüdischer Kunden in dem 'Postsparkassenamt' Wien," all in *Die Politische Ökonomie des Holocaust. Zur wirtschaftlichen Logik von Verfolgung und 'Wiedergutmachung',* ed. Dieter Stiefel (Vienna: Verlag für Geschichte und Politik, 2001), 117–148, 29–56, 149–180. Kopper, *Bankenpolitik,* chaps. 8–9. See also Harald Wixforth, *Auftakt zur Ostexpansion. Die Dresdner Bank und die Umgestaltung des Bankwesens im Sudetenland 1938/39* [Hannah-Arendt-Institut für Totalitarismusforschung, Berichte und Studien Nr. 31] (Dresden: Hannah-Arendt-Institut für Totalitarismusforschung, 2001).

39. Copy of Dresdner Bank to Allianz, 17 March 1942, sent by Hilgard to Alzheimer on 19 March 1942, FHA, AZ 8.1/1. See also Feldman, *Allianz,* 392–394.

40. Böhmische Escompte-Bank to Director Gustav Overbeck, 26 October 1939, U.S. National Archives (hereafter USNA), Roll T-83/193, 5573–5574.

41. Böhmische Union-Bank, Filiale Bratislava to SA Gruppenführer Manfred von Killinger, 26 September 1940, Bank Austria/Creditanstalt/Rechtsabteilung rot/Box 9 – Union-Bank, Pressburg/Mappe XII.

42. Feldman, *Allianz,* 413.

43. Friedrich Görnandt, Vorstandsmitglied der Südosteuropäischen Getreide-Handels-Aktiengesellschaft to Bankdirektor Dr. Hans Friedl, Creditanstalt-Bankverein, 10 November 1942, Bank Austria/Creditanstalt/Beteiligungen/Getreide AG/Südosteuropäische Getreide AG.

44. Ibid.

45. Görnandt to Friedl, 12 February 1942, ibid.

46. Jonathan Steinberg, *The Deutsche Bank and Its Gold Transactions during the Second World War* (Munich: Beck, 1999); and Johannes Bähr, *Der Goldhandel der Dresdner Bank im Zweiten Weltkrieg. Ein Bericht des Hannah-Arendt Instituts* (Leipzig: Kiepenheuer und Witsch, 1999).

47. See Feldman, *Allianz,* 401–414.

48. The documentation is to be found in the Historisches Archiv der Deutschen Bank, F119/79, 85, F122/1. On Topf, see the very well-researched and balanced article by Monika Dickhaus, "Kredite für den Holocaust – Die Deutsche Bank und J. A. Topf und Söhne, Erfurt 1933–1945," in *Banken und "Arisierungen" in Mitteleuropa während des Nationalsozialismus. Geld und Kapital. Jahrbuch der Gesellschaft für mitteleuropäische Banken- und Sparkassengeschichte,* ed. Dieter Ziegler (Stuttgart: Steiner Verlag, 2002), 211–234.

49. I have made some effort to do so in Feldman, *Allianz,* chap. 9.

50. See the fine study by Jonathan Wiesen, *West German Industry and the Challenge of the Nazi Past, 1945–1955* (Chapel Hill: University of North Carolina Press, 2001).

51. Tim Mason, "The Primacy of Politics: Politics and Economics in National Socialist Germany," in *Nazism and the Third Reich,* ed. Henry A. Turner (New York: Quadrangle Books, 1972), 175–200.

Chapter Two

BANKS AND BUSINESS POLITICS IN NAZI GERMANY

—————⟨∞∞⟩—————

Harold James

IN THE EARLY 1930S, Germany faced a general political and economic crisis. That crisis reshaped politics in a very obvious and destructive way. It also resulted in profound organizational changes in corporate bureaucracies that have been largely ignored by historical analysts who often assume that there is a single agent—such as *the* Dresdner Bank, *the* Deutsche Bank, IG Farben, and so on—and are blind to the organizational complexity of institutions in a state of profound crisis. This essay investigates the way in which organizational changes affected business policy and, in particular, facilitated increased engagement and collaboration with the Nazi regime. This was an engagement that initially looked unlikely, given the anticapitalist (and especially anti–finance capitalist) direction of Nazi thinking.

As a way of focusing such a discussion, this essay considers four bankers as examples of how the practice of banking changed, as different generations of business managers succeeded each other, and of how profoundly business values changed. The first, Georg Solmssen, was a major figure in the Weimar Republic. The last, Hermann Abs, is undoubtedly the most famous German banker of the twentieth century. The other two, Ritter von Halt and Walter Pohle, are barely known.

The Background

The reordered economy of Nazi Germany, with greatly increased regulation of business life, was developed on the basis of a number of corporate scandals. The most spectacular case was in Austria, where the unraveling of the Creditanstalt in 1931, which owned some three-fifths of Austrian businesses, involved a major political scandal, and where Austrian Nazis after 1938 made much of anticorruption politics (while implementing their new and more brutal methods of corruption). Germany experienced developments that were quite similar.

The reputation and influence of all German banks had been considerably weakened by the great banking crisis of July 1931. The worst affected was the Darmstädter und Nationalbank (or Danatbank), led by the charismatic Jakob Goldschmidt, who had appeared to Germans as well as to foreign observers to be the incarnation of the power and attraction of the German mixed banking model. The report of the British Macmillan Committee, which held Goldschmidt up as a model, was by an odd coincidence published on 13 July 1931, the day when the Danat closed its doors. The basic weakness of the Danat lay in a combination of a massive overextension of loans to a single borrower, the apparently very successful and dynamic Bremen firm of Nordwolle, with large-scale purchases of its own shares in order to support its price in a weakening market. The firm was then swept away by an international wave of panic that followed the collapse in May of the Viennese Creditanstalt. The Danat was merged in the course of a state rescue operation with the almost equally damaged Dresdner Bank, and the old management of both banks was replaced. The fact that the state de facto owned the new Dresdner Bank, and that the replacement of the board was not complete by 30 January 1933, almost inevitably gave the Nazi party substantial influence over the bank.

Danat was the weakest German bank, but it was not the only bank affected. There was, in fact, a general weakness in German universal banking, which had originated in the aftermath of World War I and inflation. Banks had lost most of their capital, and were reestablished in 1924 on a precariously narrow capital basis. Competitive pressures, in large measure the result of Goldschmidt's aggressive management of Danat, forced them to borrow, largely abroad, and to extend loans on a small capitalization, and with liquidity ratios substantially below the prewar levels. In addition, they were exposed to a substantial currency risk, as their liabilities (the foreign loans) were in dollars, pounds, or Swiss francs, while their assets were largely German and denominated in Reichsmark. Thus, any doubt about the currency, such as developed in the aftermath of protracted reparations negotiations of 1929–1930, and then as a consequence of the political crisis of the Weimar Republic, would quickly translate into lack of confidence in banks. Banking weakness and doubts about the currency were in fact intertwined in a way that anticipates some of the currency crises of the 1990s—in particular, the Asian crisis of 1997—that are now discussed in the literature as "twin crises."[1]

The Deutsche Bank had not been as badly affected by the crisis, but it also depended on government money, and had to deposit 72 million RM of its shares with the Deutsche Golddiskontobank, a subsidiary of the central bank, the Deutsche Reichsbank. A bitter controversy was fueled by the management of the failed banks as to whether Deutsche Bank had not deliberately worsened the crisis in order to hurt its competitors. This version, actively propagated by Jakob Goldschmidt, was later repeated by the then Chancellor, Heinrich Brüning, in his posthumously published memoirs.[2]

Certainly, in the eighteen months that followed the banking crisis, Deutsche Bank's senior management remained frightened and vulnerable to attack and denunciation, as well as commercially weakened. The crisis of 1931 seemed to teach the general lesson that a banking system only harmed the rest of the economy. Would it not, the critics argued, be more efficient if the state directly realized its objectives by administrative fiat?

At the end of January 1933, Adolf Hitler became Chancellor of Germany. He created a party dictatorship around the monopoly of power of the National Socialist German Workers' Party (NSDAP) that would last until Germany's defeat by the Allies in 1945. The new regime aimed at complete control of the economic, social, political, and cultural life of the nation. In economics, it interpreted the depression as evidence of the failure of the private market economy and of the necessity of state intervention. Although already earlier in the Weimar Republic there had been a great deal of government intervention, for instance in the housing market and in wage policy, the depression brought a call for new controls and regulation; the German government imposed restrictions on international capital movement and a partial debt moratorium for agriculture.

The depression, with its enormous human suffering, the almost seven million unemployed, bankrupt farmers, and closed banks, seemed unambiguous evidence that the unplanned individualistic market economy and also "finance capitalism" did not work. Banks had called in many loans in order to protect their severely endangered liquidity, and earned the hatred of many small and medium-sized enterprises. At the same time, in order to remain in business, banks had demanded, received, and become dependent on, state subsidies.

The National Socialist "New Order" inherited from the depression governments a network of controls and proceeded to make it ever more extensive. In 1934, the regime inaugurated a system of managed trade as well as the allocation of raw materials, and the restriction of dividend payments; after 1936 came a far-reaching regulation of prices. Jewish property initially was subject to apparently spontaneous attacks from local fanatics, then to official discrimination and, in the end, to expropriation. With the exception of the racially motivated attack on Jewish possessions, the fundamental principle of private ownership was left untouched.

In the story of Germany's way out of depression and into the economics of control, it is difficult to distinguish clearly what followed more or less inevitably from the financial and economic catastrophes of the depression, what followed from organizational change, and what originated in the political vision of the new masters of Germany. The capital market, for instance, became smaller, and less relevant to economic activity. Bank loans recovered much more slowly than did the rest of the economy from the world depression. But both these phenomena were characteristic not only of Germany and dictatorship, but of the development of the whole European economy.

If banks existed more and more to channel private savings into state debt, was there any justification at all for their continued independent activity? In the directed economy, did not banks belong to the apparently discredited world of the individualistic nineteenth century past? Such was the tenor of the arguments put forward by the believers in the new economic doctrines of management and control through party and state. Banking, particularly as it had developed in Germany, is concerned with identifying and assessing risks in a capital market, or, more generally, in evaluating the future. In the 1930s, many politically inspired commentators believed that the state could do all these tasks better, and above all more closely in accordance with the dominant social and political doctrines of the time. And this is where the character of the new regime made a distinct difference. Hitler had defined the new doctrines unambiguously in a series of programmatic writings and speeches. He frequently declared "unalterable" the twenty-five point NSDAP party program of 1920, which included the demand for the "breaking of the servitude of interest" and (Point 13) "the nationalization of all businesses which have been formed into trusts."[3]

In the Deutsche Bank, the chief spokesman (in practice, chief executive or *Sprecher*) Oscar Wassermann had been in charge of the bank's overall policy in the late 1920s, and was widely blamed for the 1931 crisis. He was also subject to attack as a Jew and a Zionist. Chancellor Heinrich Brüning, for instance, remained throughout his life convinced that Wassermann had contributed to the catastrophe by refusing to help prop up the Danat Bank before its closure on 13 July 1931. In fact, two non-Jewish members of the Board of Managing Directors bore a heavier responsibility than Wassermann for the mismanagement of the Deutsche Bank's business. Werner Kehl resigned from the Board because of the large speculative foreign exchange positions of the Düsseldorf branch in 1931, which fell within his regional domain.[4] Emil Georg von Stauss was held to account for the bank's losses on loans to the fraudulently managed Schultheiss-Patzenhofer brewery, over whose supervisory board he had presided.

Then, in April and May 1933, a new purge of the Deutsche Bank Board of Managing Directors began, carried out for very different reasons. Here the New Germany made itself felt. In the absence of Wassermann, Reichsbank President Schacht had spoken on 6 April 1933 with two leading figures in the bank, Georg Solmssen and the Chairman of the Supervisory Board, Franz Urbig, and suggested the removal of some of the Jewish members of the Managing Board. Wassermann initially agreed to leave by the end of 1933, but on May 20, his colleagues decided to announce the resignation already before the bank's annual general meeting scheduled for June 1. The bank's *Sprecher* was thus pushed out prematurely.[5]

Georg Solmssen

Who managed this purge? An enigmatic figure, Georg Solmssen, played a major part. He came from a banking dynasty, and one of his uncles had founded and built up the Disconto Gesellschaft, which merged in 1928 with Deutsche Bank. Solmssen himself had converted to Christianity and changed his name. In the Weimar Republic, he had been a tireless advocate of increased credit to German agriculture, and an equally militant opponent of the mergers and acquisition business of Jakob Goldschmidt, whom he felt to be endangering business morality in Germany. In June 1931, he had given a powerful warning of the forces that seemed to be submerging central Europe:

Behind the mass misery there is an ever increasing threat that the dam will break, that at the moment still divides the economic order in Central Europe, with its cultural world built on the basis of personal rights, and a culture of depersonalization. If this dam breaks, a new period in human history will begin, marked by blood and tears. The ethic of existence, a mental world based on thousand year old moral and religious beliefs is in danger of falling victim to a new doctrine which makes man into a machine. This doctrine, because it does not understand its own development, is prostrate before an exaggeratedly venerated technology.[6]

In 1933 Solmssen saw more clearly than anyone else in the banking industry what was happening. He had long been worried about how modernity would destroy tradition. But this was a new illumination. Before 1933, Solmssen, a conservative German who believed wholeheartedly in the idea of a German national cause, had worried much more about the radical and half-baked economic and political ideas of the Nazis than about their anti-Semitism. He told the agrarian leader von Batocki, who had made the argument of the center-right that Hitler and his party might be educated by being brought into governmental responsibility, that

> I would point to the necessity of mobilizing against the dangers contained in the National Socialist program. This is so excessive, agitatorial and unrealistic, in economic matters, especially in regard to financial issues, that in my view something must be done to illuminate the contents and ensure that those circles who are attracted by the national ideas of the party, and who believe that the government inadequately represents the national idea, should move away from the extremists and toward a truly conservative party based on the Conservative People's Party. What about Nazi anti-Semitism?[7]

In 1930, Solmssen treated this issue as less than serious: "I entirely disregard the anti-Semitic statements of the party because they will come to nothing, and regard it as enough to resist the economic declarations."[8]

In 1933 the situation was obviously quite different. A letter Solmssen wrote on 9 April 1933, to Franz Urbig is both moving and chillingly prophetic. It is worth quoting at length:

Dear Herr Urbig,

The exclusion of Jews from state service, which has now been accomplished through legislation, raises the question of what consequences this measure—which was accepted as self-evident by the educated classes—will bring for the private sector. I fear that we are only at the beginning of a conscious and planned development, which is aimed at the indiscriminate economic and moral destruction of all members of the Jewish race living in Germany. The complete passivity of the classes which do not belong to the National Socialist Party, the lack of any feeling of solidarity on the part of those who have up to now worked in business shoulder to shoulder with Jewish colleagues, the ever more evident pressure to draw personal advantages from the free positions created by the purges, the silence about the shame and humiliation imposed on those who although innocent see their honor and existence destroyed from one day to the next: all this is evidence of a position so hopeless that it would be wrong not to confront facts straightforwardly, or to make them appear harmless. In any case, those affected have apparently been abandoned by those who were professionally close to them, and they have the right to think of themselves. They should no longer let the enterprise to which they have devoted their lives determine their actions—unless that enterprise treats them with the same loyalty that it expected of them. Among our colleagues too, the question of solidarity has been raised. My impression was that this suggestion met only a luke-warm response in the Managing Board (perhaps because of its non-homogenous composition); and that if it were to be realized it would take the form of a gesture rather than complete resistance, and as a result would be doomed to failure. I recognize that in the decisive deliberations, differences will be made between different members of the Managing Board who happen to be on the list of proscription. But I have the feeling that although I am viewed as someone whose activity is thought of positively, and although I may be honored as the representative of a now seventy year long tradition, I too will be abandoned once my inclusion in a 'cleansing action' is demanded by the appropriate outside authorities. I must be clear about this....[9]

Solmssen left Germany, first for Switzerland, and then for the United States, where his old enemy Jakob Goldschmidt had also taken refuge. He found the United States business culture entirely unsympathetic, and returned to Switzerland, where he died in Lugano in 1957.

Karl Ritter von Halt

Let us now turn to the first member of the NSDAP appointed to the board of Deutsche Bank, Karl Ritter von Halt. His appointment came about as a result of the turbulence of personnel politics. Frequently, pressure to change personnel policy came not from the outside but from the banks' own employees. A bank inevitably responds to the sentiments and instincts of the mass of its employees, and to their conception of the way the institution should function. Bank employees were prominent among the white-collar workers who, mobilized by pay cuts, job losses, and the threat of proletarianization, formed a major part of Nazi electoral and membership support in the depression era. After 1933 came the opportunists. It was clearly tempting after the Nazi revolution to use party membership as part of a bid for promotion. Usually this was not a successful strategy, and the bank's management clearly both resented and resisted it. Karl Ernst Sippell, the director responsible for personnel issues, reprimanded the offenders quite bluntly. He told one ambitious National Socialist in charge of the Bochum branch: "as a National Socialist he should have increased duties and not merely more privileges," and refused to allow the inclusion of quotations from *Mein Kampf* in the work regulations for the Bochum branch of the bank.[10]

Such conflicts illustrate the extent to which the German Zeitgeist had been transformed. The social and political climate encouraged denunciations, not just on racial or political grounds. Very rapidly, Germany became a country of informers who took their knowledge and their petty gossip to the Gestapo and the party, but also to business managers.[11] The files of the Deutsche Bank reflect the challenges faced by the institution in the new age. One of the directors of the Leipzig branch complained that the other director had engaged in an affair with his housekeeper, was driving her to meetings and social occasions, was alienating customers, and was also making bad loans. The denouncer quoted the housekeeper involved as saying: "When Herr V. is sick, she is obliged to lie in bed with him. Herr V. demands the same thing when he comes home drunk. She needs to wean him off bringing street whores back home." The complaint concluded, "It is thus not a matter of a 'lady,' but of a 'relationship.'" But Sippell took the line that "the Bank cannot concern itself with the personal lives of its branch directors," and obliged the denouncer (and not the alleged fornicator) to move to a much less desirable branch.[12]

Moral, political, and racial complaints continued to accumulate. It is hardly surprising that Sippell had soon found the strain of dealing with both the new social climate and the party's personnel demands intolerable. He felt humiliated and burnt out, and believed that he could no longer continue to manage the personnel department *(Personaldezernat)*. The bank realized that the issues involved required the direction of someone who was himself a trusted party member.[13] In

December 1935, a new Personnel Director, Karl Ritter von Halt, was appointed. He had come from the Munich private bank Aufhäuser.[14] Halt filled the intended role perfectly: he had been a war hero in the Great War, had been wounded on three separate occasions, and had received a Bavarian knighthood.[15] He also was awarded the Austrian Military Cross, Third Class, and the Bavarian Military Cross, Fourth Class.[16] After the War he had distinguished himself principally as a horseman and athlete, and above all he was a member of the NSDAP. In 1936, he organized the winter Olympic Games in Garmisch, and made sports a major part of the life of each Deutsche Bank employee. In Berlin, he frequented the Hotel Kaiserhof, located close to the Reich Chancellery, where many of the most powerful Nazi leaders liked to relax.[17] In 1938, he was promoted to the Managing Board *(Vorstand)* of the bank.

Von Halt's appointment constituted a defensive move by the Deutsche Bank in the face of the new Zeitgeist as much as accommodation. He successfully tamed part of the National Socialist threat inside the bank. After protracted negotiations with the German Labor Front (DAF) and the Berlin party *Gauleitung,* he was allowed to dismiss the National Socialist Factory Cell Organization (Nationalsozialistische Betriebszellenorganisation, or NSBO) representative Franz Hertel, who had been the keynote speaker of the 1933 works assembly, and who had tried to make himself the head of a movement to reform the bank completely in accordance with National Socialist revolutionary doctrine. After World War II, a Deutsche Bank submission to the court *(Spruchkammer)* dealing with Hertel's "denazification" stated that he had frequently worked with the Gestapo: "He managed to declare even slight anti-fascist statements, or the avoidance of a Hitler salute, or the reading of non-Nazi newspapers, or insufficient donations to the party, as the expression of an anti-fascist attitude, and to persecute and even remove such people." In order to remove Hertel, the bank provided enthusiastic testimonials, and a large cash payment (20,000 RM, over forty times his monthly salary). Hertel rapidly became a Hauptsturmführer in the SS, and went on to a grand-scale career as an aryanizer. At first he worked in the Haupttreuhandstelle Ost, the institution that took over Polish and Jewish property in Poland. He then took over for himself a large department store in Prague (the Haus der Geschenke) and then bought Czech Jewish real estate. After the war, he tried unsuccessfully to petition for compensation for the loss of his Czech property.[18]

Walter Pohle

Halt never did banking business for Deutsche Bank. But there were Nazi bankers, and perhaps the most dynamic (and destructive) of them was a young man named Walter Pohle. Pohle took a prominent part in what became briefly a major part of the bank's activity in 1937–1938, namely the transfer of Jewish companies into Aryan hands. He played a much greater part in the Deutsche Bank's expansion outside Germany, a story that is in large measure also a history of aryanization.

Walter Pohle was the main figure in seizing Czech assets. He was an energetic young man who had briefly been employed by the Reich Economics Ministry before joining Deutsche Bank, at first as an intern *(Volontär)*. At the outset, the Deutsche Bank believed that it might be very helpful to employ someone with good contacts with the department in the Economics Ministry responsible for regulating banking (Geld-Bank und Börsenwesen). In a highly politicized economy, winning political contacts was crucial to the ability to do business. Pohle was promoted with exceptional rapidity, from the position of intern with a modest annual stipend of RM 300 to that of holder of power of attorney *(Prokurist)* in 1937. In 1938 he became a deputy director, with a salary of RM 15,000. This promotion occurred despite an odd interlude in January 1937, when he was arrested by the Gestapo and held for two days. The Gestapo eventually informed the Deutsche Bank's legal department that Pohle had "without his knowledge become involved in a stupid business and the affair is now provisionally closed."[19]

The dismembering of Czechoslovakia[20] in 1938–1939, from the September 1938 Munich Agreement to the invasion of Bohemia and Moravia in March 1939, was a crucial part of German economic expansion. Czechoslovakia had an industrial base that represented a substantial addition to Germany's armaments economy. In order to use this new potential, German policy makers aimed at a restructuring of ownership. The Czech lands were also home to a number of banks with German-Jewish histories, and with substantial industrial holdings. These banks, and indeed the whole Czech banking system, had been weakened by the depression, and there were many complaints that the country was overbanked. During the depression, many banks had acquired substantial industrial holdings as their customers found themselves in difficulties.[21] In the eyes of the German economic planners, the Czech banks might lend themselves to the goal of a reorientation of the Czech economy and its integration in German economic mobilization for war.

A strong German position was built up in the months following the first stage of the dismemberment of the Czech state at Munich, providing a base for further economic imperialism after March 1939. After the Munich Agreement, the German government sent lists of Jewish firms in the Sudetenland to the banks, together with a demand that the banks should manage the process of aryanization.[22] In addition, the Deutsche Bank prepared a detailed guide to the industrial structure and the character of the major companies of the Sudetenland, as well as of the rest of Bohemia and Moravia.[23] Expansion did not stop here. On 21 October 1938, just three weeks after the German invasion of the Sudetenland, Hitler ordered preparations by the army that would enable Germany "to conquer 'rump-Tschechei' at any time, if it were to pursue, say, a policy hostile to Germany."[24] After the German occupation of Bohemia and Moravia on 15 March 1939, aryanization became a transparent device for the establishment of German preponderance and the "Germanization" *(Eindeutschung)* of Czech business; for that reason, rather than any deep-seated moral objection, Czech industrialists and the Czech government of Emil Hácha voiced increasing hostility to the German policy, and demanded measures for the confiscation of Jewish assets "where disturbances of public order might occur."[25] The resulting clashes between German and Czech concepts produced a further brutalization in German Jewish policy in the Czech territories.

There can be no doubt that German political authorities provided the ultimate driving force in this process of establishing German control. But the major German banks, and especially the Dresdner Bank and the Deutsche Bank, played an important role as accessories. Their motivation was complex. In part, they were driven by competitive calculations. If they neglected expansion in the new territories, they would lose out to their German rivals. Deutsche Bank noted and complained about each instance when it felt that the military regime or the party was favoring Dresdner Bank unfairly. In some part, the banks were also driven by tax concessions and other subsidies from the German government. Moreover, the process of expansion developed a dynamic of its own; as the German banks established their hold over Czech business, the young, ideologically driven managers who were now placed on the frontier of German imperialism saw a chance to make a name and reputation, and they developed their own initiatives. Such spontaneous ideas, emanating from the middle levels of the banking hierarchy rather than from the Berlin executives, eventually fitted in perfectly with the turn to radicalization in occupation policy in September and October 1941, after Reinhard Heydrich came to Prague.

After the Munich Agreement of 30 September 1938, and the annexation of the Sudetenland by the German Reich, the Deutsche Bank took over sixteen branches of a Czech bank with a large German-speaking customer base, the Ceská Banká Union or Böhmische Union-Bank (BUB), as part of a reordering of Sudeten banking under the direction of the Reich Economics Ministry. It had originally been interested in acquiring the Sudeten-German branches of a larger and more successful Czech-German bank, the Böhmische Escompte Bank (Bebca), but in early October 1938, German Bank Commissar Friedrich Ernst agreed to allocate the branches of the Escompte Bank to Dresdner Bank.[26] The Deutsche Bank's chief negotiator was Walter Pohle, but it is clear that Pohle was looking from an early stage at a much bolder goal than simply the acquisition of a few banks in the economically marginal Sudetenland.

The bank's *Prokurist,* Dr. F. Kavan, who remained in this position through the whole of the occupation, prepared an account of the events of the German invasion of the Sudetenland in September 1938, and then that of Czechoslovakia in March 1939 and the takeover of BUB. Walter Pohle appeared at the BUB in Prague on 13 March 1939, two days *before* the German invasion, declared himself to be a senior official and "confidential agent" of Deutsche Bank, and started negotiations about the financial claims of Deutsche Bank following the transfer of BUB's Sudeten-German branches. Clearly, the political atmosphere was already growing more tense. On 10 March, the federal Czech government in Prague tried to launch a preemptive strike against Slovak separatism, and to dissolve the Slovak government. By 11–12 March, there was street fighting in Bratislava, and German minorities flew swastika flags and staged riots in Jihlava (Iglau) and Brno (Brünn). On 13 March, Hitler summoned his ally, the Slovak separatist leader Father Tiso, to Berlin.

In retrospect, it was clear at least to Kavan that Pohle, who subsequently came to be the dominating personality in the BUB, knew about the impending invasion. Immediately after the invasion, German military officials demanded a greater German influence over the BUB. On 16 or 17 March, Pohle put in another "forceful appearance," saying that BUB was a Jewish enterprise and must, therefore, both in its own interest and in that of Deutsche Bank as major creditor arising out of the transaction of the cession of the Sudeten branches, be pronounced an aryanized enterprise as quickly as possible.[27] Pohle's rival at Dresdner Bank, von Lüdinghausen, behaved in a similar way, arriving in military uniform in the Bebca offices shortly after the German invasion.

According to Kavan, Pohle, who was protected by the Gestapo, immediately dismissed the Jewish directors and appointed the previous director of the auditing division, Joseph Krebs, who had German nationality, as the new director. The supervisory board meeting of 16 March 1939, began with a declaration by Otto Freund "that his serv- ice contract is not being renewed and that he will remain at the bank's disposal as long at it wishes." Such an action was certainly not legal under the bank's existing articles of association. Who had the legal authority not to renew the contract? Freund also stated that Stein and Schubert "have resigned, which information was registered with regret." At the next meeting of the supervisory board, the existing eighteen members resigned en bloc; only four members returned in the reconstituted supervisory board.[28] Freund, the previous principal direc- tor, was arrested fourteen days later by the German police, and soon died in prison, allegedly by his own hand. The board members who resigned were replaced by Deutsche Bank officials, or by people who were acceptable to the occupation regime. The *Tantiemen* (payments to directors by virtue of their membership on other supervisory boards) of the former Jewish directors were now to be paid directly into the bank. Pohle himself simply moved to the BUB, after first securing from Deutsche Bank's personnel department the possibility of keeping open a return to his old bank at the end of his adventure in Prague. In June 1939, Pohle announced the dismissal of the non-Aryan members of the auditing department. But in January 1940, he reported that of the 917 employees still remaining, thirty-eight were Jewish.[29] After World War II, the Deutsche Bank estimated that in all some four hundred Jewish employees had been dismissed.[30]

Apart from participating in a reordering of the industrial capital of the Czech lands, the BUB managed many aspects of the economic destruction of Czech Jews, such as the transfer of accounts and assets to Gestapo-run accounts, and the seizure and sale of jewelry and precious metals. The involvement of Deutsche Bank was driven largely by the relentless energy of Walter Pohle, an energy so relentless that in 1942 Pohle clashed with the Four Year Plan authorities and was given repri- mands by the Gestapo and the Deutsche Bank headquarters in Berlin. The activism of the bank in the Czech territories provides a strange contrast with the Deutsche Bank's passivity in the Polish lands where, largely at the initiative of the bank's Berlin management, it took no action on government demands that it should take over the leading Polish bank, the Bank Handlowy.

Pohle himself was captured by Czechs as the last German soldiers left Prague, and died in a Czech prison from the effects of prison food on a long-standing digestive disorder.

Hermann Josef Abs

The last vignette concerns the most controversial figure in modern German banking history. David Rockefeller called Hermann Abs the "greatest banker of the twentieth century," and Abs played a major role in postwar West German rebuilding, in the reconstruction of the Deutsche Bank and German industry, and also in politics. He came from the same Rhineland Catholic milieu as Konrad Adenauer, and was Adenauer's leading foreign policy adviser in the 1950s. In particular, he played a leading role in the settlement of financial issues resulting from the war, in negotiating the London debt agreement, and also in advocating a financial settlement with Israel.

His postwar prominence is undoubtedly the major reason his prewar career is of such interest. He joined the Deutsche Bank in 1938, after the death of the Deutsche Bank's director in charge of the bank's foreign business. The Deutsche Bank had apparently asked Reichsbank President Schacht who was likely to succeed Schlieper as the German leader of debt negotiations on the Standstill Committee. When they found that Schacht favored Abs, then a partner of Delbrück Schickler, they resolved to hire Abs.

As a director of the Deutsche Bank, Abs managed the foreign expansion of the bank; he was thus responsible for the acquisition of the Austrian Creditanstalt, as well as for the difficult negotiations over the BUB. The Creditanstalt was the most famous Austrian investment bank, and held many important long-term industrial assets. It had been founded in 1855, and had a major capital participation of the Rothschild family, so that it was often held to be a "Rothschild bank." Its international fame became even greater after May 1931, when its failure precipitated a general banking and financial crisis in Austria that then spread to the whole of central Europe, and eventually brought down German banks as well. It was rescued by an expensive intervention of the Austrian state, and in 1934 it was merged with another crisis-torn Austrian bank, the

Wiener Bankverein. The Creditanstalt combined two sets of banking businesses. It was a gigantic industrial holding company whose assets had collapsed in value during the depression and had brought the bank to ruin. This part of the bank would be vital in any plan for the rearrangement of Austrian business. Secondly, the Creditanstalt had wide-ranging contacts in the former Habsburg territories and beyond, in southeast and Balkan Europe, and also played an important part in international trade and finance.[31]

Its pre-1938 management was regarded with suspicion by the German and Austrian Nazis because of the extent of the bank's linkage with the Austrian political system. Two members of the managing board were Jewish. One, Franz Rottenberg, left the bank almost immediately after the Anschluss, and a second, Oscar Pollack, stayed for just a few months. Board president Josef Joham also resigned, leaving only one board member who was an engineer rather than a banker. Then the chairman of the supervisory board resigned. The new Nazi authorities in Austria complained that their predecessors had failed to proceed with sufficient vigor against the allegedly criminal actions that had led to the failure of the bank in 1931.[32]

Immediately after the Anschluss of 12 March 1938, Eduard Mosler, the spokesman of Deutsche Bank's managing board, tried to see Bank Commissar Ernst to tell him "that we are currently considering establishing branches in Austria on the basis of annexation by Germany, but that a decision in this regard is still dependent on discussions with the Austrian Creditanstalt-Wiener Bankverein concerning a different type of close collaboration with a bank with which we have been close friends for a very long time."[33] A few days later, the Deutsche Bank sent Abs, together with two other bank officials, Hellmuth Pollems and Walter Pohle. The attractions of the Creditanstalt did not lie principally in its Austrian business alone. For the Deutsche Bank, the acquisition of the Creditanstalt would be the beginning of a drive to build contacts in an area of Europe that was increasingly subject to German political and economic pressure.

The Creditanstalt began the discussions by saying that "in the light of the friendship that already exists and the many years during which the Deutsche Bank has been represented on the C.A. board of directors, it would welcome the support of the Deutsche Bank in order to be able, as a result, to continue in the future to meet the requirements of the Austrian economy as an independent institution operating in accordance with economic standpoints." That would be "the best solution economically." A participation of the Deutsche Bank in the Creditanstalt ran into opposition from the new Nazi government of Austria. Economics Minister Hans Fischböck announced his reservations. Fischböck, a member of the NSDAP and a former manager of the ill-fated Bodenkreditanstalt and of the Creditanstalt in Austria, had been the economic adviser to the Austrian Nazi leader Arthur Seyss-Inquart. In March 1938, he was appointed Minister of Trade, and in May became Minister of Finance.[34] This impression was confirmed when the dismissed president of Austria's Nationalbank, Viktor Kienböck, told Abs of his interview with Wilhelm Keppler, Hitler's economic adviser and "Reichsbeauftragter für Österreich," on 12 April: "very nasty atmosphere against the Deutsche Bank," he noted. Keppler had said to him: "D.B., with robbery in mind, has arrived in Vienna with twenty men to take over the C.A." Kienböck had apparently then told Keppler that Abs was very new and unburdened by matters with which Keppler might have reproached D.B. in the past. Keppler said: "Abs was still the best of them all."[35]

Deutsche Bank representatives were certainly quick off the mark in establishing the appearance of control. The general meeting of the Creditanstalt on 25 March 1938 was chaired by Abs. One day later, on 26 March, a contract was drawn up regulating relations between the two banks, according to which: "given a corresponding material relationship between the Deutsche Bank and the C.A., Deutsche Bank is prepared to conduct its southeast Europe business as far as possible through Vienna. The C.A. was told in this connection that the precondition was a minimum 75 per cent holding, because then Deutsche Bank must also be able to amend the articles of association without having to rely on the agreement of the other shareholders."[36] Branches of the Deutsche Bank in the Altreich immediately began to advertise their close connection with the Creditanstalt. For instance, the Cologne branch wrote to its customers: "we are able to say that we have at our disposal exact knowledge of all relevant circumstances within Austria."[37] The full implementation of the Deutsche Bank's proposal for control of the Creditanstalt occurred only in 1942.

Abs carried out the largest aryanization operation of the Deutsche Bank, the sale of Norddeutsche Leder (formerly Adler und Oppenheimer). The special complexity of the case lay in the nature of the family's control of the firm through a Dutch holding company. Abs had been appointed chairman of the supervisory board of Adler und Oppenheimer in 1938, with the goal of preparing a sale. At first he negotiated with a number of international companies, including the big British-Dutch multinational, Unilever. The German authorities opposed this kind of transaction, and the sale had not been completed by the time the war broke out. After the invasion of the Netherlands, the Deutsche Bank bought the shares, and then resold them in a public flotation.

Abs also did a substantial amount of his own business, such as the aryanization of S. Fischer Verlag, where he managed the transfer to a leading anti-Nazi figure, Peter Suhrkamp. He also aryanized the small west German part of the giant Czech-German industrial empire of the Petscheks, engineering a sale to his father and brother. He bought back some of the external German debt (the Kreuger loan) and made a large arbitrage profit (the difference between the very low price of German debt abroad, and its face value price within Germany) on the deal on his own account.[38] He was paid CHF 786,800 by Dresdner Bank in 1944 through a Swiss account, even though the Deutsche Bank's contract precluded the control over bank accounts with other institutions, and German law prohibited the possession of foreign accounts.[39]

Abs was also on the fringes of the German resistance. There are, perhaps surprisingly, buried in the Deutsche Bank's archives, some records of Abs's contacts with some of the regime's opponents. In June 1940, Abs's secretary noted that Adam von Trott zu Solz had called "on the basis of your arrangement with him" and "regretted very much, that you were so pressed for time, and hoped that you might have a quarter of an hour for him."[40] Trott, a member of the German Foreign Office, had recently returned from a trip to the United States where he had visited prominent German émigrés and also tried to persuade the Roosevelt administration that a substantial anti-Nazi opposition existed within Germany, an opposition that might be encouraged by a conciliatory foreign policy. Once back in Germany, he tried to find men of reputation whom he could present to American and British contacts as representatives of an anti-Hitler opposition. He contacted Hjalmar Schacht and Hans von Dohnanyi, as well as Abs.[41]

From 1940, Abs repeatedly met the lawyer Helmuth James von Moltke in Berlin, almost always in the company of Peter Count Yorck von Wartenburg. Moltke liked Abs, and wanted to draw him closer to the conspiracy, inviting him to meetings at Kreisau. He wrote to his wife: "Abs has improved. He has arrived to such an extent that he no longer needs to be vain and ambitious. He is simply now the *primus inter pares* of German bankers." The meetings became much more frequent after June 1941, when Moltke was quick to recognize the difficulty of defeating the USSR. In May 1943, Abs was again invited to visit Kreisau, but for one reason or another could not go.[42]

Abs had already excited the attention of the SS because of the wide range of his foreign contacts. After the Deutsche Bank had launched an official complaint about the activities of an Amsterdam bank that was close to the SS, the Rebholz Bankierkantoor, an SS report complained that Abs had written to Reichsbank Vice-President Emil Puhl. The SS report mentions that "Abs has, as is well known, strong Catholic links," and concluded: "Because the Reichssicherheitshauptamt has a great interest in Abs, RSH III D will be informed of the contents of Abs's letter to Pohl [sic: Puhl]."[43]

Abs did not join the resistance. But he undoubtedly had a wide range of contacts that, given the political uncertainty at the time, might be seen as a kind of insurance policy.

Conclusion

Here, then, are four quite different types of banker: a nationalist, conservative traditionalist, who discovered with a shock in 1933 that his Jewish family history mattered; an enthusiastic and naive sportsman, who signed on in all simplicity to the values of the new Germany; a relentlessly ambitious manager, who saw Nazi ideology as a great chance to extend his own influence; and a highly intelligent, cynical, and cautious poker player. Whatever their intentions, all four contributed to the realization of the goals of National Socialism.

There can be no doubt that the senior managers of the Deutsche Bank knew about their environment, about the course and conduct of the war, and also about some of the criminal aspects of the regime. They were aware of the network of concentration camps across Germany; this was no secret. On the other hand, the regime kept a veil of mystery and euphemism around its murderous policies directed against racially defined minorities: Jews, Slavs, Gypsies. At least one of the purposes of this semi-secrecy was to bind the perpetrators of crimes, and those who acquiesced in them, more closely to the regime. As a result, documents that survive from this period give the historian little direct evidence about the extent of knowledge about the Holocaust. In the case of the Deutsche Bank, for instance, there are numerous files relating to the accounts and property of ethnic Germans *(Volksdeutsche)* resettled in Łódź (known as Litzmannstadt under the Germans), but no written indications whatsoever about the fate of the previous owners of the property transferred, or of the fate of the inhabitants of the Łódź ghetto. Did no one at the time give any thought to this?

In some cases, however, individual bankers made the consequences and repercussions of German political decisions more damaging and pernicious for the victims than they would otherwise have been. This was especially true when relatively junior bank officials operated in occupied Europe, seizing goods and assets whose loss made their legitimate possessors even more vulnerable. The bank, especially after September 1938, became part of the machine of German imperialism, and its employees the agents of a brutal political process. The older managers of the bank regarded such behavior with considerable suspicion. Even during the Nazi dictatorship, one member of the Deutsche Bank's managing board had commented on the most destructively energetic of the Deutsche Bank's "new men," Walter Pohle:

> He undoubtedly possesses a great deal of vigor, appetite for work, and eagerness to assume responsibility, but in addition an unbridled ambition from which his management style suffers. We were able in the Creditanstalt case to gain some idea of the stupidities into which his ambition leads him astray and of how, even in a hopeless situation, he cannot muster the insight to admit his mistake. He is temporarily lacking in the self-discipline required for the development of personal maturity, being very much inclined to see things only from the standpoint of commercial success, never mind how that success has been achieved.[44]

In conscious or unconscious calculations of how adaptation to the "New Germany" would affect the financial and social standing of bankers, most financiers could only come to the conclusion that whatever happened, they were bound to lose as representatives of a world and a style of business that the new regime had declared to be obsolete and discredited. German banking had traditionally depended on large networks of contacts, both formal and informal, both national and international, in which commitments were made on the basis of trust and honor. This social and cosmopolitan environment corresponded to one of the primary economic functions of banks, as collectors and transmitters of large quantities of information. To the National Socialists this appeared simply as a discredited old-boy network. But the new Nazi ideology, which had a substantially egalitarian dimension, was not just something that came from the outside, from the state or the party organization. The new doctrine convinced many of the bank's employees and a substantial part of the National Socialist revolution that this financial institution was driven by a dynamic internal to the bank bureaucracy.

Faced with this change of intellectual climate, bankers became more and more passive. The bank's leading figures did not participate in the resistance or in plots against Hitler. It is interesting to note that of Germany's old elites, soldiers, diplomats, and civil servants, and to some extent churchmen, were involved in the resistance; but there were almost no businessmen and no bankers. It seems to me too easy to say that this was because bankers simply kept their heads down and wanted to make money. Unlike generals and diplomats, who still felt valued and important under the dictatorship, bankers were fundamentally regarded as parasitical. To the extent to which they internalized this criticism, it constituted a brake on effective political action. Soldiers and generals occupied a more prominent position. Correspondingly, many committed greater crimes than any banker sitting at a desk, dealing with the balance of debit and credit, could possibly undertake; but the soldiers' and generals' moral possibilities and choices were also greater. They were more likely than bankers to be villains, but more likely also to have the historic opportunity of being heroes. Their moral spectrum was longer; it encompassed the ruthless brutality and the atrocities of the Eastern Front, but also the heroism of 20 July 1944. The two Deutsche Bank managers who were condemned by the People's Court, on the other hand, were not heroes; they were simply very unlucky. Hermann J. Abs, without doubt the most dynamic and imaginative of the Deutsche Bank's managing directors during the war, was happy to attack, in only a slightly veiled form, the entire trading policy of National Socialist Germany. But when he had contacts with the men of the resistance, he self-consciously decided not to be a hero. Should it be the historian's role to condemn him for this?

In the course of their progressive marginalization, many bankers retreated into that environment with which they were most familiar: the comfortable certainties of a rational economic world. They went on behaving in a traditional way in a world that had become strange and irrational. It may seem to many subsequent observers extraordinary that bankers, businessmen, and civil servants criticized the regime most vehemently in the 1930s about relatively mundane characteristics, such as its tendency to run large budget deficits, and not its spectacular inhumanity. There can be no doubt that this vision was the product of an extreme moral shortsightedness. The banking world was trapped in this by the regime, and by the way it presented itself to

Germans. National Socialism claimed insistently and militantly that it was the embodiment of the common good, and that others represented merely narrow self-interest. Told repeatedly that they had nothing to say about the social and political ordering of society, that the social vision of the business community was nothing more than rampant egoism, bankers tried ever harder not to look beyond the ends of their own noses. The result was that bankers too played their part in Germany's moral catastrophe.

Notes

1. Graciela L. Kaminsky and Carmen M. Reinhart, "The Twin Crises: The Causes of Banking and Balance-of-Payments Problems," Board of Governors of the Federal Reserve System International Finance Discussion Papers, no. 544, March 1996.
2. Brüning apparently had found it hard to write the section on the banking crisis. Whereas most of the manuscript was complete in the 1930s, Brüning wrote the banking section in the 1950s, while consulting Goldschmidt, who had fled from the Nazis to New York. See Rudolf Morsey, *Zur Entstehung, Authentizität und Kritik von Brünings Memoiren 1918–1934* (Opladen: Westdeutscher Verlag, 1975); Stephen A. Schuker, "Ambivalent Exile: Heinrich Brüning and America's Good War," in *Zerrissene Zwischenkriegszeit: Wirtschaftshistorische Beiträge. Knut Borchardt zum 65. Geburtstag,* ed. Christoph Buchheim, Harold James, and Michael Hutter (Baden-Baden: Nomos Verlagsgesellschaft, 1994), 329–356.
3. See Yitzhak Arad, Israel Gutman, and Abraham Margoliot, eds., *Documents on the Holocaust* (Lincoln: University of Nebraska Press, 1999), 15–18.
4. *Frankfurter Zeitung,* 9 December 1932.
5. Report of Urbig of July 1933, Bundesarchiv (hereafter BA): R 8119 F, P55. See also Christopher Kopper, *Zwischen Marktwirtschaft und Dirigismus. Staat, Banken und Bankenpolitik im "Dritten Reich" von 1933 bis 1939* (Bonn: Bouvier, 1995), 132ff.
6. Meeting of the Extended Committee of the German Associatoin of Banks and Bankers, 27 June 1931, BA: R2/13260.
7. Solmssen to Harms, 17 October 1930, Historisches Archiv der Deutschen Bank (hereafter HADB): B198.
8. Ibid.
9. Solmssen to Urbig, 9 April 1933, HADB: P1/14.
10. Sippell note for Kimmich, 29 September 1934, HADB: RWB, 54.
11. See, in general, Robert Gellately, *The Gestapo and German Society: Enforcing Racial Policy 1933–1945* (Oxford: Oxford University Press, 1990), especially 130–158.
12. Winkelmann to Managing Board, 3 September 1934, HADB: RWB, 54; Winkelmann to Sippell, 9 September 1934, HADB: RWB, 54.

13. Sippell memorandum of 6 December 1935, HADB: RWB, 54; also Rösler letter to Maximilian Müller-Jabusch, 1 March 1951, HADB: RWB, 54.

14. Von Halt had joined the NSDAP in May 1933: Bundesarchiv-Berlin Document Center (hereafter BDC): party membership number 3204950.

15. Hermann Hess, *Ritter von Halt. Der Sportler und Soldat* (Berlin: Batschau, 1936), 126–129. I owe this reference to Carl-Ludwig Holtfrerich.

16. von Halt file, BDC.

17. Tregaskes to Dougherty, 1 February 1945, United States National Archives (hereafter USNA): RG 260/2/148/16, OMGUS.

18. Deutsche Bank submission, 1 August 1947, HADB: P2/H2; Süddeutsche Zeitung, 2 November 1964.

19. 10 July 1934; 21 January 1937, 22 January and 27. January memoranda, BA: ZE/14060.

20. The name was changed in October 1938 to Czecho-Slovakia.

21. František Vencovský et al., *Dějiny Bankovnictví v Českých Zemích* (Prague: Bankovní Institut, 1999), 242–245.

22. Stauss to Regierungspräsident Fritz Krebs, 7 March 1939, BA: R8119 F, P24419.

23. Deutsche Bank, *Böhmen und Mähren im deutschen Wirtschaftsraum* (n.p., (1938?).

24. Klaus Hildebrand, *Das vergangene Reich: Deutsche Aussenpolitik von Bismarck bis Hitler* (Stuttgart: Deutsche Verlags-Anstalt, 1995), 606.

25. Miroslav Karny, Jaroslava Milotova, and Margita Karna, eds., *Deutsche Politik im "Protektorat Böhmen und Mähren" unter Reinhard Heydrich 1941–1942: Eine Dokumentation* (Berlin: Metropol, 1997), 45.

26. Abs note, 8 October 1938, OMGUS FINAD 2/47/2; also Abs statement, 10 October 1945, Exhibit 195; see also Kopper, *Zwischen Marktwirtschaft und Dirigismus,* 345–348.

27. Czech Republic Finance Ministry (hereafter CFM): BUB reference files, 28 November 1950, affidavit of Dr. F. Kavan.

28. Minutes of the Aufsichtsrat of 16 March 1939 and 12 April 1939, CFM: BUB files (CFM), 67/1830.

29. Minutes of the Aufsichtsrat of 27 June 1939 and 29 September 1939, CFM: 67/1830; minutes of the Engerer Ausschuss, 26 January 1940.

30. Handschriftliche Abschrift betr. Entnazifizierungsverfahren, 4 January 1947, HADB: NL38/3.

31. On the Creditanstalt, see Dieter Stiefel, *Finanzdiplomatie und Weltwirtschaftskrise: Die Krise der Credit-Anstalt für Handel und Gewerbe 1931* (Frankfurt: Fritz Knapp, 1989); Herbert Matis and Fritz Weber, "Economic Anschluss and German Grossmachtpolitik: The Take-Over of the Austrian Credit-Anstalt in 1938," in *European Industry and Banking Between the Wars: A Review of Bank-Industry Relations,* ed. P. L. Cottrell, Hakan Lindgren, and Alice Teichova (Leicester: Leicester University Press, 1992), 109–126.

32. See "Rechnungshof: Strafverfahren und Haftungsansprüche gegen ehemalige Vorstandsmitglieder der Credit-Anstalt," 15 September 1938, Austrian State Archive (hereafter ÖstA): 4/2-92/2165/2/8.

33. Mosler note, 14 March 1938, HADB: B203.

34. Note, 31 March 1938, HADB: B51.

35. Abs note, 13 April 1938, HADB: B51.

36. Note, 31 March 1938, HADB: B51.

37. Deutsche Bank branch Cologne, BA: R8119 F, P6507.

38. See Lothar Gall, "A Man for All Seasons: Hermann Josef Abs im Dritten Reich," *Zeitschrift für Unternehmensgeschichte* 44 (1998): 123–175.

39. Marc Perrenoud et al., *La place financière et les banques suisses à l'époque du national-socialisme* (Zurich: Chronos, 2002), 419–422.

40. Note of 27 June 1940, BA: R 8119 F, P24130.

41. Giles MacDonogh, *A Good German: Adam von Trott zu Solz* (London and New York: Quartet Books, 1989), 164.

42. Beate Ruhm von Oppen, ed., *Helmuth James von Moltke: Briefe an Freya* (Munich: Beck, 1988), 261, 265, 481.

43. Instituut voor Oorlogsdokumentatie, Amsterdam, 77–85 (RSSPF), 65 Aa.

44. Note, 10 June 1942, HADB: B192.

Chapter Three

THE CHEMISTRY OF BUSINESS-STATE RELATIONS IN THE THIRD REICH

━━━━━━━ ∞∞∞ ━━━━━━━

Peter Hayes

BUSINESS-STATE RELATIONS in the chemical industry under Nazism were structured by the prominence inevitably assigned to this branch of production by the Nazi goals of autarky and armament. To reduce Germany's dependence on imported raw materials and amass a modern, well equipped military force, Hitler's regime needed the inventiveness and manufacturing capacity of the nation's chemicals firms. Convincing them to turn their efforts in these directions, however, meant overcoming traditional market reasoning, since products derived from domestically available resources often could not compete in price and/or quality with substances made elsewhere, and reliance on proffered government purchases or subsidies entailed high political risks. The Third Reich thus presented the industry with both high prospective profits and considerable pressure, and the combination proved irresistible in the aftermath of a depression and in the context of a dictatorship. My book on the giant IG Farben concern, originally published in 1987, thus portrayed that firm as becoming ever more deeply implicated in the criminality of the Nazi regime between 1933 and 1945, yet always on the defensive against it, as both lured and lashed into serving Hitlerian purposes.[1] Now, having completed a study of the Degussa corporation in the same period, I am struck by the degree to which the history of that rather different sort of chemicals enterprise duplicates the general pattern seen earlier, but also illustrates the idiomatic variations that arose in relations between particular firms and the Nazi state.[2]

Though headquartered in the same city, represented on each other's supervisory boards, linked through numerous agreements regarding production and sales, and increasingly inclined as time passed to step on each other's toes, IG Farben and Degussa entered the Nazi era divergent in scale and scope, heritage and culture, prospects and purposes. Farben was Europe's largest private corporation, a remarkably inventive and bureaucratic behemoth formed in 1925 by the merger of eight primarily organic chemicals firms that dated from the 1860s. Capitalized at one (U.S.) billion Reichsmarks and commanding a web of hundreds of subsidiaries and branches, its total workforce and sales nearly trebled between 1928 and 1943, when they peaked at 333,000 people and three (U.S.) billion Reichsmarks, respectively. Although the giant concern concentrated on carbon-based chemicals, the range of these connected it to virtually every branch of modern industrial production, from automobiles to mass media and medicines. It also mined coal and manufactured aluminum, explosives, steel, and synthetic fibers.[3] By contrast, since Degussa's incorporation in 1873, it had been essentially an exploiter of niches, specializing in smelting precious metals; supplying the jewelry, dental, fountain pen, and porcelain industries; making inorganic compounds (especially cyanides); and marketing the output of many smaller firms, including the nation's principal producers of charcoal and distillates from wood. In 1927, it drew half of its gross profits from a single product, sodium perborate, the active ingredient in the phenomenally successful detergent Persil.[4] Between 1925 and 1943, as the enterprise's capitalization, sales, workforce, and subsidiaries all burgeoned, it rose from being the tenth largest chemicals firm in Germany to perhaps the third or fourth largest.[5] But it remained by most indices only one-tenth the size of the colossus that loomed over the opposite side of Frankfurt am Main's city center.

Despite these outward disparities, the two firms evolved under Nazism along parallel lines for analogous reasons. Above all, the distinctive growth strategies that each had adopted prior to the Third Reich proved remarkably compatible with that regime's objectives and the opportunities it created during the 1930s. Farben's development had been propelled by the success of its forerunner firms in synthesizing vegetable dyes, notably indigo, and in obtaining nitrogen for fertilizers and explosives from the air via a high-pressure process called hydrogenation. These two massive research efforts not only had freed Germany from expensive imports, but also yielded enormous export earnings, until foreign imitators caught up with German technology.

On the basis of this experience, Carl Bosch, the head of Farben's managing board from 1925 to 1935, formulated the iron law of the firm's growth as follows: "A great research accomplishment requires ten years to reach the production stage; for ten more years it brings returns; in the next ten years, it sags. Then another problem already must have been solved. What we earn on a successful discovery has to be poured into the preparation of a new product."[6] During the late 1920s, as Farben's monopoly over nitrogen production waned, its intended successor was to be liquid fuels derived from coal, also by hydrogenation, a project to which the firm devoted between four and five hundred million Reichsmarks.[7] But steady reductions in the cost per liter of output lagged behind falling international prices for crude oil, so the advent of the Nazi regime coincided with a delicate juncture in Farben's history. While the firm's designated flagship product could not fulfill its market-conquering role, its appointed successor, another coal-based innovation called Buna rubber, had not emerged from the development stage.

Whereas the Nazi regime's desire to promote domestic substitutes for imported materials thus promised to carry Farben through this awkward passage, the advantages to Degussa of Hitler's ascent were both similar and broader. Under Ernst Busemann, the dominant figure on that firm's managing board even before he became its first official chairman in 1930, the strategic watchword was diversification. Convinced that the precious metals field offered little growth potential and that dependence on a single buyer of sodium perborate exposed his firm to long-term dangers, Busemann had begun in the late 1920s investing the substantial profits from Persil in a chain of corporate acquisitions. Though many of these merely rounded off Degussa's holdings in the precious metals, specialty piping, ceramic dyes, and wood carbonization and distillation fields, others took the enterprise into new sectors of production, such as imitation leather and carbon black *(Ruß)*, a soot-like granular organic product used in making inks and pigments. Moreover, because detergent sales proved almost depression-proof, Busemann still had plenty of desire and money to extend Degussa's operations in 1933, when Hitler's regime began not only encouraging the development of a form of carbon black that could replace American imports as an additive to increase the durability of rubber tires, but also putting pressure on Jewish industrialists to sell their companies and leave Germany.

Both IG Farben and Degussa therefore found the economic environment of the early Nazi years highly favorable in several respects.

Threats to exclude Jewish-owned firms from government contracts smoothed the way for the two enterprises jointly to buy up the Chemische-Pharmazeutische Fabrik Bad Homburg AG in 1933, and for Degussa to take over the Degea AG (earlier and later again known as the Auergesellschaft), the nation's leading producer of gas masks and rare, especially radioactive earths.[8] Official decrees also kept competitors at bay while Degussa applied its research breakthroughs regarding carbon black.[9] Meanwhile, a government price-and-purchase guarantee stemmed Farben's hemorrhaging losses on fuel-from-coal, and the regime dragooned ten mining firms into forming the Brown Coal Gasoline Corporation (Brabag) and paying IG Farben substantial license fees for its production process.[10] Other forms of state-stimulated demand quickly increased the giant combine's sales of synthetic fibers, light metals, nitrogen, and plastics, and revived the research and development effort on synthetic rubber. Both Farben and Degussa saw orders mount for their output of solvents, lacquers, resins, and related preliminary products as a result of the general economic upturn and increased military spending. The latter also produced striking rises in Degussa's income from acetoncyanhydrin, the basic component of Plexiglas for airplane cockpits and ship portholes; metallic sodium, used in making tetraethyl lead for high-performance fuel; hydrogen peroxide, essential to manufacturing synthetic fibers and propelling U-boats and torpedoes; pentaerythrite, a derivative of formaldehyde that served as an important intermediate product for munitions; and the steel-hardening processes sold by the firm's Durferrit division.[11]

In September 1936, Degussa closed its most profitable business year since World War I, and its books recorded that, for the first time in the enterprise's history, the precious metals and perborate operations together provided barely half of its total profits.[12] Three years later, its tax returns registered increases since 1932–1933 in the corporation's total worth by 29 percent, in its surplus of assets over liabilities by over 100 percent, and in net profits by 140 percent.[13] Farben's resurgence was slower, but eventually slightly more pronounced, so that by 1939 its sales, gross and net profits, and workforce all had climbed to two to two and one-half times their levels in 1933, and annual investments in new plants had risen roughly tenfold.[14]

Lucrative as these trends were, they occurred, at least in part, against the better judgment of the firms' leaders. The depression remained too fresh a memory to be erased by the Nazi boom. On the contrary, the boom's very rapidity, and the fact that it was not accompanied by a revival of the overseas sales that long had been the backbone of both Farben's and Degussa's profitability, raised the specter of excessive investment in plant and machinery akin to that of the late 1920s, which had proved disastrous to German industry when the bottom fell out of demand from 1930 until 1932. Moreover, the Reich was so insistent on more output at faster rates that companies benefiting from the arms and autarky drives found themselves chasing their own tails, and losing. By 1937–1938, both Farben and Degussa confronted liquidity crises brought on by government-fostered investment projections that had vastly outrun the firms' deployable reserves. But Farben's efforts to tailor its expansion more closely to "normal" market prospects achieved even brief and partial success only with regard to synthetic rubber, and Degussa's struggles to rein in carbon black production and to stem the growth of its increasingly indebted Auer subsidiary, four-fifths of whose business was with the German military, came to virtually nothing.[15]

Whenever either enterprise argued the case for prudence to the officials of the Army Weapons Office or the Four Year Plan, the reply was, sooner or later, the same upbraiding and conversation-stopping one: what business could not accomplish, the state would undertake, since private enterprise was a means, not an end, and there was, in the Führer's words, "no such thing as a commercial balance of expenditures and profits ... only a national balance of being and not being."[16] Well before the regime lent force to these pronouncements by compelling the major German steel firms to underwrite the Reichswerke Hermann Göring in the summer of 1937, most of the nation's corporations already were enmeshed in an allocative system that left them almost incapable of asserting their own interests against those of the state, lest they lose priority access to vital supplies and see more compliant competitors rewarded.[17] Months earlier, in fact, Degussa's supervisory board chairman had grasped the nature of the Nazi "steered economy" *(gelenkte Wirtschaft)* and summarized it with a reference to the cameralist past that it echoed: "it is a euphemism to speak of the 'self-administration' of business.... Socialization of industry is rejected. The initiative of individual entrepreneurs is not to be restricted and leading people are to be well paid, but ... the executive will work in the future in the truest sense 'for the King of Prussia,' only now one says: for the people's community."[18]

The resulting situation, in which corporate executives increasingly felt called upon to justify private enterprise (and themselves) by demonstrating its (and their) worth to the regime, had two salient and fateful consequences for Degussa and IG Farben: the militarization of their output and their implication in the persecution of the Jews. The former development is easily captured in a few statistics. In 1933, traditionally consumer-oriented product lines (dyes, pharmaceuticals, photographic supplies, and nitrogen for fertilizers) accounted for 70 percent of Farben's sales; ten years later, they provided only 30 percent, having been superseded by such mainstays of the Nazi economy as light metals for aircraft, nitrogen for munitions, and synthetic fibers, fuel, and rubber.[19] At Degussa, the transformation was only slightly less extreme. Whereas the precious metals and bleaching and detergent agents divisions had yielded over 60 percent of Degussa's sales in 1932–1933, their share fell to 38 percent by 1941–1942; carbon black, metal hardeners, and the organic products of wood distillation, on the other hand, all of which had important military applications, went from providing roughly 30 percent of the corporation's turnover to almost 48 percent. Moreover, within the bleaching and detergent sector, output of sodium perborate and related products tumbled by two-thirds, while that of peroxides for use in fabricating synthetic fibers and powering the V-I and V-II rockets more than doubled.[20] To be sure, the profit margins on the ascendant products were narrower than on the traditional ones, as a result of the new investment required and the ceilings set by government contracts, but that fact merely underscores the degree to which both enterprises were being turned into purveyors to the Nazi state.

Profitability, and the regime's adeptness at blurring the lines between government and corporate functions (delegating the former to private firms while threatening to assume the latter if necessary) had much to do, however, with the way in which Degussa and Farben were drawn into mounting complicity in the Holocaust. Both enterprises became implicated in pillaging and exploiting the Jews largely as part of efforts to preserve vital monopoly positions against possible encroachment. Especially after the turn of 1937–1938, when the Reich's program of dispossessing Jews within its reach took blatant and official form, the primarily defensive quality of Degussa's and Farben's participation in so-called aryanizations emerged unmistakably. The targeted companies were active almost exclusively in the two German firms' traditional core spheres, namely dyes and nitrogen, precious metals and related products, and located either within the expanding borders of the Reich or in the Protectorate of Bohemia-Moravia, where such installations might have become sources of domestic competition if not absorbed. When interests of this sort were engaged, Degussa turned out to be capable of particular ruthlessness; in one instance the firm actually instructed the Gestapo on how legally to seize control of a desired enterprise. Equally striking, however, is the rarity of such rapacity. Degussa and Farben generally pursued Jewish-owned factories when passivity would have posed a threat to their competitive positions and profitability, rather than for the sake of immediate returns.[21]

This reactive, yet future-oriented causal pattern also animated Degussa's second form of participation in the plundering of the European Jews, namely, its role in processing the precious metals stolen from them. The practice began in the aftermath of the pogrom of November 1938, when the Nazi regime established a system of requiring the Jews of Greater Germany to turn in virtually all of their gold, silver, and platinum possessions to the state-run pawnshops in return for nominal compensation.[22] Objects that could not be resold at a profit for the Reich were then earmarked for shipment to precious metals refineries, where they were to be converted at a small commission into bars usable by the German National Bank or saleable at a narrow, government-fixed markup to industrial customers. Limited as the potential income for performing these services was, Degussa pursued them eagerly, since any other course would have thrown into question the firm's position since 1935 as the executor of the national rationing system for precious metals, and amounted to an abandonment of market share. Moreover, because Degussa's intake and inventory of such goods had been falling steadily since 1934 as a result of the Nazi regime's financial and trading policies, the so-called Jewish Metal Action *(Judenmetallaktion)* offered a rare opportunity to revive the operations of the firm's most underutilized sector. Accordingly, the firm took the lead in brokering agreements with the smaller German refiners and with the state that enabled Degussa to process 50 percent of the platinum, 56 percent of the silver, and 80 percent of the gold taken from the Jews of Germany and Austria in 1939–1941.[23] From the 79.5 U.S. tons of silver and 1.3 U.S. tons of gold that, as a result, "passed through" the enterprise's refineries, it pocketed some 490,000 RM in fees and commissions, which corresponds to roughly U.S. $2,000,000 in contemporary values. The resulting gross profits, however, were considerably smaller, coming to perhaps 60,000 RM or about U.S. $240,000.[24]

Its appetite thus whetted, and with no alternative to cooperation that did not seem to chance forfeiting its preeminence in the precious metals industry, Degussa became the predominant smelter and refiner for the Reich in the far more extensive pillaging of Jews throughout occupied Europe after 1941. From this process, the company appears to have made gross profits of at least two million Reichsmarks, or U.S. $8 million in today's currency. Such a sum certainly contributed to the firm's indifference to the origins of the metals involved, of which the managers at Degussa's refineries, especially in Berlin, became increasingly cognizant.[25] But, once again, the principal motive for doing what the regime asked was less immediate income than ingratiation. Degussa's leaders had nothing to gain (but honor, and that only depending on which side won the war) from refusing to carry out tasks that the state was bound to request of the predominant firm in the industry, but they did have something to lose, namely that very standing, if the regime had to look elsewhere for assistance. And Nazi victories had made Degussa's market position more valuable than ever: in the first few months of 1941 alone, conquered Belgium and France provided the firm with more gold and silver to reprocess and/or resell for the Reich than did the entire Greater German Jewish Metal Action over two and one-half years.[26] All told, gold and silver stolen from Jews accounted for less than one-tenth of the gross profits earned by Degussa's precious metals division from 1940 to 1944. But the firm took part unhesitatingly in processing these materials, lest demurring endanger far greater gains.

A similar narrative lies behind Degussa's and Farben's implication in two other aspects of the Holocaust: the sale of Zyklon B, the fumigant used to asphyxiate the victims of the gas chambers at Auschwitz and Maidanek; and the brutal exploitation of forced laborers at the enterprises' factories. In these regards, too, the preservation of lucrative monopoly positions militated against even perceiving, let alone acting on, the consequences of corporate behavior. Degesch, the jointly owned subsidiary of Degussa and Farben that owned the patents for Zyklon B, had not been an unusually profitable enterprise prior to 1939, but it dominated the field of vaporizing pesticides within the Reich, from which the proceeds rose exponentially after the war began as the number of barracks and U-boats in need of delousing proliferated.[27] With sales of the substance, almost entirely to the military, coming to 3.6 million Reichsmarks in 1942–1943, and the net income amounting to roughly two-thirds of Degesch's annual profits, too much was at stake for the head of the company, a Degussa employee named Gerhard Peters, to risk looking deeply into the use being made of the mere 105,000 Reichsmarks worth of the material delivered to Auschwitz in 1942–1944.[28] Though he was told by SS-Obersturmführer Kurt Gerstein in mid-1943 that Zyklon was being applied to kill "inferior" people, Peters made no attempt to follow up on the information.[29] Had he done so or tried to interdict the supply, he would have run afoul of Bruno Tesch, the fervent and well-connected Nazi who owned Tesch & Stabenow and lived off its income as Degesch's exclusive sales agent to the SS and the German military.[30] Prudence counseled pretending to know nothing, for fear of jeopardizing the future of the firm, or Peters's own position in it.

With regard to forced labor, the leaders of both Farben and Degussa saw their choice as between resorting to it or failing to achieve the regime's output targets for two closely related products, synthetic rubber and carbon black, respectively, that the enterprises considered indispensable to their postwar prospects. Reluctance to antagonize the government's planning agencies, in fact, motivated the firms' acceptances in 1940–1941 of state mandates to locate new installations for these substances in Upper Silesia, where the prevailing labor shortage was one among many adverse factors that made the locations initially unappealing. Eagerness to underline newfound dedication to these projects, which the regime desired but the companies had long resisted, then swept away any lingering reticence about relying on labor provided by the SS, once the locations of the new factories (Farben's at Auschwitz and a Degussa subsidiary's at Gleiwitz) had been chosen.[31] Thereafter, the facts that the laborers were leased on a daily basis and primarily to perform the temporary task of building the plants reinforced the local managers' completely instrumental attitude toward the prisoners consigned to them. At Gleiwitz, the very low attrition rate among female workers engaged in actual production suggests that the firm showed some solicitude toward them; but a much higher share of the male construction workers there either died erecting the site or, after being so weakened by that process, were "selected" for return to concentration camps. At Farben's huge Auschwitz site, known as Monowitz, and the concern's nearby coal mines, 25–30,000 people were consumed in this fashion, which corresponds to a mortality rate of 70–85 percent.

Contrary to popular opinion, however, it was not the putative cheapness of these laborers that made them attractive to either firm. Mistreatment both before and after they arrived at the factories assured that they seldom could generate sufficient return to offset the per capita fees paid to the SS and the costs of barracks, fencing, and guards charged to the employers. Indeed, the most recent and thorough study of Farben's Monowitz installation concludes not only that such workers were unprofitable to the firm, but also that they completed only 15 percent of the work on the site, which was never finished in any case and might have made more rapid progress without them.[32] What made Farben and Degussa contract for such laborers was their political value in the context of the unavailability of other workers. Engaging forced labor functioned as proof that each firm was doing its utmost to achieve the production goals laid down by the regime, and thus that each was worthy of retaining its unchallenged hold on manufacturing a commodity essential to both the "people's community" and each corporation's future.

In order to secure their positions within the Nazi economic order, Farben and Degussa thus proved willing literally, as the German expression goes, "to walk over corpses," and the same long-term reasoning undergirded a final notable congruence in the two firms' histories during the war years. Flush with the proceeds of military demand, but worried about their postwar staying power and competitiveness, each enterprise embarked in 1941 on building new, gargantuan, integrated (and never finished) manufacturing centers.[33] These were intended to supersede older and less flexible installations, that is, to rationalize and streamline output so as to reduce unit costs and permit the most efficient possible changeovers of production runs as market conditions dictated. Moreover, their locations near the center of a German-dominated Europe (Degussa located its new *Konzernwerk* at Fürstenberg an der Oder, today's Eisenhüttenstadt, near the current border with Poland, and Farben upgraded Auschwitz from a synthetic rubber plant to a mammoth complex pivoting on acetylene chemistry) reflected political as well as economic considerations. Each Frankfurt-based firm was signaling its adaptation not only to the new dimensions of the German home economy, especially to the resultant problem of transportation costs, but also to the regime's "Drive to the East," and thus offering one more demonstration of corporate reliability.

For German industry under the Nazi regime, and especially for the chemical companies that came so constantly in contact and conflict with it, the overriding behavioral guidelines from 1933 to 1945 were pithily summarized by the two successive chairmen of Degussa's managing board. Ernst Busemann, who presided over the corporation until he succumbed to cancer as World War II was beginning, formulated his touchstone principle in clichéd, canny, and pragmatically self-excusing fashion. Having early recognized the imbalance of power between business and the state in the Third Reich, he concluded, as did most of his peers in the course of the 1930s, that "it is pointless to swim against the stream."[34] His successor, Hermann Schlosser, invoked two other justifications for always doing as Berlin bade, which also acquired widespread currency: the obligations of "comradeship" in wartime; and the likelihood that "the trend epitomized by the Hermann-Göring-Werke will only be reinforced, if private enterprise fails to take advantage of its chances."[35] Both men, in short, articulated the prevailing corporate version of the "flaccid loyalism" that, according to Pierre Ayçoberry, pervaded German elites during the Nazi era, the view that business decisions were dictated by political duties and economic necessities that left limited room for maneuver or choice.[36]

In fairness, it must be said that the constraints on the leaders of the chemical industry were substantial between 1933 and 1945. The Nazi economic and political systems astutely applied, as David Schoenbaum brilliantly noted long ago, "the carrot-and-stick principle that was the de facto constitutional premise of the Third Reich," and in this context "submission was the precondition for success."[37] Indeed, so narrow was the decision-making range left to corporate executives, as long as profitability remained their objective, that the most insightful and well researched recent study of Daimler-Benz proceeds from the premise that "different managers would not have made substantially different choices." Their options, in effect, were predetermined by the interaction of Nazi policy and commercial rationality.[38]

And yet, if much of this essay buttresses contemporaries' and scholars' views that business-state relations in the Third Reich operated within a tight, politically determined framework, I am unable to regard the particular persons who came to direct IG Farben and Degussa between 1933 and 1945 as historically inconsequential. In particular, the leadership successions at Farben in 1935 and Degussa in 1939 altered the degree to which either could present a united front toward state demands in any matter. Neither Hermann Schmitz, the financial wizard who took over at Farben, nor Hermann Schlosser, the master of marketing agreements who moved into the top post at Degussa, possessed the authority of their predecessors over their more technically and scientifically trained colleagues. Both men, therefore, had great difficulty preventing subordinates from pursuing pet initiatives in collusion with either some government agency that allegedly had insisted on them (a recurrent phenomenon at the increasingly atomized Farben combine) or the Henkel company's gathering effort in 1940–1942 to turn Degussa into a rival of Farben in several fields. The attributes that ultimately assured each man's ascent (Schmitz's ability to meet the enormous capital requirements of IG Farben's mushrooming growth, and Schlosser's political connections in Frankfurt) were not enough to guarantee intramural deference. As a result, the polycracy so often noted as characteristic of Nazi government also marked the chemical firms that dealt with it.

Moreover, the men who led these two firms during the war years conceived of their positions in fashions that hastened the degradation of managers, to borrow a memorable metaphor, from drivers of the corporate bus to mere collectors of its fares.[39] Unable and temperamentally disinclined to stand up to his goal-directed colleagues, Schmitz concentrated on the hows rather than the whats of corporate policy and sank increasingly into a fatalism that shattered his nerves during the final, convulsive Nazi years, stamped his almost helpless attitude during his postwar trial for war crimes, and left him a shadow of his former self thereafter.[40] Schlosser, on the other hand, reflexively understood his business role as a mere civilian platform for exercising the soldierly virtues he had imbibed during front service in World War I. He justified every imposition from Berlin as an order from on high, treated the "overrunning" of the Reich as an "unfortunate" outcome to the fighting, never showed the slightest remorse or reservation about what he had felt compelled or obligated to do, and thus had a clean conscience as he returned to prominence in the firm during the early years of the West German Federal Republic.[41]

In their own, distinctive ways, Schmitz and Schlosser illustrated how virtually an entire generation of German business leaders could fail the challenge to morality and political responsibility posed by Nazism. Of course, their devotion to a narrative of passivity and reactiveness, to a description of their own actions that emphasized duty and powerlessness, national obligation and obedience, was a product of history, especially of the military nostalgia and nationalist resentment that grew up among such people during the 1920s. It was also a result of the depression's effect on their self-confidence, of the regime's ruthlessness and ever-present threat to bypass them, of the climate of "working toward the Führer" that Nazism cultivated, and of the self-centeredness that inclines most individuals in most times and places to understand the world primarily in terms of what is happening to them. But whatever its source, the inadequacies exhibited by Schmitz and Schlosser constitute an indispensable element in the chemistry of business-state relations during the Third Reich, and a key reason why the initiative in these relations always remained with the Nazi regime.

Notes

1. Peter Hayes, *Industry and Ideology: IG Farben in the Nazi Era*, 2nd ed. (New York: Cambridge University Press, 2001).

2. Peter Hayes, *From Cooperation to Complicity: Degussa in the Third Reich* (New York: Cambridge University Press, forthcoming); in German: *Mitgegangen, Mitgehangen: Degussa im Dritten Reich* (Munich: Beck Verlag, forthcoming).

3. See Hayes, *Industry and Ideology*, 16–18, 325–327.

4. On the early history of Degussa, see Mechtild Wolf, *Im Zeichen von Sonne und Mond: von der Frankfurter Münzscheiderei zum Weltunternehmen Degussa AG* (Frankfurt am Main: Degussa, 1993); and Heinz Mayer-Wegelin, *Aller Anfang ist Schwer* (Frankfurt am Main: Degussa, 1973), especially 60 (on the share of profits from Persil).

5. For Degussa's relative standing in 1927, see Hannes Siegrist, "Deutsche Großunternehmen vom späten 19. Jahrhundert bis zur Weimarer Republik," *Geschichte und Gesellschaft* 6 (1980): Anhang II, 97.

6. Quoted in Josef Winschuh, *Männer, Traditionen, Signale* (Berlin: F. Osmer, 1940), 102–103.

7. Helmuth Tammen, *Die I. G. Farbenindustrie Aktiengesellschaft (1925–1933): ein Chemiekonzern in der Weimarer Republik* (Berlin: H. Tammen, 1978), 50–52.

8. On these and Degussa's numerous but smaller-scale so-called aryanizations in subsequent years, see Peter Hayes, "Die Arisierungen der Degussa AG: Geschichte und Bilanz," in *"Arisierung" im Nationalsozialismus: Volksgemeinschaft, Raub und Gedächtnis*, ed. Peter Hayes and Irmtrud Wojak (Frankfurt am Main: Campus, 2000), 85–123; and idem, "The Degussa AG and the Holocaust," in *Lessons and Legacies V: The Holocaust and Justice*, ed. Ronald Smelser (Evanston: Northwestern University Press, 2002), 145–151.

9. See Peter Hayes, "Market Assessment and Domestic Political Risk: The Case of Degussa and Carbon Black in Germany, 1933–39," in *European Multinationals and Dictatorship*, ed. Per Hansen and Christopher Kobrak (New York: Berghahn Books, 2003).

10. See Hayes, *Industry and Ideology*, 115–120, 133–135.

11. See Hayes, *From Cooperation to Complicity*, chap. 4.

12. See Degussa Unternehmensarchiv (hereafter DUA): Biographische Unterlagen (hereafter BU), Dr. Fritz Roessler, "Zur Geschichte der Scheideanstalt," Abschrift, 102, 116–120, 125; and RFI 4.2/74, Abschluß vom 30. September 1936.

13. See Hayes, *From Cooperation to Complicity*, appendix B; and DUA, RFI 4.8/5, Bilanz per 30. September 1934, Anlage 2, and Bilanzen per 30. September 1939, Anlage 2.

14. Hayes, *Industry and Ideology*, 17, 42, 158, 180.

15. See ibid., 188–193, 205–206; and Hayes, *From Cooperation to Complicity*, chap. 4.

16. See Hayes, *Industry and Ideology*, 163–169, 171–172. The quoted remarks are Hitler's, cited in J. P. Stern, *Hitler: The Führer and the People* (Berkeley: University of California Press, 1975), 134.

17. See Richard J. Overy, *War and Economy in the Third Reich* (Oxford: Clarendon Press, 1994), 93–118; and Avraham Barkai, *Nazi Economics* (New Haven: Yale University Press, 1990).

18. DUA: BU Fritz Roessler, "Zur Geschichte der Scheideanstalt" [1937], 100, 128–129.

19. See Hayes, *Industry and Ideology*, 326–327; and Gottfried Plumpe, *Die I.G. Far-benindustrie AG: Wirtschaft, Technik und Politik 1904–1945* (Berlin: Duncker & Humbolt, 1990), 296–338, 550, and 592.

20. See Hayes, *From Cooperation to Complicity*, appendices F–G.

21. See ibid., chap. 3; "Die Arisierungen der Degussa AG," in *"Arisierung" im National-sozialismus,* ed. Hayes and Wojak, 85–123; and Hayes, *Industry and Ideology*, 219–226, 244–248.

22. On this and what follows, unless otherwise indicated, see Hayes, *From Cooperation to Complicity*, chap. 5; idem, "Degussa AG and the Holocaust," 152–154; and Ralf Banken, "Der Edelmetallsektor und die Verwertung konfiszierten jüdischen Ver-mögens im 'Dritten Reich,'" *Jahrbuch für Wirtschaftsgeschichte* 39 (1999): 135–162.

23. DUA: GEH 5/5, Degussa to the Reichskommissar für die Preisbildung, 27 August 1941, contains a summary report.

24. Calculated on the basis of the fee structure outlined in DUA: GEH 6/11, memo-randa by R. Hirtes, 9 and 15 June 1939. I have estimated the present dollar value of the income by dividing the number of RM by 2.5, the official exchange rate of the time, and multiplying by ten.

25. On the quantities of gold and silver, the sums of money involved, and indications of knowledge on the part of Degussa's managers, see Hayes, "Degussa AG and the Holocaust," 154–157. However, since that article was written, I have refined some of the statistics presented there; see Hayes, *From Cooperation to Complicity*, chap. 5.

26. DUA: GEH 6/10 and 6/20, documents prepared for the Belgian Military Mission in Frankfurt in 1946–47, and GEH 6/11, French tally of 6 February 1941.

27. See Hayes, *From Cooperation to Complicity*, chap. 7.

28. DUA: BET 9/43, Gewinn- und Verlustrechnung, Heerdt & Lingler; Anlagen zum Geschäftsbericht der Degesch für 1943; Bericht über die Prüfung des Jahres-abschlusses vom 31. Dezember 1943, 10 August 1944; and Beantwortung der Fragen in der Anweisung der amer. Militärregierung für Deutschland betr. Dekartell-isierung, Anlage zu 6a; BET 10/7, Aufteilung des Brutto-Erlöses 1930–44, and Gewinn- und Verlustrechnung für 1944; and SCH 1/44, Scherf to Oberstaats-anwalt beim Landgericht Frankfurt, 1 March 1948, which tallies total shipments of Zyklon B to Auschwitz in 1942–1944 at 23,053.5 kilograms.

29. See DUA: BU Dr. Gerhard Peters, especially the Third Judgment of the Schwurg-ericht Frankfurt, 27 May 1955.

30. On Tesch and his firm, see Jürgen Kalthoff and Martin Werner, *Die Händler des Zyklon B: Tesch & Stabenow: eine Firmengeschichte zwischen Hamburg und Auschwitz* (Hamburg: VSA, 1998).

31. On this and what follows, see Hayes, *Industry and Ideology*, xii–xvi, 347–353; idem, "Degussa AG and the Holocaust," 158–163; and idem, *From Cooperation to Complicity*, chap. 6.

32. Bernd C. Wagner, *IG Auschwitz: Zwangsarbeit und Vernichtung von Häftlingen des Lagers Monowitz 1941–1945* (Munich: K.G. Saur, 2000), 265–275, 290–291.

33. See Hayes, *From Cooperation to Complicity*, chap. 6; and idem, *Industry and Ideol-ogy*, 347–358.

34. DUA: IW 22.5/4-5, Busemann to Herzog, 30 July 1937.

35. On the former sentiment, see, for example, DUA: BU Hermann Schlosser, Ansprache … anlässlich des Richtfestes des Degussabetriebs in Stierstadt, 5 Sep-tember 1944; for the quotation, DUA, TLE 1/23, Schlosser's memo entitled

"Grosswirtschaftsraum Deutschland," 6 July 1940, 3. That his views were widespread in his generation of German industrialists is suggested by Cornelia Rauh-Kühne, "Hans Constantin Paulssen: Sozialpartnerschaft aus dem Geiste der Kriegskameradschaft," in *Deutsche Unternehmer zwischen Kriegswirtschaft und Wiederaufbau,* ed. Paul Erker and Toni Pierenkemper (Munich: Oldenbourg, 1999), 109–192.

36. Pierre Ayçoberry, *The Social History of the Third Reich, 1933–1945* (New York: Norton, 1999), 137.

37. David Schoenbaum, *Hitler's Social Revolution: Class and Status in Nazi Germany, 1933–1939* (New York: Doubleday, 1967), 116, 277. See also Peter Hayes, "Industry under the Swastika," in *Enterprise in the Period of Fascism in Europe,* ed. Harold James and Jakob Tanner (Aldershot: Ashgate, 2002), 26–37.

38. Neil Gregor, *Daimler-Benz in the Third Reich* (New Haven: Yale University Press, 1998), 14–15.

39. See Richard Grunberger, *The 12-Year Reich: A Social History of Nazi Germany, 1933–1945* (New York: Holt, Rinehart, Winston, 1971), 184.

40. See Hayes, *Industry and Ideology,* 368–372.

41. See Hayes, *From Cooperation to Complicity,* chap. 8.

Chapter Four

THE BUSINESS OF GENOCIDE
The SS, Slavery, and the Concentration Camps

Michael Thad Allen

MOST SLAVE LABOR in Nazi Germany took place under the aegis of German corporations. Concentration camp prisoners represented only a small minority of compulsory laborers in Germany's wartime workforce, that is, "only" about 700,000 at the height of wartime production. In comparison, millions of prisoners of war and slave laborers conscripted in the East made up over 25 percent of the German workforce by 1945. The SS served as a labor lord, to be sure, but it was, to mix metaphors, the handmaiden of slavery in the German war economy, not its initiator. It has been widely assumed that the SS sought to use its captive pool of slave labor in order to increase its influence over German corporations and, indeed, to "control the German economy." But, in fact, well-known German companies such as Volkswagen or IG Farben came to the SS looking for labor. Business partnerships between them and the SS solidified only at the very end of the Third Reich The first tentative projects, involving no more than a few thousand prisoners, did not begin until 1941, when labor was desperately scarce. A network of slave labor in SS "satellites" of the major concentration camps did not really begin to spread throughout Germany until late 1943 and early 1944. After this point, scarcely any German factory of importance had not applied for concentration camp prisoners.

There is a reason why the process of mobilizing forced and slave labor was so halting and slow, for even after the German transition to total war, the SS tried constantly to keep its prisoners for its own special projects. Its motives for doing so have likewise been misunderstood. Many have commonly assumed that the SS embarked upon slave-labor ventures out of pure greed. Rudolf Vrba, for example, who escaped from Auschwitz, spoke of the "commercialism of Auschwitz" and the SS's desire to extract the ultimate profit. This was the original meaning of the "Holocaust industry": "Killings were carried out with an efficiency which few time-and-motion experts would fault, and they paid rich dividends."[1] Later historians such as Robert Koehl suggested a similar straightforward motive: "[SS businessmen] can [not] be described as ideologically motivated [but] as very ruthless entrepreneurs who, quite clear-eyed, saw opportunities for profit in the exploitation of concentration camp labor."[2]

To counter these assumptions, I would like to make an example of Kurt Wisselinck, an SS manager who, in 1944, went out of his way to intervene in SS corporate operations at the Gross-Rosen camp. First of all, his motives would seem to have nothing to do with profit; in fact, the management of the camp complained that his meddling endangered the efficiency of their works. Gross-Rosen had come to Wisselinck's attention because SS apprentices had complained. Upon closer investigation, Wisselinck reported: "The apprentices complain that they are being withheld additional portions of potatoes with the justification that there are no more left, while it can be observed that the prisoners receive the additional food."[3]

Anyone who has seen documentary film footage knows what many prisoners looked like in 1944. Mortality statistics, which fluctuated wildly, were running at about 10 percent a year at Gross-Rosen and were carefully tracked by SS management. A steady diet, even of leftovers, might have even benefited production. In fact, Gross-Rosen's managers wrote that this was so, but to no avail. Wisselinck mobilized the entire apparatus of SS bureaucracy against Gross-Rosen's cook: he wrote reports, compiled statistics, called in his superior, and in the end demanded the "rationalization" of the camp's kitchen to ensure that such "embezzlement" could not happen again.

If efficiency could so easily be compromised over a few potatoes, what, then, were the motives of SS business entrepreneurs? Wisselinck again proves exemplary, for in the spring of 1944 he wrote a lengthy memorandum with no apparent recipient other than himself. It began: "The business undertakings of the *Schutzstaffel* are the best means to ... break through to new directions in the area of applied socialism. We must live socialism as the deed! Through our example [we must] spur other corporations forward ... in order to see the growth of a healthy, satisfied, and happy Volk."[4] He went on to declare that SS companies had to provide settlements, or housing developments *(Siedlungen),* that would encourage Aryan families "rich in children." The SS had to bind families to their "Motherland." Before Hitler's rise to power, Wisselinck claimed, "primitive housing" had proved a "breeding ground of immorality" and a "feeding trough [*Nährboden*] of Marxism." He also blamed banks, thus condemning communism and capitalism in the same breath. Ideals like these could make the distribution of leftover potatoes seem like an issue of national renaissance.

Widespread willingness to believe that the likes of Wisselinck were "one-dimensional men," pursuing vacuous careerism or pure, material self-interest, simply cannot account for his actions. Furthermore, popular preoccupation with what Hannah Arendt called the "banality of evil" cannot capture his own heroic self-image. In 1944, with German-occupied Western Europe on the brink of invasion and Red Army offensives imminent in the East, Wisselinck, a compulsive doodler, took the time to turn out a sketch (fig. 4.1), which provides an excellent self-representation of SS industrial management. The handsome, square-jawed man drawn on office stationery gazes sidelong down a

FIGURE 4.1: Sketch, 1944. United States National Archives Microfilm collection, T-976/18

string of telephone poles with focused intensity. Rings around his eyes betray fatigue, but his determination is undimmed. He holds a telephone to his ear, and it is impossible to say whether he is giving or receiving orders; but the pose, ready for action, portrays virtues that the SS managers wished to see in themselves. The man is dynamic, the master of modern technology and, with his high forehead and perfectly straight nose, a model of Teutonic racial fortitude.

The drawing shows a heroic ambiance in managerial tasks imagined by SS officers, the kind that led Wisselinck to intervene angrily at Gross-Rosen. At the same time, it illustrates the trivial paper pushing that filled their days, even as they presided over the life and death of human beings. Taken together with his musings about the mission of SS corporate ventures, we must view Wisselinck as an exemplar of the SS spirit of mission that animated its corporate investments.

Phase 1: Economic Crisis and Unemployment, 1933–1936

There is not enough space in this essay to consider every single SS corporate venture. The first grew out of pet projects undertaken by members of Heinrich Himmler's Personal Staff, an institution within the SS that served him directly. Their founders were usually personal acquaintances or cronies of the Reichsführer-SS. The first, the Nordland publishing house founded in the last weeks of 1934, issued some two hundred publications over the next ten years and promised to "bring the SS world view to the SS membership and to the people."[5] The SS could have easily contracted with existing publishers, but Himmler saw his organization as the vanguard of cultural renewal, a mission too lofty to trust to private industry. Such cultural and political pretensions provided one of the few constants of SS enterprise for the next decade, and more often than not led SS business executives to override more traditional motives such as profit, often to the detriment of the corporations they led.

Commenting on the executives who ran Himmler's companies, one historian remarks: "These men can neither be described as ideologically motivated nor as misfits of the depression, but simply as very ruthless entrepreneurs who, quite clear-eyed, saw opportunities for profit."[6] This is true to the extent that SS executives certainly did not count as "misfits" in German society, but it overlooks the extent to which an underlying ideological mission guided the industrial empire of the SS. Even as the Third Reich crumbled under Allied bombs in 1944, some SS managers were unwavering in their ideological zeal and commitment to the corporate mission of the SS. To quote Kurt Wisselinck's impassioned, if turbid, prose once again: "We must live socialism as the deed! Through our example [we must] spur other corporations forward … in order to see the growth of a healthy, satisfied, and happy *Volk*."[7] In the same year an SS corporate lawyer wrote a somewhat less impassioned tract intended to serve as supplementary material for a business course at an SS officer training program. It nevertheless left little doubt about the ideological drive of SS corporations:

> Why does the SS pursue business? This question is thrown at us especially by those who think in purely capitalist terms and look unfavorably on public enterprise or at least on enterprises that have a public character. The time of liberal economics promoted the primacy of business. That is, first comes the economy and then the state. In contrast, National Socialism stands on the principle that the state commands the economy; the state is not there for the economy, but the economy is there for the state.[8]

Paradoxically, then, the SS set out to invest capital in the name of National Socialism's own brand of anticapitalism. At the time these SS men wrote their manifestos, SS business transactions had long come to include a bizarre trade in broken and exhausted prisoners in a network of slavery that spread throughout Europe.

In the early years, between 1933 and 1936, the SS was not yet engaged in the business of genocide. During this period the SS founded several companies in addition to the Nordland Verlag mentioned above, among them a building cooperative, a foundation for the protection of German cultural monuments, a photographic studio, and what would remain ever after Himmler's darling: the Allach Porcelain Manufactory. Perhaps most improbable of all, Anton Loibl, one of Hitler's chauffeurs and a self-styled independent inventor, convinced Himmler in September 1936 to invest in a research and development house for "technical articles of all kinds," though he himself held only a bogus patent for a bicycle pedal light.[9] Accountants later brought in by Oswald Pohl, who later supervised all SS businesses, referred to these early SS companies as "worse than wretched."[10]

None, at first, used slave labor, but this did not mean that the SS refrained from experimentation with slave labor in the years 1934–1936. Already by mid-1934, when the Inspectorate of Concentration Camps was established, camp staff were selecting, from among inmates, skilled craftsmen who could make personal effects, tend their gardens, and do other personal favors. In this form, prison labor was a more or less organized effort in graft to benefit the camp's staff. The SS also entertained larger, more systematic plans to exploit the labor of prisoners. For instance, the Gestapo proposed to use political prisoners to drain the moors of Emsland, but a coalition of private corporations and state municipal and national agencies actually opposed such projects. Germany was suffering from widespread unemployment, and it seemed a crime to give work to Germany's political "opponents" instead of reserving all possible jobs for law-abiding German citizens.

Perhaps the most important use of concentration camp labor during this early phase was for the purpose of terror. Inside the camps, work conformed to the primacy of policing, that is, the enforcement of discipline, and not so much to profit or economic efficiency. But terror, policing, and discipline were no less "pragmatic" in the eyes of the SS. In daily practice, the camp SS used prison labor as an occasion to beat and demoralize inmates. SS men either did this personally or relied upon prisoner-foremen called *Kapos,* some of whom developed a reputation for cruelty that exceeded that of their captors. Work details also kept prisoners constantly working and continually exhausted. Menial tasks such as digging ditches made prisoners amenable to control, and less likely to mount resistance or plot escape. One official of the Reich Ministry of Justice formulated this functional role quite bluntly: "One of the most valuable tools for securing the safe incarceration of the criminal is [to make him] work all day long, from morning to night, every week, month, and year of his imprisonment. This leaves him no time for stupid thoughts [*dumme Gedanken*] and, as an added bonus, helps to raise discipline within the institution."[11]

Beyond the efficacy of control, the concentration camps designed work details chiefly to punish and mock their political enemies. The first *Kommandanten* assigned prisoners to labor details according to their political transgressions, not their skills or abilities, reserving the hardest labor for the most unforgivable political or racial enemies (communists and Jews, for instance). The first Inspector of Concentration Camps, Theodor Eicke, issued service regulations that demanded that "Prisoners, without exception, are obligated to carry out physical labor. Status, profession, and background will not be taken into account."[12] Eicke's watchmen kept their eye less on productive organization than on security and punishment, and they usually sought to maximize the demeaning nature of labor, making a mockery of the prisoners' toil, and insulting their integrity.

Phase 2: Full Employment and Führer Buildings, 1936–1939

Only during the period from 1936 to 1939 did SS industry and slave labor begin to merge into anything resembling an industrial empire. Now a pressing labor shortage, rather than unemployment, arose as the central problem of the German economy. Earlier objections on behalf of private industry and Reich labor agencies were rendered moot. The camps also acquired a new political function during this period. In the early years, concentration camps were nothing more than a successful dictatorship's bloody (but scarcely unusual) tools for gaining and maintaining power. At the end of 1935, the Justice Ministry even considered eliminating them.[13] Only with new foundational principles did they evolve into the system of terror that has become a symbol of Nazi rule. They became a uniquely National Socialist institution, and began to incarcerate new kinds of prisoners. The Gestapo began to target "professional" criminals, "habitual" criminals, and "asocials," all loosely defined groups identified not so much by actual misdeeds as by a speciously defined "nature." In a context that conflated biology, culture, and politics, crimes against property, inconvenient political viewpoints, or deviance of any kind could be taken as evidence of transgression against the "race." The concentration camps, as Eicke and Himmler argued, must vigilantly protect what Michael Burleigh and Wolfgang Wippermann have called the "racial state."[14]

Racial-biological definitions of citizenship were also inherently economic, defining prisoners in terms that gauged the worth of individuals by their use-value to the body politic. These found more common, slang expression in terms such as "ballast existences," "unnecessary eaters," and so forth. The SS, along with German planners, considered such individuals a threat to national output. From 1936 to 1939, SS industries claimed the task of laying hands on such "fallow work power" *(brachliegende Arbeitskräfte)*, and driving prisoners to useful, "communal" service to the Reich, against their "nature," as it were.[15]

The SS concentrated on a sector of the economy that was neglected precisely because it lay outside the massive rearmament drive that Nazi Germany embarked upon in 1935. This was the building-supply industry. Paul Jaskot has pointed out that initiatives to combine concentration camps with large-scale industry seem to have originated in Thüringen. There, a regional geological surveyor suggested the location of Buchenwald near suitable clay deposits, and the Interior Minister urged that "camp inmates should be occupied within the framework of the Four-Year Plan with the production of bricks."[16] Perhaps at this suggestion, the SS quickly organized brick factories within several newly founded camps. Here, Albert Speer, Hitler's favorite architect, was the strongest ally of the SS. Since 1934, Speer had been preparing massive projects as monuments to Hitler's "Thousand Year Reich," among them the Reich Chancellery, the Nuremberg Party Rally Grounds, and other so-called "Führer Buildings."

The pressing labor shortage and the high value of architectural monuments created a congenial setting for what the historian Gregor Janssen called Speer's "dangerous embrace" with the SS.[17] The strongest evidence suggests that Hitler personally brought Speer and Himmler together sometime between the end of 1937 and the beginning of 1938, while the Inspector of Concentration Camps (IKL) was surveying sites for prison industries. Speer was placing huge orders for bricks, dressed granite, marble, and limestone, all raw materials that required labor-intensive production. Both Speer and Himmler sensed that they could use each other to mutual benefit.

In April 1938, the SS founded the German Earth and Stone Works, and Albert Speer offered an advance payment of 9.5 million Reichsmarks for brick and stone, which amounted to an interest-free loan. A welter of organizations shared in this initiative. Hamburg placed orders similar to those of Speer, and the German Workers' Front promised a loan of 700,000 Reichsmarks.[18] From the summer of 1936 to the outbreak of war in 1939 the Inspectorate of Concentration Camps founded no less than five new concentration camps: Sachsenhausen (1936), Buchenwald (1937), Flossenbürg (1938), Mauthausen (1939), and Ravensbrück (1939). Others, such as Neuengamme, Natzweiler, and Gross-Rosen, grew out of industrial satellite camps established next to quarries or clay pits.

In these endeavors, ironically, the SS tried to make contempt for profit into a virtue: "The SS fundamentally avoids business endeavor for the sole purpose of earning money," wrote Oswald Pohl, the chief administrator of all SS industry in 1941. "The very fact of our cultural goals leads our companies down certain paths that a purely private businessman would never dare, and this causes losses from time to time." Should some ventures actually make money, "it is the will of the Reichsführer SS that profits from lucrative corporations be diverted to cover the losses of others. These must labor under the constraints of their non-capitalistic [*nicht privatwirtschaftliche*] end goals. At times these goals damn our corporations to years of future losses."[19] The German Earth and Stone Works would supposedly fulfill this mission by providing the raw materials necessary for the monuments to Hitler's rule. Blithe disregard for profitability and hopelessly vague pretensions to "culture" spurred the SS into a plethora of industries before war in 1939. Himmler's agrarian fantasies found expression in an Experiment Station for Alimentation, supposed to conduct scientific experiments. One improbable venture, as publicized by the SS newspaper *Das Schwarze Korps*, was a new "pepper mill" and greenhouse cultivation process supposed to enable Nazi Germany's "independence in spices."[20] This served the cause of autarky because spices came predominantly from English overseas colonies.

These efforts quickly displayed the same amateurish and fraudulent business practices typical of the first SS companies. Any concerted effort to centralize and professionalize SS management began only after these first ventures proved abject disasters. For example, the SS "Experiment Stations" ended up investing in bogus patents just as had the Loibl GmbH. And the brick machinery and kilns installed at Sachsenhausen were so faulty that fuel generators threatened to explode; the German Earth and Stone Works also invested in a newly invented brick-mold press before bothering to test available clay, which turned out to be unsuitable. In this company and in others, account books were penciled in on loose-leaf piles, if they were kept at all.

Starting in 1939, Oswald Pohl began to impose order. Pohl had joined Himmler only in 1933 after a successful career as a Navy paymaster, but he was a long-standing and ambitious Nazi who once remarked, "I was a National Socialist before National Socialism came into being."[21] From 1933 to 1938, Pohl worked tirelessly on administering the exponentially growing budgets of the SS. He was Himmler's most competent financial officer and had established cordial relations with the Reich Finance Ministry and the Reich Ministry of the Interior. He acted swiftly. In June 1939, he fired the original top managers of the German Earth and Stone Works (Arthur Ahrens and Clemens Tietjen), and by September he created the Administration and Business Main Office (*Verwaltungs und Wirtschaftshauptamt*, or VuWHA) in an effort to consolidate all SS enterprises. As a Main Office chief, he was responsible to Himmler alone, and he spent the bulk of 1939 cleaning house. In May, for instance, he also founded the German Equipment Works to coordinate "the special business enterprises ... in connection with the concentration camps."[22] These were the scattered workshops maintained ad hoc by the *Kommandanten*. Now they, too, would have to submit to centralized management. In late 1939 at Ravensbrück, a women's camp, Pohl also founded a garment factory because he deemed such industry most suitable for "women's work."

The Administration and Business Main Office recruited a young cadre of dedicated officers, mostly accountants and lawyers with experience in business law. In captivity after the war, some of these SS men described themselves as "new leading managers [who] came in many cases out of idealism to the economic undertakings of the VuWHA and did not allow themselves to be led astray from their motives. One believed that one could find something exemplary here."[23] They began to impose a limited measure of order upon industries that had, at first, been founded willy-nilly, often with embarrassing losses. By 26 July 1940, Pohl founded a long-promised holding company, christened the German Commercial Operations (*Deutsche Wirtschaftsbetriebe,* or DWB) for all SS enterprises. "The Führer Principle," he wrote to Reich ministries, "is applied in the industries of the SS with the same rigor and same effectiveness as in the [SS] administrative sector."[24] The German Commercial Operations registered carrying a loss of over 100,000 RM. Little more than a year later, on 4 September 1941, Pohl proudly announced the "final organizational form" of all these industrial enterprises, the culmination of a two-year effort. He stressed the "fulfillment of tasks that fall to the Reichsführer SS as the Chief of German Police, such as the concentration camp industries," including "leadership of corporations that promote the National Socialist world view [Weltanschauung]" and "tasks ordered by the Reichskommissar for the Reinforcement of Germandom."[25]

Phase 3: The New Order, War, and "Final Victory," 1939–1942

Pohl's efforts to clean up SS business practice had occurred in tandem with the outbreak of war. Like the rearmaments campaign of the mid-1930s, war now transformed the German Commercial Operations, but in ways that have rarely received the attention they deserve. In announcing the "final organizational form" of SS business enterprise, Pohl alluded to the Reichskommissar for the Reinforcement of Germandom (RKF), a grandiloquent title that fell to Himmler on 7 October 1939, shortly after the conquest of Poland. Himmler began to plan a vast ring of utopian Aryan settlements in German-occupied Poland. These would "surround" *(einkesseln)* native Polish and Jewish populations in order to "gradually crush them to death economically and biologically."[26]

Far from responding to pragmatic calculations of the war economy, Himmler and Pohl sought to expand the SS slave-labor empire well into 1942 in the name of this racial-supremacist social engineering project. In 1940 Himmler had named Pohl "General Trustee for Building Supply Production in the East."[27] The DWB founded the East German Building Supply Works to coordinate brick and cement factories seized from Jews. Likewise, the DWB also confiscated furniture companies from Jews in Bohemia and retooled them to produce "settler furniture." In January 1942, Himmler demanded the immediate expansion of the German Commercial Operations to meet a minimum of 80 percent of the settlement construction needs of the SS: "If we do not," Himmler warned, "we will never … get houses for our SS men in the Reich, nor will I, as Reichskommissar for the Reinforcement of Germandom, be able to erect the homes that we will need in order to make the East German."[28] To this end, by the summer of 1941, Pohl had reorganized the civil engineering corps of the SS by luring a top engineer from the Luftwaffe, Dr. Hans Kammler, who was hired as General Advisor for Settlement in the staff of the Reichskommissar for the Reinforcement of Germandom.[29]

By the beginning months of 1942, Pohl and Kammler had gone a long way toward a vertically integrated building combine. Hans Kammler's engineering corps would lead SS Building Brigades, meant to employ upwards of 160,000 prisoners: "POW's, Jews, and otherwise incarcerated foreigners, etc.," as Kammler himself put it.[30] Pohl and Kammler worked feverishly on this project in late 1941 and early 1942, submitting a budget of 13 billion Reichsmarks in January. Despite this sizable sum, Himmler asked Pohl and Kammler to think bigger. The scale of their plans is dumbfounding, especially when one considers that the German economy was in the midst of a painful transition to total war mobilization in the early months of 1942. Kammler, nonetheless, dutifully projected over double the initial volume for settlement building. Yet, Himmler's handwritten notes chided the engineer's needless parsimony: he crossed out an estimate of 20 to 30 billion Reichsmarks and penciled 80 to 120 billion in the margin.[31] This amounted to 50 percent or more of Germany's gross domestic product in 1942. By comparison, Germany's total industrial investment in 1942 was only 5.9 billion, a figure surpassed only in 1953. Even in 1955, total industrial investment was no larger than 9.3 billion.[32] Their final report reached Himmler on 5 March 1942.

The above also explains Himmler's well-known allusion to "great industrial projects" in his order to Richard Glücks, Inspector of Concentration Camps, on 26 January 1942: "[I]n the coming days I will send ... 100,000 Jews and up to 50,000 Jewesses. In the next few weeks the concentration camps will be assigned great industrial tasks. SS Major General Pohl will inform you of the details."[33] Historians have often suspected that Himmler's statement was mere camouflage, meant to conceal his real purpose of sending German Jews east to the killing camps. Likewise, others have speculated that the SS meant to use these Jewish workers in a bid to build up armaments factories in the concentration camps in order to transform itself into a self-contained "state within the state." In any case, there can be little doubt that Himmler intended these prisoners to serve the massive construction program for Aryan settlements proposed for the east.

This should not obscure the fact that the killing never ceased. In fact, slave labor and genocide continued simultaneously throughout the remaining years of the Nazi regime. It is important to note here that the 150,000 "Jews and Jewesses" referred to by Himmler represented only a small portion of even the Western European Jews. The SS never intended to set aside as many Jews for labor as it intended to murder outright, but this 150,000 almost exactly matched estimates for Kammler's newly proposed SS Building Brigades slated to build Himmler's racial supremacist utopia in the east.

In their most megalomaniacal dimensions, these visions of racial imperialism became known as the New Order. Himmler's ambitions were limited only by the advance of German arms, and quickly encompassed the conquered territory of the Soviet Union as well. Kammler and Pohl were to build the New Order using slave labor. Only with a completely integrated slave labor empire, Himmler believed, could the racial and cultural mission of the SS succeed after the war:

> The war will have no meaning when, 20 years hence, we have not undertaken a totally German settlement of the occupied territories.... If we do not provide the bricks here, if we do not fill our camps full with slaves [to] build our cities, our towns, our farmsteads, we will not have the money after the long

years of war in order to furnish the settlements in such a fashion that truly German men can live in them and can take root in the first generation.[34]

In 1940–1941, the SS founded Maidanek near Lublin, Auschwitz in Upper Silesia, and Stutthof near Danzig. From the beginning, the DWB integrated slave labor with regional plans for Aryan settlements. Stutthof alone, the smallest of the three camps, foresaw space for twenty-five thousand prisoners; this in itself would have doubled the previous captive labor force of the Inspectorate of Concentration Camps, "with whom we can then complete the build-up of settlements in the Gau Danzig-West Prussia," as Himmler put it.[35] The German Commercial Operations expanded the Allach porcelain works by confiscating the Victoria AG from Jewish owners in Bohemia and Moravia. Allach began firing practical items for everyday use to augment its former specialization in SS memorabilia and kitsch. The pull of the New Order was further evident in preexisting industries that had little to do with building supply. The Textile and Leather Utilization GmbH (Textil- und Lederverwertung GmbH, or TexLed), for example, still sought to contribute straw mats "for the purposes of shading residential gardens" as well as matting for plaster work and facades.[36]

Phase 4: Total War, 1942–1945

The more grandiose the "peace-building" plans of Pohl, Kammler, and Himmler became, the more grim Germany's prospects in war became. As already mentioned, Kammler and Pohl generated their plans and budgets amidst a general transition to total war, and the total mobilization of the economy redirected the industrial empire of the SS one final time. Nevertheless, there were some disturbing continuities: the handmaiden of SS influence in the German economy remained Albert Speer. In February 1942, Hitler appointed Speer to the position of Reich Minister for Armaments and Munitions.

Fritz Todt, Speer's predecessor, had paid a visit to Hitler on 8 February. Most secondhand accounts of this meeting suggest that he wished to impress upon Hitler that Germany was hopelessly outmatched by the combined industrial might of the United States, the Soviet Union, and Great Britain. This news was so unpalatable that the two ended up in a shouting contest. After the meeting, Todt's plane mysteriously crashed, killing him instantly. Although many speculate that he was sabotaged as the bearer of bad tidings, most evidence suggests nothing more than an accident.[37] Whatever the substance of Todt's meeting with Hitler, however, it is certain that big, structural changes in the German war economy were afoot. Speer would carry them out.

After 1945, Speer claimed to be an architect and artist, but he hardly arrived in the armaments ministry as a freelance aesthete. By 1942, he had already long proven his skill in exactly those areas that suited him for the centralized direction of industry. For years he had coordinated tight timetables for the production and delivery of raw materials on construction projects such as the monumental "Führer Buildings." Like Todt, he understood the complexity and inseparability of machines, labor, and organization, and he managed all effectively. Human labor remained "the only completely unsolved administrative problem in my newly erected house," as Speer commented upon his appointment as Minister for Armaments and Munitions.[38] Hitler recognized this as well, and, less than two weeks after Speer's entry into office, the Eastern Workers Decrees laid the foundation for the forced conscription of Eastern European civilians (the Reich Labor Action). Thus, the transition to total war intensified the pace of industrial production and, at the same time, escalated the coercion used by German management. Thus, by the spring of 1942, the armaments ministry and private German companies had already begun to travel down the "twisted road to Auschwitz," a road they and the SS would litter with corpses.

Key figures within Speer's armaments ministry soon approached the SS for potential partnerships in joint slave-labor ventures. Until this time, German corporations had made few contacts with SS companies and, as a rule, a peculiar breed of company had first entered what few dealings there were. Typically, these were other state-owned or at least state-controlled corporations. During 1941, noteworthy SS-corporate involvement was limited to the construction of a light-metals foundry for Volkswagen (owned by the German Workers Front of Robert Ley), an aircraft engine works of Steyr-Daimler-Puch at Graz, a subsidiary of the Hermann-Göring Works, and the Heinkel Aircraft Works in Oranienburg near Sachsenhausen. Heinkel had been a private corporation but came under state ownership in the 1930s. The most well known case of slave labor in the German war economy, IG Farben's synthetic rubber factory at Auschwitz, remains the exception that proves the rule. IG Farben was a private cartel, but its synthetic fuel and rubber programs relied almost entirely on state contracts. Thus, all firms outside the SS that deployed concentration camp prisoners had become almost entirely the creatures of National Socialist economic policy.

These first projects also followed a distinct pattern: they were initiated by individuals outside both the SS and the regular channels of the armaments ministry. German managers often sought personal deals with the SS, arranged as favors among a few individuals, in what we might now call networking. When approached, Himmler would usually promise the moon and the stars, but Pohl and the IKL could seldom deliver, and usually disappointed all involved. Nevertheless, public and private corporations kept asking for more slave labor. In fact, the historian Mark Spoerer, who surveyed thirty-three known case histories of industries that employed concentration camp prisoners, found only one, the Akkumulatorenfabrik AG Stöcken, a battery factory for U-boats, in which any evidence suggests that the SS or any state authority forced a firm to deploy slave labor against its will. On the other hand, twenty-two, including sixteen private corporations, eventually initiated such dealings of their own accord. It also bears mention that the evidence in the case of the Akkumulatorenfabrik AG is extraordinarily weak and stems from postwar interrogations in which the firm's managers claimed that SS men pressured them into war crimes.[39]

Speer's armaments ministry approached the concentration camps in the consistent pattern set in late 1941 by Volkswagen, IG Farben, Heinkel, and Steyr-Daimler-Puch. In other words, the armaments industry, not Himmler or Pohl, took the initiative. A top official from Speer's ministry, Walter Schieber, expressly stated to the chief of the SS Main Office, Gottlob Berger, that he wanted to work with the SS "in all possible ways," and it was Schieber who laid the groundwork for pilot factories at Neuengamme and Buchenwald by the first weeks of March 1942.[40] At the same time, on 3 March, Himmler ordered Pohl to incorporate the Inspectorate of Concentration Camps within his existing main offices.

After declaring the "final organizational form" of all SS industrial enterprises in late 1941, Pohl planned a consolidation of his offices in early 1942, announcing the new Business Administration Main Office (*Wirtschaftsverwaltungshauptamt*, or WVHA), on 1 February 1942. This Main Office initially merged the Main Office of Budgets and Buildings, formerly Pohl's office for construction and financial budgets, and the SS companies under Pohl's Administration and Business Main Office. The Inspector of Concentration Camps had remained autonomous since its founding and was markedly absent from Pohl's deliberations of December and January. Thus, Himmler's order to take over the concentration camps was a new initiative meant to create a slave labor preserve for the German war effort. The IKL became the Office Group D of the WVHA.

Pohl greeted this new initiative with enthusiasm: "[T]he fetters of discoordinated administration must be shed in the concentration camps and will be hailed everywhere as progress."[41] The WVHA initially promised Speer twenty-five thousand prisoners, a large number, but still a minority of the prisoners the SS had intended to dedicate to the Building Brigades and its own German Commercial Operations, or DWB.[42] But by the fall of 1942 and early 1943, despite initial optimism on both sides, initial pilot projects had already grown increasingly dubious, largely due to incompetent management in the SS. Each party began to blame the other for delays and mishaps. Small wonder, then, that a small carbine assembly plant at Buchenwald, scheduled for start-up in April 1942, proved "technically impossible" by June.[43] By 20 September, Speer actually asked Hitler to limit SS influence in these affairs: "I have called to the Führer's attention that I see in the demands of RFSS Himmler a desire to exercise a measurable influence over [concentration-camp] factories.... The Führer agrees that the RFSS expects to derive advantages for the equipment of his military divisions by putting CC prisoners at the disposal of armaments industries."[44]

The vexed relationship between Speer and the SS has created the abiding impression, promoted by no one more than Speer himself, that the SS was intent upon making a bid to become "independent in armaments," and that Speer played a near-heroic role for preventing this. To the contrary, neither Speer nor Himmler ever broke off their "dangerous embrace." Moreover, Himmler's overarching motives never really changed, even as he sought to put SS labor reserves at the disposal of the German war effort. In 1943, he wrote to Speer with some irritation regarding continuing troubles at the carbine factory at Buchenwald:

> I have clarified once again to these gentlemen [the managers of the carbine factory] that in the coming peace I have completely different ambitions than to become a competitor in this sector. I see the tasks of the SS in peacetime, as you well know, in the area of settlements and every other sector where I might promote families well endowed with children and whose healthy lives I might encourage.[45]

If Himmler's motives remained more or less constant, so too did Speer's. As at the year's beginning, so too in September of 1942 a relentless labor shortage continued to draw the Armaments Minister toward the concentration camps' labor reserves. September had thrown the entire German war effort into tumult. The Plenipotentiary for the Reich Labor Action, Fritz Sauckel, first began to miss promised deliveries of conscripted Eastern European workers. Summer offensives had stalled. Everyone sought new solutions to long-standing problems. If Speer would have us believe that he was heading off SS "infiltration," it is curious that five days before his late September meetings with Hitler, Speer also received Oswald Pohl and the chief of SS engineers, Hans Kammler, with whom it "was agreed upon that inmates of concentration camps will be made available for armaments industries."[46] Speer's September discussions were part of plans to recruit, not curb, the SS slave labor empire.

Pohl's own report to Himmler of meetings with Speer expressed enthusiastic cooperation: "Reich Minister Speer expects the immediate mobilization of fifty thousand Jews who are fit to work."[47] Speer was now asking for twice the number of prisoners promised in the spring, which the SS had never been able to deliver. Regarding these fifty thousand Jews, Pohl added cynically: "The necessary laborers, primarily from Auschwitz … who are fit to work must therefore interrupt their immigration to the east and undertake some armaments work."[48] It is therefore no accident that Speer approved the release of scarce building materials for the expansion of Auschwitz at this very meeting. Though the memorandum does mention "SS Armaments Works" to be enclosed within the concentration camps, conspicuously absent in Pohl's own internal memorandum to Himmler is any reference to intentions to make SS companies the direct and sole suppliers of the Waffen SS.

Only one thing had changed, and this was Himmler's grim recognition that "final victory," and thus the SS's cherished "Peace Building Program," was still a long way off. Now, like many other German industrial enterprises, the German Commercial Operations sought to preserve their capacity by serving the war effort in order to reconvert to a "normal" peace economy after total war had ended. The radical difference lay in what vision of "peace" the SS had in mind. On the other hand, here too Speer proved accommodating. Only half of Pohl's communication about his meetings with Speer's ministry in September dealt with armaments, while exclamation points sprinkled the second half, far overreaching any excitement over proposed "SS Armaments Works": "We are ready! I have discussed the organization of Building Brigades [with Speer]…. In our Building Brigades I see the beginnings of our later Peace Building Brigades that will develop and build. It will

Work!"[49] The German Earth and Stone Works would also supply roofing tiles and bricks; the German Equipment Works, another SS company, would provide window and door frames. In this way the SS could help repair damaged cities in the short term while building up its capacity to embark upon settlement construction after "final victory." The long-term intentions of the SS never wavered.

Ironically, SS corporations proved unable to navigate this transition and swiftly declined in importance. The SS's furniture factories increasingly emphasized practical bunks, tables, and beds for barracks instead of "settlement furniture," and they also secured contracts to manufacture casings for airplane radios. The Allach Porcelain Manufacture made perhaps the most absurd statement regarding the German Commercial Operations' transition to total war. Its top manager, Rudolf Dippe, reported, "The production of war-essential dishes and crockery in the year 1943 corresponds to 52.1 percent of total output."[50] But such things were hardly "decisive" for the war effort. By 1944, his chief auditor wrote, "The result of our audits is clear; the SS companies are insolvent."[51] In 1938–1939, Oswald Pohl had taken over insolvent SS enterprises in an effort to impose central coordination. By war's end, Pohl and the DWB ended where they had begun.

Nevertheless, it would be a mistake to consider the WVHA merely a bit player in the German war economy. Although SS factories contributed but little to that economy, private industry and the armaments ministry alike came to the SS as slave labor lord, especially in 1944. The chief manager of labor allocations, Gerhard Maurer, received glowing praise. "It has been reported to me that we owe the smooth operation of this action [the SS Labor Action] essentially to your competence and cooperation," wrote the head of German aircraft production in the spring of 1943.[52] "[I]n the last weeks I have had to rely upon the support of SS-Colonel Maurer ... almost daily," another manager wrote to Pohl, "I feel it is my duty to communicate to you that without the before mentioned support the full operations could never have been mastered at its current level, not even close."[53] Hans Kammler, chief of SS engineers, helped build underground armaments factories, among them the caverns in the Harz Mountains where the V-2 rockets were manufactured. Karl Otto Saur, an engineer and armaments ministry official who had originally expressed reluctance to work with the SS in 1942, praised Kammler in no less glowing terms than did those who praised Maurer: "It is clear that the assignments of Kammler must continue with all the energy of this man."[54] Joseph Goebbels wrote in his diary, "In the deployment of these new weapons one must recognize that it is always only one individual who has really achieved a great and unique thing ... Kammler."[55] This was an all too typical SS relationship with private corporations and Nazi ministries seeking slave labor.

The Business of Genocide

The foregoing analysis only suggests how slave labor in the Third Reich had become a business of genocide. Slavery was directly tied to the Holocaust and could not have functioned without the constant influx and "liquidation" of prisoners. Of course, all laborers worked under the threat of the concentration camps, which anchored the German war effort much like the Gulag system did for the Soviet Union, providing a powerful negative incentive in an economy that had few positive incentives to offer. But slave labor became a business of genocide in much more direct ways than this. The SS maintained its camps in a constant state of deterioration; sanitation was poor at best, the food supply miserable. In fact, already by the summer of 1941, epidemics and the attrition of inmates had caused a labor shortage within the SS's own DWB, in spite of the relatively small scale of operations at that time that was estimated at a maximum of sixty thousand total working prisoners (while later the SS Labor Action encompassed up to seven hundred thousand).

The SS compensated for this by organizing both the constant influx of new prisoners in tandem with systematic killing. By late 1942, Gerhard Maurer and the Inspector of Concentration Camps ordered camp doctors to remove and replace weak, sick, or injured prisoners. The fate that awaited them was common knowledge. As a foreman once snorted to a Jewish laborer near Auschwitz, "Whether you stinking Jews work or not, you'll go one way or another into the crematorium and go through the oven."[56] The SS thus coupled the preservation of working prisoners with the liquidation of the sick and weak. Hans Kammler serves as an example once again. He and his subordinates were well aware that they could complete their projects only by using absolute terror. When a member of Speer's ministry complained that prisoners had sought to escape a labor detail, Kammler retorted: "It's always the case with these people [i.e., prisoners] when they notice that they are not being driven hard enough. I let 30 hang in special treatment [*Sonderbehandlung*]. Since the hanging, things proceed in a little better order. It's the old joke: if people notice that they are not being held in a firm grip, then they try to get away with all possible things."[57] Although not all private firms emulated the SS, many did. That the National Socialist state managed industrial work in tandem with murder (murder that was itself no less industrialized) still remains part of the abiding uniqueness of the Holocaust.

Notes

1. Rudolf Vrba, *I Cannot Forgive* (New York: Grove Press, 1986), 266.

2. Robert Koehl, *The Black Corps: The Structure and Power Struggles of the Nazi SS* (Madison: University of Wisconsin Press, 1983), 170.

3. Wisselinck, "Ernährung und Ausbildung der Lehrlinge: Deutsche Erd- und Stein-werke Grantiwerk Gross-Rosen," 2–7 March 1944, United States National Archives Microfilm Collection (hereafter USNA): T-976, Roll 18.

4. Wisselinck, "Die SS-Siedlungen bzw. die Werksiedlungen in den wirtschaftlichen Unternehmungen der Schutstaffel," 17 May 1944, USNA: T-976, Roll 18.

5. Enno Georg, *Die wirtschaftlichen Unternehmungen der SS* (Stuttgart: Deutsche Verlags-Anstalt, 1963), 15.

6. Koehl, *The Black Korps,* 170.

7. Wisselinck, "Die SS-Siedlungen bzw. die Werksiedlungen in den wirtschaftlichen Unternehmungen der Schutstaffel," 17 May 1944, USNA: T-976, Roll 18.

8. Nuremberg Trial Documents—Nazi Organizations (hereafter NO)-1016, Leo Volk, "Organisation und Aufgaben der Amtsgruppe W." In the trial Protocol 58, prosecutor Robins stated that this report was written for Leo Volk by Heinz Fanslau. NO-1016 includes a cover letter by Fanslau, who sent the manifesto in Volk's absence, but it is unclear that Fanslau wrote the document alone. It is likely that the two men (or more) collaborated.

9. Unsigned reports and balance sheets on Anton Loibl GmbH cover the years 1936–1941. NO-542 Salpeter, undated (mid-1939), "Tasks, Organization and Finance Plan of Office III-W of the RFSS."

10. NO-542 Salpeter, "Tasks, Organization and Finance Plan of Office III-W of the RFSS."

11. Staatssekretär des RJM-Berlin, Dr. Jur. Roland Freisler, "Arbeitseinsatz im Straf-vollzug"(Title Article for 13 September 1940), *Deutsche Justiz* 102 (1940): 1021–1025.

12. Theodor Eicke, 1 October 1933, "Disziplinar- u. Strafordnung für das Gefangenen-lager (Dachau)" and "Dienstvorschriften für die Begleitpersonen und Gefangenen-bewachung," Bundesarchiv Potsdam (hereafter BAP) Microfilm PL5: 42053.

13. Here and below I follow the analysis of Karin Orth, *Das System der national-sozialistischen Konzentrationslager. Eine politische Organisationsgeschichte* (Hamburg: Hamburger Edition HIS Verlagsgesellschaft, 1999), esp. 32–33.

14. See Michael Burleigh and Wolfgang Wippermann, *The Racial State: Germany, 1933–1945* (New York: Cambridge University Press, 1991).

15. Walter Salpeter to Reichsfinanzministerium Dr. Asseyar, 5 February 1941, "Steuerpflicht der DEST," USNA: T-976, Roll 25.

16. Thüringen's regional Interior Minister, Hellmuth Gommlich, from 24 April 1937, quoted in Paul Jaskot, *The Architecture of Oppression: The SS, Forced Labor and the Nazi Monumental Building Economy* (New York: Routledge, 2000), 21. Here and below I follow much of Jaskot's analysis.

17. Gregor Janssen, *Das Ministerium Speer. Deutschlands Rüstung im Krieg* (Berlin: Verlag Ullstein, 1968).

18. Reichsschatzmeister, 17 June 1938, "Kreditbeschaffung für Zwecke der Klinkerwerke Buchenwald bei Weimar," Institut für Zeitgeschichte (hereafter IfZ), Fa 183. Undated report (1940), "DESt," Bundesarchiv Koblenz (hereafter BAK), NS3/625.

19. Pohl to Reichskommissar für die Preisbildung, 19 September 1941, "Erklärung nach §22 KWVO der dem VuWHA angeschlossenen Gesellschaften," USNA: T-976, Roll 3.

20. "SS erschließt Neuland. Wo in Deutschland der Pfeffer wächst," *Das Schwarze Korps*, 22 September 1938, 4.

21. NO-1224, Oswald Pohl, 24 June 1932, "Why am I a National Socialist and why an SA man?"

22. NO-542, Salpeter, undated (mid-1939), "Tasks, Organization and Finance Plan of Office III-W of the RFSS."

23. "Mindener Bericht," printed in Walter Naasner, *SS-Wirtschaft und SS-Verwaltung. 'Das SS-Wirtschafts-Verwaltungshauptamt und die unter seiner Dienstaufsicht stehenden wirtschaftlichen Unternehmungen' und weitere Dokumente* (Düsseldorf: Droste, 1998), 78.

24. Pohl to Reichskommissar für die Preisbildung, 19 September 1941, "Erklärung nach §22 KWVO der dem VuWHA angeschlossenen Gesellschaften," USNA: T-976, Roll 3. This was prepared by Hans Hohberg.

25. Dr. Leo Volk, signed by Pohl, 4 September 1941, "Stichworte zu den Ausführungen des Gruppenführers für die Ansprache bei der Amtschefsitzung," USNA: T-976, Roll 35. See also, Volk to Pohl, 1 September 1941, "Umorganisation der Ämter," T-976, Roll 35. Noteworthy is the absence of any armaments factories or mention of self-sufficiency for the W-SS, which the SS was neither striving for nor interested in.

26. SS officer quoted in Josef Marszalek, *Majdanek: Konzentrationslager Lublin* (Warsaw: Verlag Interpress, 1984), 18.

27. NO-1043, Leo Volk (?), undated, from 1940, "Generaltreuhändlers für Baustofferzeugungsstätten im Ostraum im Jahre 1940."

28. Himmler, reply to Pohl and Kammler, 31 January 1942, BAK: NS19: 2065. Note here again the total absence of preoccupation with SS armaments factories.

29. Wolff to Gen. Kastner-Kirdorf, Chef d. Luftwaffenpersonalamtes, 6 March 1941, Berlin Document Center (hereafter BDC): SS Personal-Akte Hans Kammler. "Gutachten" from 31 May 1941 signed by the Reichsminister der Luftfahrt und Oberbefehlshaber der Luftwaffe, Luftwaffenverwaltungsamt, BDC SS Personal-Akte Hans Kammler. Kammler must have agreed to work for the HAHB immediately (for his official personnel card lists him as an officer of the Amt II already in August 1940).

30. NO-1292, Kammler to Glücks, 10 March 1942, "Einsatz von Häftlingen, Kriegsgefangenen, Juden usw. für die Durchführung des Bauprogrammes des SS-WVHA, Amtsgruppe C 1942."

31. Himmler's notes on Kammler to Himmler, 10 February 1942, "Aufstellung von SS-Baubrigaden für die Durchführung von Bauaufgaben des RFSS im Kriege und Frieden," BAK: NS19/2065.

32. I thank Mark Spoerer for these estimates of German gross domestic product. See also Christoph Buchheim, "Die Wirtschaftsentwicklung im Dritten Reich: mehr Desaster als Wunder. Eine Erwiderung auf Werner Abelshauser," *Vierteljahrshefte für Zeitgeschichte* 49 (2001): 659.

33. Himmler to Richard Glücks, 26 January 1942, BDC: Hängeordner 643. See also Arthur Liebehenschel to all *Konzentrationslager,* 19 January 1942, "Überstellung von Juden," printed in Harry Stein, *Juden in Buchenwald* (Weimar: Gedenkstätte Buchenwald, 1992), 119. This decree orders the immediate transfer of the "number of Jews able to work to the POW Camp Lublin as reported by teletype" (received on the 26th). It mentions a teletype from 8 December. Note that this predated serious talks of *Konzentrationslager* armaments works with Speer or Walter Schieber. I thank Peter Witte for providing this document.

34. Himmler's speech on 9 June 1942, quoted in Götz Aly, *'Endlösung': Völkerverschiebung und der Mord an den europäischen Juden.* (Frankfurt am Main: S. Fischer, 1995), 292.

35. Himmler to Pohl, 19 December 41, BAK, NS 3/52, quoted in Orth, *Das System der nationalsozialistischen Konzentrationslager,* 154–156.

36. Amtsrat Scheck, "Vermerk über die Gesellschaft für Textil- und Lederverwertung, GmbH. Dachau und Ravensbrück," BAP: 23.01 Rechnungshof des Deutschen Reiches: 5636. See also NO-1918, Georg Lörner and Volk to Reichsjustizministerium, 21 March 1942. Compare a similar statement about the SS Kleiderkasse, which was managed by the same men. "Kleiderkasse der Schutzstaffel," 23 June 1941, BAK: NS3/954.

37. Franz Seidler, *Fritz Todt: Baumeister des Dritten Reiches* (Frankfurt am Main: Verlag Ullstein, 1988), 365–391.

38. Janssen, *Das Ministerium Speer,* 63.

39. Spoerer, "Profitierten Unternehmen von KZ-Arbeit? eine kritische Analyse der Literatur." *Historische Zeitschrift* 268 (1999): 84. Compare Hans-Hermann Schröder, "Das erste Konzentrationslager in Hannover: das Lager bei der Akkumulatorenfabrik in Stöcken," in *Konzentrationslager in Hannover: KZ-Arbeit und Rüstungsindustrie in der Spätphase des Zweiten Weltkriegs, Teil I,* ed. Rainer Fröbe et al. (Hildesheim: August Lax, 1985), 52–54, and also Dokumentenanhang, 3–5, 590–593, which emphasizes all the initiative of armaments ministry official Walter Schieber.

40. NO-2448, Gottlob Berger to Himmler, 22 April 1942. NO-421, Walter Schieber, 17 March 1942, "Vermerk: Ausnutzung des KZ-Lagers Neuengamme." Janssen, *Das Ministerium Speer,* 97–98. NO-2468, Schieber to Saur, 20 March 42. Later, the armaments ministry added a flack gun at Auschwitz, a signaling device at Ravensbrück, and a pistol assembly at Neuengamme.

41. R-129, Pohl's report to Himmler, 30 April 1942.

42. NO-2549, Schieber, 20 March 1942, "Verlegung von Rüstungsfertigung in Konzentrationslager."

43. Pister to D2, 14 June 1942, "Arbeitszeiten der Häftlinge," in *Buchenwald. Mahnung und Verpflichtung*, ed. Walter Bartel et al. (Berlin: Kongress Verlag, 1960), 236–237. NO-598, Heinrich Himmler to Pohl, 7 July 1942 and reply 8 September 1942. Speer, 28 June 1942, "Chronik der Dienststellen," BAK: R3/1736, hereafter cited as "Chronik."

44. Cited after Willi Boelcke, *Deutschlands Rüstung im Zweiten Weltkrieg: Hitlers Konferenzen mit Albert Speer 1942–1945* (Frankfurt am Main: Akademische Verlagsgesellschaft, 1969), 187–188.

45. Himmler to Speer, 5 March 1943, USNA: T-175, Roll 73.

46. "Chronik," 15 September 1942.

47. Nuremberg Trial Documents—Nazi Industrialists (hereafter NI)-15392, Pohl to Himmler, memorandum of meeting on 15 September 1942 with Speer, Pohl, Schieber, Saur, Minsterialrat Steffen, Ministerialrat Briese, Kammler, 16 September 1942, "Rüstungsarbeiten. Bombenschäden."

48. Ibid. See also Florian Freund, Bertrand Perz, and Karl Stuhlpfarrer, "Der Bau des Vernichtungslagers Auschwitz-Birkenau," *Zeitgeschichte* 20 (1993): 194.

49. Ibid. A report one year later lists all of the SS independent industrial endeavors, none of which was an armaments firm: NO-551, unsigned, 30 September 1943, "Die Wirtschaftsunternehmungen der Schutzstaffel."

50. Albert Knoll, "Die Porzellanmanufaktur München-Allach: Das Lieblingskind von Heinrich Himmler," *Dachauer Hefte* 15 (1999): 124.

51. Cited after Walter Naasner, *Neue Machtzentren in der deutschen Kriegswirtschaft 1942–45* (Boppard am Rhein: Harald Boldt Verlag, 1994), 394.

52. Erhard Milch to Maurer, 13 April 1943, USNA: T-175, Roll 80.

53. NI-315, Budin's letter included in Pohl to Himmler, 17 October 1944.

54. Jägerstabbesprechung, 1 May 1944, Bundesarchiv-Militärarchiv (hereafter BAMA): RL3/6.

55. From 31 March 1945, in Elke Fröhlich, ed., *Die Tagebücher von Josef Goebbels*, Band 15 (Munich: Institut für Zeitgeschichte, 1987), 647.

56. Kommandoführer to Schutzhaftlagerführer KL Au. III, 20 April 1944, "Meldung wegen Wachvergehen," State Museum Auschwitz-Birkenau in Oswiecim, D-Au III/Golleschau, vol. 3.

57. Jägerstabbesprechung, 2 May 44, BAMA: RL3/6.

Chapter Five

CORPORATE SOCIAL RESPONSIBILITY AND THE ISSUE OF COMPENSATION
The Case of Ford and Nazi Germany

Simon Reich

THE CONVENTIONAL USE and widespread acceptance of the concept of corporate social responsibility has only become more popular globally in the course of the last decade. The whole notion fuses questions of accountability and ethics with that of transparency in influencing the behavior of major corporations in their role as conduits for progressive change. While there is skepticism expressed regarding the importance of multinational corporations as global actors in some elements of the international political economy literature, scholars, policy makers, and multilateral institutions have generally come to regard corporations as engines of prosperity and, indirectly, of democracy.[1]

In essence, corporate social responsibility asserts that major corporations have more dimensions to their role than purely the economic one of satisfying stockholder demands. Through their behavior, they may also choose to contribute to maintaining political stability, to the provision of public welfare services, and to addressing social and developmental problems across the globe. In many of the world's poorer countries, multinational corporations have a greater capacity to administer educational and medical services, feed and clothe populations, and ensure that rights are respected than do the governments who rule those countries.

The notion and underlying code of ethics generally described as corporate social responsibility attempts to imbue corporations with three core values: transparency, accountability, and integrity. Collectively, they

PHOTOGRAPH 1: Reichsführer-SS Heinrich Himmler tours the Monowitz-Buna building site in the company of SS officers and IG Farben engineers. Pictured in the front row from left to right are: Rudolf Brandt, Heinrich Himmler, Max Faust, and Rudolf Höss. Faust, who was an IG Farben engineer, was head of building operations at Monowitz-Buna. 17–18 July 1942. *Source:* United States Holocaust Memorial Museum

PHOTOGRAPH 2: The Deutsche Bank building in Cologne decorated with Nazi flags and a sign that reads: "One Reich, One People, One Leader," perhaps in honor of Austria's unification with Germany. March–April 1938. *Source:* United States Holocaust Memorial Museum

PHOTOGRAPH 3: Baldur von Schirach, accompanied by German military officers, reviews a newly opened industrial complex for the construction of automobiles in Breslau. From left to right: Undersecretary Generalmajor von Schell, von Schirach, and Reichsminister Graf Lutz Schwerin-Krossigk. 23 September 1941. *Source:* United States Holocaust Memorial Museum

PHOTOGRAPH 4: Prisoners at work in the BMW plane engine factory in Allach. Here they measure the cylinders in the final control examinations. 1940–1945. *Source:* Bayerische Motoren Werke via the United States Holocaust Memorial Museum

PHOTOGRAPH 5: Prisoners working on a rifle production line in the SS-owned munitions factory at Dachau, 1943–1944.

Source: KZ Gedenkstätte Dachau via the United States Holocaust Memorial Museum

PHOTOGRAPH 6: View of the Siemens factory chimney in the forced labor camp at Bobrek, a sub-camp of Auschwitz. Circa 1944. *Source:* United States Holocaust Memorial Museum

PHOTOGRAPH 7: View of the Monowitz-Buna complex at Auschwitz. After January 1945. *Source:* Panstwowe Muzeum w Oswiecim-Brzezinka via the United States Holocaust Memorial Museum

PHOTOGRAPH 8: View of Ford-Werke plant at Cologne, with Rhine River on right. 1939. *Source:* Ford Motor Company

PHOTOGRAPH 9: Ford-Werke truck, concealed by camouflage netting, produced at the Cologne plant for the German military under wartime production orders. Circa 1944. *Source:* Ford Motor Company

PHOTOGRAPH 10: Postwar photograph of wartime artillery damage and damaged trucks at Ford-Werke plant in Cologne. 1945. *Source:* Ford Motor Company

PHOTOGRAPH 11: Postwar photograph of forced labor barracks at Ford-Werke plant in Cologne. Circa 1945.
Source: Ford Motor Company

PHOTOGRAPH 12: Dr. Kurt Schmitt (1886–1950), general director of Allianz, 1921–1933. Circa 1925.
Source: Allianz AG

PHOTOGRAPH 13: General Director Hans Hess making a speech to employees assembled at the jubilee meeting to celebrate the 50th anniversary of Allianz. 29 May 1940.
Source: Allianz AG

PHOTOGRAPH 14: The Allianz headquarters on Mohrenstrasse 63/64 in Berlin after being severely damaged during Allied air raids on Berlin in 1944 and 1945. 1945.
Source: Allianz AG

Der Allianz-Adler

FELDPOST-NACHRICHTENDIENST
DER ALLIANZ-BETRIEBSGEMEINSCHAFTEN

Nummer 2	Berlin, September / Dezember 1943	1. Jahrgang

Kämpfer

Ölgemälde von Rudolf Lipus, Leipzig, auf der Großen Deutschen Kunstausstellung München 1943

IN DAS NEUE KAMPFJAHR 1944

Liebe Arbeitskameradinnen und -kameraden! Wieder geht ein Kriegsjahr zu Ende. Eine gewaltige Kraftentfaltung hat das deutsche Volk gezeigt. Unsere herrliche Wehrmacht hat unerhörte Ruhmestaten vollbracht, die in die Geschichte als einmalige Leistungen eingehen werden, und die Heimat kann dem Heldentum deutscher Soldaten zu Lande, zu Wasser und in der Luft ihren Dank vorläufig nur durch treueste Pflichterfüllung und unermüdliche Arbeit abstatten. Darum bedenke ein jeder, wie klein

1

PHOTOGRAPH 15: *The Allianz Eagle Military Postal Information Service* was sent to drafted employees of Allianz in the German military on a regular basis. 1944.
Source: Allianz AG

lie at the heart of what is more commonly described as good governance. Why these three? Well, they are values consistent with democratic government. Transparency focuses on what corporations do in terms of their employment and social practices, why they take the actions they do, and how these policies are implemented. Corporations invoking the concept of accountability attempt to defuse accusations that they stand outside the jurisdiction of national and international legislative bodies. Rather, accountability suggests that corporations are subject to more than the interests of their major shareholders; they are also subject to the rule of law, and are answerable to the court of public opinion. Finally, integrity portrays corporations as engaging in ethical conduct that extends beyond the immediate self-interest of any company to a broader set of enlightened values, particularly in areas of environmental degradation and labor practices.

Nonetheless, questions regarding contemporary corporate conduct proliferate. Just one notable example is the recent accusations publicly leveled against major American retailers suggesting that they knowingly purchased goods from suppliers who abused female sweatshop laborers in Saipan who had been lured from all over Asia by false promises of high wages.[2] As if such questions are not complex enough when dealing with current issues, corporations are now subject to comparable questions being raised about their behavior in the (extended) past. Inquiries regarding their exploitation of slave or forced labor, for example, have come into distinct focus, as have concerns about theft. It is the glare of globalization with the greater flow and transparency of information, however, which now subjects corporations more than ever to the court of public opinion and to the power of consumer purchasing patterns influenced by social concerns.

We are often told that corporations, as they move about the globe, are now freer of the bonds of government regulation than ever before.[3] Perhaps paradoxically, then, it is the very growth of direct investment by foreign corporations in the United States that has also created a new degree of corporate vulnerability. The existence of such foreign corporate assets, available for confiscation should court rulings go against the firms, has created the opportunity for plaintiffs from both within and outside of the United States to exercise greater financial leverage against both domestic and foreign corporations found culpable of transgressing U.S. law. The advent of new technologies such as the Internet ensures that evidence of corporate malpractice is presented to an audience on a global scale.

When shifting public attitudes are fused with greater accountability and awareness than ever before, the understandable temptation is to revisit and adjudge past corporate behavior. The purpose is often to establish whether compensation is due for corporate complicity in the confiscation of property, for abusive labor practices, or for environmental degradation. Although not the first of its kind, perhaps the landmark series of cases in this regard may be the claims brought against Swiss banks by former account holders whose possessions were seized during and in the aftermath of the Holocaust.[4] Public clamor, heightened by evidence of the banks' tampering with and destroying evidence, served only to further persuade a skeptical audience of the banks' guilt. But the importance of the episode, in retrospect, could arguably be the galvanizing effect of the Swiss banks cases on other comparable claimant cases. Many of these extend beyond the realm associated with the Holocaust to include issues of land confiscation, colonialism and, most recently, claims made by African-Americans for compensation for slavery.

Examples more clearly linked to the genesis of the Swiss banks cases concern those of German banks, such as the Deutsche Bank, and of insurance companies, such as Allianz, both discussed so extensively and effectively elsewhere in this volume. Perhaps a more complex and interesting set of cases involves the accusation of reluctant assistance, if not enthusiastic collaboration, leveled against the subsidiaries of American firms that, at least in name, operated in Germany during the Nazi period. Initiated by a combination of BBC reports and a provocative article in the *Washington Post*,[5] questions were raised on the public agenda regarding the possible collaboration in the Nazi war effort by two major American automobile producers, Ford and General Motors. Simultaneously, a lawsuit brought the issue to the legal system.[6] It is in the context of the case of Ford, as an illustration of the type of questions involved, that this essay examines the issue of the culpability of American firms in the German military effort.

Two Issues Intertwine

The question of the role of American firms in the Nazi war effort, in a sense, meets at a crossroads of two themes. The first, already mentioned, concerns that of corporate social responsibility. What does the concept imply? What does it entail? In the context of globalization, the power and influence of states has largely been adjudged to be in retreat.[7] While national legislatures retain many of their traditional roles associated with taxation, security, and welfare, an increasing number of the crucial decisions affecting the health, safety, and prosperity of the world's citizens are decided by international convention, by international organizations, and by dynamic market forces in which the world's corporations play a central role. In contrast to states, major corporations have therefore been accorded a new stature, far beyond their traditional primary economic purpose, in at least four areas:

- as agents of progressive social and economic change in their role as employers, particularly in relation to issues of wages and working conditions;
- as sources of monetary compensation for historic injustices or development projects;
- as catalysts of economic growth outside of the OECD; and
- as conduits for dealing with the environmental impact of trade, investment, and finance.

Yet, along with their proliferation and expanded mantle of responsibility, corporations have become the subject of more critical scrutiny than ever. One aspect of this is a respect for the rights of those who either have suffered historic injustices or are suffering contemporary ones at the hands of governments and corporations alike. These injustices take many forms, and include, for example, the claims of indigenous peoples who have had their land confiscated in the age of imperialism; the demands for decent working conditions by laborers subject to sweatshop rules; or the claims of victims who suffered the denial of their economic, political, and human rights as forced and slave laborers during the Nazi period. Often, corporations are considered to have been beneficiaries of inequitable and repressive systems and, correspondingly, sources for financial redress.

The second theme is that of culpability. In the aftermath of World War II, historians, anthropologists, political scientists, and sociologists sought to find explanations for the breakdown of the Weimar Republic, the onset of fascism, and the horrors of the Holocaust. Increasingly they moved away from issues relating to the personal culpability of Germans, both individually and collectively, and toward structural analyses that seemed to locate the sources of these phenomena in broader economic, political, and social conditions prevailing in Germany prior to 1933.[8]

One seemingly inevitable conclusion of this trend was the resurgence of a debate about responsibility and relativism (the *Historikerstreit*) with claims that challenged the uniqueness of the Holocaust as a singularly evil act.[9]

A second product of the apparent shift toward structural analysis and away from individual responsibility was, perhaps just as predictably, a backlash. The issue of German personal culpability was once again pitched to the forefront in the form of Daniel Jonah Goldhagen's emphatic and provocative critique of the nature of German anti-Semitism in his book *Hitler's Willing Executioners*.[10] Goldhagen's now-familiar thesis was that the virulence of anti-Semitism was unique and endemic to Germany. Tracing its historic roots, he argued that the cruelty and humiliation inflicted on the Jewish victims of the Holocaust were proof of German exceptionalism in this regard, and that the source lay in an indigenous culture that encouraged personal hatred toward Jews. Germans, as individuals, were therefore responsible for the depravity and extent of the Holocaust rather than an abstract set of economic factors or disjointed political circumstances.

When these two seemingly unrelated elements, corporate social responsibility and culpability for the crimes of the Holocaust, were joined together, one product was a revisiting of the corporate crimes of the past. The first stage of that process, analytically if not always chronologically, was to scrutinize the loss and potentially illegitimate if not illegal seizure of Jewish assets in Switzerland. The second element was a consideration of the more widespread question of the remuneration and compensation of all forced and slave laborers in Nazi Germany.[11]

This second wave focused on the activities of German firms and the German government. The process was initiated by threatened litigation, potentially in American courts, against the subsidiaries of German firms with assets in the United States on behalf of former slave and forced laborers seeking, in class-action lawsuits, compensation for past abuses. The response was to deal with the issue systematically by the initiation of negotiations between the U.S. and German governments, the legal representatives of former forced and slave laborers, and German business. These negotiations focused on creating a compensation fund for laborers, financed in principle by equal contributions from German business and the German government. This scheme subsequently proved problematic as a result of laxity in German corporate contributions. The principle of the formation of the fund was soon established, although the representatives of German business were quick to stress that companies contributing to the fund were doing so on the basis of what they regarded as a moral, and not a legal obligation.[12] Nevertheless, several issues remained highly contested: the contributory sums involved; the distribution of those contributions; exactly who was eligible to receive compensation; and how much they were to receive.[13] The pressure to conclude an agreement rapidly was intensified by the fact that those eligible for compensation are now aged and dying at a rapid rate—reputedly in excess of 10 percent a year.

With hindsight, it appears perhaps predictable that the third wave involved accusations of complicity leveled against American foreign direct investors in Germany in the Nazi period. Ford's contribution to the Allied war effort was renowned, earning the company the mantle it proudly wore of being part of the "arsenal of democracy."[14] It was then somewhat pointed, if indeed not ironic, that Ford was singled out for potentially collaborating with the Third Reich. I believe that the Ford case can only therefore be understood as part of an expanding process of accountability. This process included both the more obvious and likely collaborators identified elsewhere in this volume by Peter Hayes,[15] and the less obvious (and less likely) candidates such as Ford-Werke, the German subsidiary of the American firm.

On 4 March 1998, attorneys filed a class-action lawsuit against Ford that was subsequently dismissed.[16] Attorneys represented Elsa Iwanowa, a Belgian citizen who had been abducted from Russia as a teenager by the Nazis during World War II and forced to perform heavy labor at Ford-Werke in Cologne, Germany. This lawsuit contended that the plaintiffs, represented by Elsa Iwanowa but unknown in number at the time (although it is unclear whether other former forced laborers were eventually located), were owed compensation by Ford. They claimed that Ford was culpable for their forced labor between 1941 and 1945. Was Ford responsible? How did Ford react to the charge? It is to this case, and these questions, that I now turn.

Ford's Investment in Germany: The Pathology of a Case

I had researched a doctoral dissertation during the course of the mid-1980s that subsequently became my first book, *The Fruits of Fascism: Postwar Prosperity in Historical Perspective*.[17] This book examined the hypothesis that the contrasting patterns of development of the British and German economies could, in large part, be traced to the very different behavior of the state in these countries between the early 1930s and 1945. The dominant explanations of German development at the time took two contrasting forms. The first consisted of a macro-historic argument, a "grand sweep of history" view. I label it here the "original sin" argument because of its primary focus on Germany's economic and political structure at its formation. Could the breakdown of the Weimar Republic, for example, be linked to the initial pattern of formation of Germany, or was it a product of subsequent German domestic politics? The answer was often keenly contested among scholars offering support for their work using the highest quality of research.[18] When political scientists applied these principles to understanding German postwar economic development, they often used this literature to generate arguments consistent with this "original sin" approach.[19]

The second explanation, by contrast, rejected a focus on the prewar period, emphasizing instead that the postwar period was analytically divorced from Germany's past. Here the combination of fascism, war, and occupation had created a tabula rasa in some countries, leading to the crumbling of old, inflexible institutions, and generating the possibility of unfettered growth. Offered as a broad (and abstract) conception by Mancur Olsen in his celebrated book, *The Rise and Decline of Nations,*[20] the argument was subsequently applied to Germany in attempting to explain why the Federal Republic's economic vibrancy had turned to Euro-sclerosis by the 1980s.[21]

What lay at the heart of this debate was the issue of whether, and to what degree, periods of German history can be analytically insulated so that the events of one period can be used to explain developments in another, or if the patterns of German history are too interwoven to make the attribution of causation from one discrete period to another a justifiable and meaningful exercise. What was more remarkable, perhaps, was the way that both arguments largely ignored events in the Nazi period, as if they bore little significance in regard to subsequent developments.

My work sought to consider areas of both continuity and discontinuity between the Nazi and postwar periods. It specifically addressed what I regarded as this anomalous gap in the literature by focusing on the contrasting treatment of foreign direct investors in Britain and Germany in the 1930s and 1940s, and how those differences influenced postwar patterns of economic development. I chose to examine the auto industries in Britain and Germany for three reasons. The first was their relatively similar organizational structures in the late 1920s. The auto industry was dominated by U.S. investors (General Motors and Ford) in both Britain and Germany, although Ford was far larger than GM in Britain and, conversely, GM was far larger than Ford in Germany.[22] Domestic producers were far smaller, were fragmented by comparison, and did not effectively employ techniques of mass production. The second reason was that the industries did, in fact, look so different from each other by the time the war was over, and they experienced significant changes in Germany and far fewer in Britain between 1929 and 1945. Finally, the auto industry was an infant industry in the 1920s, but became a pivotal one in each country in the postwar period in terms of employment and exports. My initial research suggested that this industry was clearly worth examining.

I therefore compared the experiences of Ford's subsidiaries in Britain and Germany from their inception through the late 1950s, primarily using a series of company case studies. I discovered that Ford suffered from significant discrimination in the Nazi period, with the obverse being true in Britain. Not only was Ford treated fairly in Britain but it could also legitimately be concluded from my work that Ford was more favorably treated by the British state than were its domestic counterparts. The result was that the Ford subsidiary emerged as a relatively small producer in Germany, diminished if not dwarfed by the end of the war, while in Britain it was the largest producer, and arguably became dominant by the 1960s.

The book's findings generated little controversy. It did elicit some criticism among faculty from business schools who did not like the implication that authoritative, belligerent state intervention might in any way generate anything but perverse and deleterious effects on the fortunes of manufacturers. In this case I argued that the positive discrimination experienced by some of the major German domestic auto firms might, in part, explain their relative degree of success in the postwar period. Still, the book did not elicit public debate. Half a dozen years later, however, I began receiving telephone calls from lawyers from the firm of Milberg and Weiss acting on the behalf of a potential plaintiff, questioning me regarding Ford's activities during the period. I maintained my conviction that Ford's American parent had lost control of the German subsidiary by the outbreak of war, and all communication between the two companies had ceased after 1941. I concluded that Ford could not be held responsible for events at its Cologne plants between 1941 and 1945, when forced and slave labor was used there.

Undeterred by this assessment, the lawyers pursued their claims against Ford by filing a lawsuit and engaging the press, with Michael Dobbs contacting me in his capacity as a reporter for the *Washington Post.* Dobbs claimed, in conversation at the time, that he had been alerted to the issue by counsel for the plaintiffs. I reiterated my conclusion that evidence supported the view that Ford was not culpable. Dobbs, undeterred, published a piece that questioned Ford's innocence, although he did, in fairness, mention my views. As the claim took on new vitality, I was subsequently contacted by representatives of the media.

Ford's response was novel. Rather than axiomatically denying any guilt, the company promised to address the matter fully. Appointing a team of internal investigators, they devoted considerable resources and time to a very expensive enquiry that eventually lasted for over three years. I was asked to assist in an investigation by both the legal representatives of the plaintiffs and those of Ford itself. I chose to participate in Ford's investigation because I was guaranteed unfettered access to materials, and was made the promise that the report itself would be conducted with the utmost integrity in its efforts to be uncompromising, transparent, and honest in its delivery of the findings in a final report.

Investigative research teams were assembled in Dearborn, Washington, D.C., London, and Cologne. Their goal was to locate all relevant materials at various public and private archives. Another team was assigned the role of traveling to various German archives looking for materials. The project's initial goal was to meet the traditional '80/20 rule': to locate 80 percent of the materials that existed on the subject if possible. I estimate that they far exceeded this figure, collecting, collating, and indexing over ninety-eight thousand pages of materials that were all donated to the Henry Ford Museum's collection for the purpose of permitting public scrutiny subsequent to the final report's publication.

Oversight for the project was located at a central headquarters in Dearborn and administered by Elizabeth Adkins, a professional archivist employed to coordinate what quickly became an exhaustive and complicated search.[23] To ensure that the highest appropriate standards were attained in the collection and indexing of materials, Larry Dowler, a recognized authority on research methodology,[24] was retained by Ford as an independent adviser. I was asked to serve in a capacity comparable to Dowler's, my purpose being to assist in locating materials and to ensure that integrity was maintained in the reporting and representation of their substance in the final report. The report itself attempted to address three questions generated by the lawsuit:

- Was Ford-Werke treated differently from other American-owned companies in Germany, since it was not placed under Nazi control when the United States entered the war?
- Were executives of Ford Motor Company in the United States able to exercise control over Ford-Werke throughout the war years, whether through direct communication or indirectly through other European subsidiaries?
- Did Ford in the U.S. knowingly utilize unpaid, forced labor to generate enormous profits and, even if it did not, did Ford-Werke materially benefit from such labor?

The final report provided what I believe are conclusive answers to all three questions through the exhaustive presentation of data without commentary or interpretation. This data can be evaluated on the Ford web site by those interested, and so I shall provide only a brief review of any materials here.[25] What follows is an analysis, evaluation, and summary of the data rather than a presentation of it.

Setting the Context, Answering the Questions

The first of three questions listed above essentially addresses the issue of whether Ford unduly benefited from positive discrimination, a question generated by the fact that its assets were not confiscated. Did the fact that the ownership of the stock of the company formally remained with the parent in Dearborn signify that the parent had control of the subsidiary during the war? Evidence suggests the answer was that Ford did not retain control. Ford's U.S. parent neither controlled the subsidiary, nor did it unduly benefit from that status relative to other firms.

Perhaps surprisingly, given its size and scope today, Ford was not among the largest American investors in Germany. Ford-Werke was incorporated as the Ford Motor Company Aktiengesellschaft (AG)[26] on 5 January 1925, and was originally headquartered in Berlin.[27] Truck assembly began in 1926, followed by the manufacture of the Model T in June 1926. In 1929, Ford-Werke acquired a fifty-two acre tract of land on the banks of the Rhine in Cologne, and on 2 October 1930, Henry Ford laid the cornerstone of a new manufacturing plant there. The plant opened in June 1931, despite economic difficulties throughout Germany.[28] In October 1928, Ford had reorganized its European operations, and Ford-Werke became a subsidiary of Ford's British subsidiary.

A further reorganization in 1934, however, resulted in Ford-Werke reverting to its former status as a direct subsidiary of the American parent company when it assumed direct ownership of a majority of Ford-Werke shares. Although Ford's stake subsequently fluctuated over the years, it retained a majority ownership in Ford-Werke.[29]

Yet, as already mentioned, Ford was not among the major American investors in Germany at the start of World War II. Collectively, 250 American firms owned more than $450 million in assets in Germany. The top ten of those firms owned 58.5 percent of this total. Ford was ranked sixteenth by investment holdings, accounting for 1.9 percent of the total American investment.[30] A list of the top fifty-nine American firms with investments in Germany according to size of investment during the war is provided in table 5.1.

Among this list of familiar names (including Standard Oil, Singer, and General Electric), GM's investment in its subsidiary, Adam Opel, represented the second largest U.S. position in this period. GM's investment accounted for 12.18 percent of all U.S. investment, or over six times the size of the Ford investment.

Ford's relatively small investment was matched by its comparable production capacity and market share. At some points in the mid-1930s, it was only the ninth largest auto producer in Germany. From 1932 until 1937, Ford-Werke manufactured between 4 and 9 percent of Germany's total yearly motor vehicle production[31] at a time when Opel was responsible for between 40 and 50 percent of production. By the outbreak of war Ford-Werke had recovered to be the fourth largest producer in Germany.[32] Ford-Werke experienced systematic discrimination both because it was largely marginal to Nazi strategic plans and because of its foreign ownership. Nazi authorities explicitly justified this discrimination because of the company's refusal to standardize its parts so that they would be interchangeable with those of other German producers. The company justified its refusal because it wanted its parts to be interchangeable with those of other Ford subsidiaries. The effect of this discrimination was clear in the maldistribution of material resources and in the allocation of government contracts, which after 1933 became an increasing and eventually overwhelming percentage of all sales as civilian production. Civilian production was first diminished and eventually prohibited.[33]

Although its assets were not seized, and therefore Ford-Werke formally remained under the ownership of Ford USA, Ford's foreign and Jewish senior management came under increasing pressure, and both

TABLE 5.1: Investment of U.S. Companies in Germany, 1943

	Primary German Subsidiary	American Parent Company	Year Established	Amount of Investment	Percent of Total U.S. Investment
1	Deutsch-Amerikanische Petroleum-Gesellschaft	Standard Oil Co. (New Jersey)	1890	$64,990,446	14.43
2	Adam Opel Aktiengesellschaft	General Motors Corp.	1905	$54,852,486	12.18
3	F.W. Woolworth Co. GmbH	F.W. Woolworth Co.	1927	$25,727,087	5.71
4	Singer Nahmaschinen Aktiengesellschaft	International Securities Co.	1895	$20,531,679	4.56
5	Telephonefabrik Berliner AG	International Telephone & Telegraph Corp.	1900	$19,369,932	4.30
6	Singer Nahmaschinen AG	Singer Mfg. Co.	1895	$18,661,180	4.14
7	Kohlen Import & Poseidon AG	Hugo Stinnes Industries, Inc.	1920	$16,062,153	3.57
8	Aktien-Malsfabrik Landsburg AG	Corn Products Refining Co.	1871	$14,434,541	3.21
9	Nationale Radiator GmbH	American Radiator & Standard Sanitary Co.	1901	$14,393,923	3.20
10	International Harvester Company GmbH	International Harvester Co.	1908	$14,183,273	3.15
11	Deutsche Vacuum Oel AG	Socony-Vacuum Oil Co., Inc.	1900	$12,623,510	2.80
12	Kodak Aktiengesellschaft	Eastman Kodak Co.	1927	$12,200,789	2.71
13	Aktiengesellschaft fuer Anlagewerte	New Jersey Industries, Inc.	1898	$11,497,238	2.55
14	Roth-Buchner GmbH	Gillette Safety Razor Co.	1925	$9,641,011	2.14
15	Deutsche Hollerith Maschinen GmbH	International Business Machines Corp.	1934	$9,000,128	2.00
16	Ford-Werke AG	Ford Motor Co.	1925	$8,549,061	1.90
17	Ebano Asphalt-Werke Aktiengesellschaft	Pan Foreign Corp.	1928	$8,377,970	1.87
18	Deutsche Vereinigte Schuhmaschinen Gesellschaft	United Shoe Machinery Corp.	1900	$8,375,714	1.86
19	Mercedes Buromaschinen Werke AG	Underwood Elliott Fisher Co.	not stated	$7,058,547	1.57
20	Osram GmbH	International General Electric Co., Inc.	1919	$6,655,334	1.48
21	National Krupp Register-Kassen GmbH	National Cash Register Co.	1896	$6,623,235	1.47
22	Damm & Ladwig Kommandit Gesellschaft und Dulv Aktiengesellschaft	Yale & Towne Manufacturing Co.	1928	$5,297,653	1.18
23	Borvisk Kunstseiden AG	Continental "Borvisk" Co.	not stated	$5,160,025	1.15

TABLE 5.1: Investment of U.S. Companies in Germany, 1943 *(cont.)*

	Primary German Subsidiary	American Parent Company	Year Established	Amount of Investment	Percent of Total U.S. Investment
24	Mergenthaler Setzmaschinen-Fabrik GmbH	Mergenthaler Linotype Co.	1896	$3,687,116	0.82
25	Allgemeine Erdol GmbH	Jadev Corp.	1921	$2,641,659	0.59
26	Allgemeine Oel-Handels GmbH	Atlantic Refining Co.	1920	$2,602,778	0.59
27	Powers GmbH	Remington Rand, Inc.	1914	$2,593,143	0.58
28	Ritter AG	Ritter Co., Inc.	1927	$2,459,946	0.55
29	Internationale Pressluft und Elektricitats GmbH	Chicago Pneumatic Tool Co.	1905	$2,432,625	0.54
30	Steinway & Sons	Steinway & Sons	1889	$2,159,152	0.48
31	Deutsche Norton GmbH	Norton Co.	1909	$2,081,690	0.46
32	Coca-Cola GmbH	Coca-Cola Co.	1930	$2,071,661	0.45
33	Glucksklee Michgesellschaft GmbH	International Finance Co.	1925	$1,847,527	0.41
34	Ambi-Budd Presswerk, GmbH	Edward G. Budd Manufacturing Co.	1926	$1,673,962	0.37
35	Otis Aufzugswerke GmbH	Otis Elevator Co.	1931	$1,619,955	0.36
36	Gustav Lohse AG	International Affiliated Corp.	1922	$1,403,188	0.31
37	Deutsche Herskllth AG	American-Austrian Magnesite Corp.	1928	$1,400,147	0.31
38	Deutsche Libby GmbH	Libby, McNeill & Libby	1926	$1,365,489	0.30
39	Holzwarth Gasturbinen GmbH	Schilling Estate Co.	1927	$1,115,563	0.25
40	Union Special Maschinenfabrik GmbH	Union Special Machine Corp. of America	1901	$1,092,047	0.24
41	Zinnwerke Wilhelmsburg GmbH	National Lead Co.	not stated	$947,104	0.21
42	Maschinenfabriken Wagner Aktiengesellschaft	New England Industries, Inc.	1890	$855,577	0.19
43	American Express GmbH	American Express Co., Inc.	1907	$845,749	0.19
44	Kraft Kaese Werke GmbH	Kraft Cheese Co.	1927	$759,462	0.17
45	Oelwerke Julius Schindler GmbH	Pure Oil Co.	1920	$698,849	0.16
46	Westinghaus Bremsen GmbH	Westinghouse Air Brake Co.	1919	$606,870	0.13

TABLE 5.1: Investment of U.S. Companies in Germany, 1943 *(cont.)*

	Primary German Subsidiary	American Parent Company	Year Established	Amount of Investment	Percent of Total U.S. Investment
47	Watch Tower Bible & Tract Society	Watch Tower Bible & Tract Society	1903	$597,595	0.13
48	Quaker Nahrmittel GmbH	Quaker Oats Co.	1922	$586,767	0.13
49	Pfaudler-Werke AG	Pfaudler Co.	1907	$577,247	0.13
50	Intertype Sezmaschinen GmbH	Intertype Corp.	1926	$575,198	0.13
51	Standard Elektrisitats Ges. AG	International Standard Electric Corp.	1930	$465,884	0.10
52	Ota Schlesische Schurwerke Ottmuth AG	Westhold Corp.	1930	$441,100	0.10
53	Unida Schiffstreuhand GmbH	United Fruit Co.	1936	$327,639	0.07
54	Addressograph-Multigraph GmbH	Addressograph-Multigraph Corp.	1928	$305,688	0.07
55	Verkehrs & Handels Aktiengesellschaft	United Continental Corp.	1898	$266,770	0.06
56	Almco Waschereimaschinen GmbH	American Laundry Machinery Co.	1903	$253,460	0.06
57	Deutsche Worthington Gesellschaft mbH	Worthington Pump & Machinery Corp.	1893	$188,751	0.04
58	Ahr, Krath and Co.	Delta Finance Co.	not stated	$142,628	0.03
59	Warner, W.R. and Co. GmbH	Wm. R. Warner & Co., Inc.	1904	$52,671	0.01

Source: National Archives and Records Administration (hereafter USNA): RG 56, Acc. 56-68A-209, Box 38, File: TFR-500, Business Holdings in Germany of United States Firms, circa 1943 (USNA 0005992-0006838). [This chart was reproduced by Ford Motor Co. in its *Research Findings About Ford-Werke Under the Nazi Regime* (Dearborn, MI: Ford Motor Company, 2001). The names of the German subsidiaries are given as they appear in that report. Eds.]

were marginalized in the running of the company.[34] Eventually, Ford-Werke was placed under German government control on 15 May 1942. The German government named Robert Schmidt as custodian of Ford-Werke. Schmidt reported to the Reich Commissioner for the Treatment of Enemy Property.[35] The board of directors was replaced by a board of advisors appointed by the government to assist the custodian in the administration of the company. Although formally private, Ford's production was incorporated into the Nazi military apparatus. Ford thus suffered from discriminatory state practices.

The second important question addressed in the Ford report concerns whether executives of Ford Motor Company in the United States were able to exercise control over Ford-Werke during the war years, either through direct communication or indirectly through other European subsidiaries. The findings of the Ford report appear to offer a conclusive answer to this question. Nazi policies systematically set out to limit the influence of foreign business owners, and therefore weakened Ford Motor Company's control over Ford-Werke. This was combined with a series of other regulatory measures taken by the German government from 1936 onward. The Ford-Werke board meeting held in Cologne on 20 April 1938 was the last time an American or British board member attended a meeting until after the war.[36] In a letter to a senior member of Ford's (U.S.) management dated 27 November 1939, a German counterpart advised that new government rules and regulations limited the amount of information he could provide to foreigners about the company's operations, even to members of the board or shareholders. As a result, Ford-Werke was unable to call a full meeting of the board.[37]

Nonetheless, representatives of Ford and Ford-Werke communicated on issues relating to the German occupation of Europe until 1940. Ford received several reports concerning the conditions of Ford plants in the German-occupied countries of Holland, Belgium, and France.[38] In addition, routine letters about the Ford-Werke board's new membership were exchanged.[39] But the number of communications between Ford and Ford-Werke diminished significantly in 1941, although correspondence between the two entities continued until the U.S. entry into the war. The last confirmed communication until after the war between the parent and subsidiary took place on 28 November 1941.[40]

What did an independent reviewer conclude on the question of communication and control? A 1943 U.S. Department of Justice report stated that even before the outbreak of war, German authorities interfered with the parent company's control over policy at Ford-Werke by the use of pressure on the Ford-Werke management. As preparations for war intensified in the late 1930s, the report suggested that where the two conflicted, Ford's German management chose loyalty to the goals of the Nazi authorities over the interests of Ford more generally.[41]

As already mentioned, a related issue concerned whether there was any indirect contact between Ford and Ford-Werke through third party intermediaries, most pointedly other European subsidiaries. One suggestion had been made that subsidiaries based in occupied, neutral, or Axis countries might have acted in relaying information or instructions between the two. The primary candidates for countries in this intermediary role are Portugal and Spain. Ford's investigation into contact with the neutral countries suggested that while the management of the German subsidiary might have attempted to generate business with such subsidiaries, the management in Spain and Portugal refused to work with their German counterparts.[42] Contact here did not amount to U.S. parent/German subsidiary communication, let alone control.

The third question addressed in the report concerned the matter of whether Ford-Werke knowingly utilized unpaid, forced labor to generate enormous profits and, even if it did not, whether Ford-Werke materially benefited from their labor. The report sheds considerable light on these two questions. Part of the lawsuit had been focused on the issue of material gain because, purportedly, under American law, Ford would be liable for undue profits even if the firm had not wittingly participated in the use of forced and slave labor. So, was forced and slave labor used? The report was revealing in this regard, as illustrated by table 5.2.

The data in table 5.2 provide evidence suggesting that forced labor was used extensively at the Cologne plant between 1941 and 1945. The available data also reveal that forced laborers steadily grew as a percentage of the total workforce from 1942 onward, reaching a peak number (1,932 workers) and percentage (37.1 percent) in August 1944 as the German component of the workforce began to dwindle. Only a very small percentage of the workforce was composed of slave laborers.[43] On what basis were these groups distinguished by the Nazis? As the Ford report stated:

> The overall treatment of the various groups was determined by Nazi ideology and practice that placed foreigners on a scale according to race, nationality and gender. The foreign workforce included: laborers, recruited from German allies, who were paid and treated better than any other group of

TABLE 5.2: Number of Workers at Ford-Werke, January 1941–December 1944*

Date	Russian or Eastern Workers	Italian POWs	Other Foreign Workers	POWs	Total Foreign Workers	Total Work-force	Percentage of Foreign Workers
Jan 1941	–	–	n.a.	n.a.	n.a.	3863	n.a.
Feb 1941	–	–	n.a.	n.a.	n.a.	3810	n.a.
Mar 1941	–	–	n.a.	n.a.	n.a.	3724	n.a.
Apr 1941	–	–	n.a.	n.a.	n.a.	3732	n.a.
May 1941	–	–	n.a.	n.a.	n.a.	3651	n.a.
Jun 1941	–	–	n.a.	n.a.	n.a.	3647	n.a.
Jul 1941	–	–	n.a.	n.a.	n.a.	3663	n.a.
Aug 1941	–	–	n.a.	n.a.	n.a.	3581	n.a.
Sep 1941	–	–	n.a.	n.a.	n.a.	3605	n.a.
Oct 1941	–	–	n.a.	n.a.	n.a.	3609	n.a.
Nov 1941	–	–	n.a.	n.a.	n.a.	3500	n.a.
Dec 1941	–	–	n.a.	n.a.	n.a.	3476	n.a.
Jan 1942	–	–	n.a.	n.a.	n.a.	3435	n.a.
Feb 1942	–	–	n.a.	n.a.	n.a.	3471	n.a.
Mar 1942	–	–	n.a.	n.a.	n.a.	3500	n.a.
Apr 1942	314**	–	n.a.	n.a.	n.a.	3594	n.a.
May 1942	320	–	94	94	508	3978	12.8
Jun 1942	621	–	101	92	814	4182	19.5
Jul 1942	610	–	103	90	803	4143	19.4
Aug 1942	567	–	n.a.	91	n.a.	4104	n.a.
Sep 1942	570	–	n.a.	89	n.a.	4172	n.a.
Oct 1942	715	–	n.a.	89	n.a.	4512	n.a.
Nov 1942	679	–	n.a.	83	n.a.	4613	n.a.
Dec 1942	677	–	n.a.	85	n.a.	4648	n.a.
Jan 1943	677	–	448	86	1211	4625	26.2
Feb 1943	670	–	575	84	1329	4579	29.0
Mar 1943	711	–	488	81	1280	4816	26.6
Apr 1943	671	–	518	80	1269	4855	26.1
May 1943	751	–	526	79	1356	4998	27.1
Jun 1943	749	–	n.a.	79	n.a.	4985	n.a.
Jul 1943	753	–	n.a.	79	n.a.	5115	n.a.
Aug 1943	743	–	696	–	1439	5137	28.0
Sep 1943	749	–	570	–	1319	5108	25.8
Oct 1943	900	–	489	–	1389	5306	26.2
Nov 1943	777	568	478	–	1823	5783	31.5
Dec 1943	789	559	458	–	1806	5711	31.6
Jan 1944	788	552	465	–	1805	5600	32.2
Feb 1944	789	554	420	–	1763	5298	33.3
Mar 1944	790	533	420	–	1743	5198	33.5
Apr 1944	786	505	400	–	1691	5175	32.7
May 1944	795	486	527	–	1808	5138	35.2
Jun 1944	870	497	536	–	1903	5223	36.4
Jul 1944	881	490	549	–	1920	5199	36.9
Aug 1944	882	496	554	–	1932	5208	37.1

TABLE 5.2: Number of Workers at Ford-Werke, January 1941–December 1944 *(cont.)*

Date	Russian or Eastern Workers	Italian POWs	Other Foreign Workers	POWs	Total Foreign Workers	Total Work-force	Percentage of Foreign Workers
Sep 1944	n.a.	–	n.a.	–	n.a.	n.a.	n.a.
Oct 1944	n.a.	–	n.a.	–	n.a.	n.a.	n.a.
Nov 1944	n.a.	–	n.a.	–	n.a.	n.a.	n.a.
Dec 1944	865[***]	–	n.a.	–	n.a.	n.a.	n.a.

[*]Ford-Werke Records, Financial Ledger, January 1942–September 1944 (FW 0007011-0007890). These figures are repeated in a postwar summary report prepared by Vitger; see FMC, AR-75-62-616, Box 79, Cologne 1939-1945 Reports—Custodian, no date (FMC 0001017).

[**]The figures for Russian workers in April 1942 come from IWM, FD 4369/45, Folder B, handwritten staff report, 27 April and 4 May 1942 (IWM 0000297). The figures for "Other Foreign Workers" from May through July 1942 come from IWM, FD 4369/45, Folder B, staff reports from 15 May to 17 July 1942 (IWM 0000283-0000292).

[***]Ford-Werke Records, Financial Ledger, December 1944–December 1946, Balance Sheet, 31 December 1944 (FW 0008273). The ledger does not specify the nationality of these workers, referring to them only as "foreign civil workers." The placement of the line item, the use of the term "civil," and the actual number of workers, however, are all consistent with their identification as Russian civilian workers. Little other information could be found on the workforce during the period from October through December 1944, when Ford-Werke was dispersing equipment and some workers to other locations.

Note: The entry "n.a." indicates that there was not enough information available to provide meaningful statistics.

Sources: This table was compiled from two sources:

- The first is a financial ledger from Ford-Werke internal records. The ledger contains monthly balance sheets reporting employment statistics for the period from 1941 to 1944. In some cases, these statistics are broken into different categories of foreign workers at the plant; in other cases, there are no breakdowns.[*]
- In a few instances, these ledger figures were supplemented by numbers from periodic staff reports prepared by Ford-Werke production departments. These staff reports were located in a collection of British Royal Air Force bombing survey records held by the Imperial War Museum in London.[**]

Both of these sources generally agree on the number of foreign workers reported each month. Where the reported numbers differ widely, only the figures from the ledgers have been included in this table.

foreign workers; prisoners of war (POWs), who received only token wages; forced workers (civilians) taken from occupied territory in Western and Eastern Europe, the latter receiving lower wages and worse treatment than their Western counterparts; Italian military internees sent to Germany after Italy's surrender in September 1943; and concentration camp inmates used as unpaid slave laborers.[44]

Western civilian workers were therefore paid the most, about the same as their German counterparts. Those from Eastern Europe, overwhelmingly Russians, were paid less. POWs were initially paid less than Western civilians but later received more. Slave laborers were paid nothing at all. Of the thousands of workers at the Ford plant, very few were slave laborers from concentration camps. As the Ford report concluded:

> In August 1944, shortly after concentration camp labor was made available to the automotive industry, 50 men from Buchenwald arrived at Ford-Werke. At any given time from August 1944 through February 1945, about 50 or fewer Buchenwald prisoners worked at Ford-Werke. All together, at least 65 different men were assigned there at one time or another.[45]

So the use of slave laborers was very limited, and that of forced laborers far more extensive. But did Ford materially benefit? In attempting to answer that question, Ford employed specialists from Price Waterhouse Cooper to conduct an internal audit. This was no easy task given the limited data, the vagaries of translating sixty-year-old German accounting entries and techniques into modern auditing methods accessible to a contemporary audience, and the calculations necessitated by aged currency conversions.

An examination of the effects of war damages, operating profits and losses, and the debilitating effects of government taxes and controls, provides a complex picture of Ford-Werke's financial affairs. But the combination of these various figures collectively suggests that neither the American parent company nor the German subsidiary benefited financially from the use of subsidized labor at its German plant.[46] What is clear is that all dividends were blocked from 1939 onwards. Furthermore, in partial recognition of its losses, Ford received compensation in the postwar period from a variety of sources, including the U.S. government itself.[47]

Conclusion

This essay has two purposes. The first is to inform the reader about the context, issues, and events pertaining to American investment in Nazi Germany. This can be done, to some extent, by answering central questions concerning the fortunes of Ford's German subsidiary. Indeed, in some ways, Ford serves as a fair test of the proposition that some German subsidiaries of American investors enjoyed favorable treatment at the hands of the Nazis. After all, no American investor should have found greater favor with the Nazis than Ford-Werke, given Henry Ford's pronounced and publicized views on both the supposed influence of Jews and on his advocacy of American nonintervention in the war.[48] Some have chosen to focus on these issues, concluding that Ford-Werke must therefore have been well treated by the Nazis. The evidence suggests otherwise. An extensive internal investigation provides evidence that Ford did not control its Cologne plant, knew little of what was happening there, and did not realize any material benefit. Even one of the most likely of U.S. investors to benefit, according to one set of criteria, did not benefit, and this suggests that Henry Ford's attitudes did not improve Ford-Werke's fortunes.

The second intent of this essay is to examine the current nature of a firm's response to the accusation of possible historical wrongdoing. Without warning, Ford was publicly and legally accused of what amounted to collaborative behavior at worst, unscrupulous behavior at best. Relying on little more than circumstantial evidence, lawyers for the plaintiffs and the media were willing to condemn the company for labor abuse, an area of clear vulnerability in the age of globalization, transparency, and the ethos of corporate social responsibility. This reflex is understandable, given the history of corporate malfeasance. Firms or their subsidiaries often do not behave as though they have a moral conscience. They respond flexibly to the demands of capitalism, adapting to the vagaries of a variety of political systems. Certainly, the indigenous management at Ford-Werke did so, whether it was because they supported the aims of the Nazis, feared for their jobs and lives, or were simply trying to keep the subsidiary in existence and free of governmental seizure.

Interestingly, faced with these claims, the contemporary Ford parent firm rejected the defensive posture of denial that could have been anticipated under these circumstances. Rather, and perhaps surprisingly (in view of the skepticism about the behavior of corporations when accused of wrongdoing), Ford conducted an exhaustive, credible, and transparent investigation. As I have elsewhere noted, Ford company officials reacted to this public scrutiny by promising an exhaustive and uncompromising assessment regarding accusations about profiteering, collaboration, and the use of forced and slave labor, resisting the public clamor for immediate answers. They decided that the report was to be purely descriptive in addressing these claims, not interpretative or even a historical narrative, allowing interested readers to draw their own conclusions.[49] That the findings do not support the suggestions of wrongdoing is not grounds for ignoring them.

This strategy therefore paid off for the company. Although the firm had to endure years of questioning from the press without being able to supply "sound bite" answers, Ford eventually drew applause from the media and a broader audience of concerned civic leaders for the way it acted. Even the most ardent of critics, such as Edwin Black, columnist and author of a book critical of IBM's behavior in the Nazi period,[50] supported the company's findings.

One conclusion that can be drawn is that this transparent approach worked to the company's benefit. Rather than obfuscate, it methodically addressed the central question head-on, and did so effectively. There is always the possibility of "the smoking gun" appearing in the form of countervailing evidence such as, for example, material showing that the parent firm did communicate with the subsidiary. But the likelihood has diminished as a result of Ford's exhaustive search. Furthermore, even if such evidence were to emerge, it would be hard to argue persuasively that the company had not exhausted every means to locate such data. In effect, it is the integrity of the process, as much as the substantive findings, that has benefited the company so successfully in the court of public opinion. And that, as much as anything, may be the main benefit of the ethos of corporate social responsibility.

Notes

1. See, for example, John Dunning, "Governments and Multinational Enterprises: From Confrontation to Co-operation?" *Millennium* 20, no. 2 (1991): 225–244; *World Investment Report 1994: Transnational Corporations, Employment and the Workplace,* chap. 3: "Globalization, Integrated International Production and the World Economy," 117–160; UNCTC, *World Investment Report: Transnational Corporations as Engines of Growth* (UN/CTC/130, 1992), chap. 6, "TNCs, Technology and Growth," 131–162.

2. For this and related stories, see "Sweatshops Under the American Flag," *New York Times,* 10 May 2002, A-34.

3. For a challenge to this view, see Paul Doremus, William Keller, Louis Pauly, and Simon Reich, *The Myth of the Global Corporation* (Princeton: Princeton University Press, 1998).

4. See Elazar Barkan, *The Guilt of Nations: Restitution and Negotiating Historical Injustices* (New York: Norton, 2000), 88–111.

5. Michael Dobbs, "Ford and GM Scrutinized for Alleged Nazi Collaboration: Firms Deny Researchers' Claims On Aiding German War Effort," *Washington Post,* 30 November 1998, A1.

6. Elsa Iwanowa et al. v. Ford Motor Company and Ford-Werke AG, U.S. District Court for the District of New Jersey, Civil Action No. 98-959, 4 March 1998.

7. See, for example, Susan Strange, *Mad Money: When Markets Outgrow Governments* (Ann Arbor: University of Michigan Press, 1998).

8. For a variety of approaches, see Hans-Ulrich Wehler, *The German Empire 1871–1918* (Dover: Berg Publishers, 1985); Geoff Eley, *From Unification to Nazism: Reinterpreting the German Past* (Boston: Allen and Unwin, 1986); and David P. Calleo, *The German Problem Reconsidered: Germany and the World Order, 1870 to the Present* (New York: Cambridge University Press, 1978).

9. See, for example, Charles Maier, *The Unmasterable Past: History, Holocaust, and the German National Identity* (Cambridge: Harvard University Press, 1988); and Richard J. Evans, *In Hitler's Shadow: West German Historians and the Attempt to Escape from the Nazi Past* (London: I.B. Tauris, 1989).

10. Daniel Jonah Goldhagen, *Hitler's Willing Executioners: Ordinary Germans and the Holocaust* (New York: Knopf, 1996).

11. For a breakdown of the foreign workforce, see Ford Motor Company, *Research Findings About Ford-Werke Under the Nazi Regime* (Dearborn, MI: Ford Motor Company, December 2001), iv.

12. This point was made by Wolfgang Gibowski, who represented the German companies in the negotiations. See his comments in a chapter entitled "The German Economy Foundation Initiative: Remembrance, Responsibility, and the Future," in *The German Remembrance Fund and the Issue of Forced and Slave Labor,* ed. Genevieve Libonati (Washington, D.C.: Friedrich-Ebert-Stiftung, 2001), 76.

13. For a description of the details, see Dieter Kastrup, "Foreword" and Dieter Dettke, "The German Remembrance Fund and the Issue of Forced and Slave Labor," both in Libonati, *The German Remembrance Fund.*

14. See Dobbs, "Ford and GM Scrutinized for Alleged Nazi Collaboration." For a description of the history of Ford's involvement in the Allied war effort, see Allen

Nevins and Frank Ernest Hill, *Ford: Decline and Rebirth, 1933–1962* (New York: Charles Scribner's Sons, 1962); Simon Reich, *The Fruits of Fascism: Postwar Prosperity in Historical Perspective* (Ithaca: Cornell University Press, 1990); and Mira Wilkins and Frank Ernest Hill, *American Business Abroad: Ford on Six Continents* (Detroit: Wayne State University Press, 1964).

15. For a fuller analysis, see Peter Hayes, *Industry and Ideology: IG Farben in the Nazi Era* (Cambridge: Cambridge University Press, 1987).

16. Elsa Iwanowa et al. v. Ford Motor Company.

17. Reich, *The Fruits of Fascism.*

18. See as examples of this extensive literature, Volker Berghahn, *Germany and the Approach of War in 1914* (New York: St. Martins Press, 1973); Geoff Eley, *From Unification to Nazism,* and his *Reshaping the German Right: Radical Nationalism and Political Change after Bismarck* (New Haven: Yale University Press, 1980); Fritz Fischer, *Germany's Aims in the First World War* (New York: Norton, 1967), and idem, *The War of Illusions,* (New York: Norton, 1975); Alexander Gerschenkron, *Economic Backwardness in Historical Perspective* (Cambridge: Harvard University Press, 1962); John A. Moses, *The Politics of Illusion: The Fischer Controversy in German Historiography* (New York: Barnes and Noble, 1975); and Wehler, *The German Empire 1871–1918.*

19. See, for example, Christopher S. Allen, "The Underdevelopment of Keynesianism in the Federal Republic of Germany," in *The Political Power of Economic Ideas: Keynesianism Across Nations,* ed. Peter A. Hall (Princeton: Princeton University Press, 1989).

20. Mancur Olson, *The Rise and Decline of Nations: Economic Growth, Stagflation and Social Rigidities* (New Haven: Yale University Press, 1982).

21. See, for example, Simon Bulmer, ed., *The Changing Agenda of West German Public Policy* (Aldershot: Dartmouth Publishing Company, 1989).

22. For figures suggesting that Opel was responsible for over 50 percent of sales at some points, see "Organizational and Management Basic Data Book: Ford of Germany," Cologne, Germany, Ford-Werke AG 1951–1952, AR-75-63-430: 93, Ford Industrial Files. For figures showing that Opel commanded 42 percent of the market at points in the 1930s, see "The Importance of German Passenger Cars and Truck Factories, 1935," Accession 38, Box 33, Edison Institute, and letter, Diestel to Sorensen, 2 March 1936, Accession 38, Box 33, Edison Institute.

23. Elizabeth W. Adkins, a certified archivist, was manager of Ford Motor Company Archives Services at the time this project was launched. She had twenty years of experience in managing business archives, and has served in leadership roles in the Society of American Archivists, the Academy of Certified Archivists, and the International Council on Archives.

24. Lawrence Dowler is a librarian, archivist, and historian. His thirty-year career includes sixteen years at Harvard University and twelve years at Yale University. He played a leading role in developing and implementing national standards for describing primary sources. At Harvard, he led an effort to create a "gateway" to research resources within the university and beyond, and subsequently published a book, *Gateways to Knowledge* (Cambridge: M.I.T. Press, 1997) on these issues. He has published more than twenty-five other books, chapters, and articles.

25. Those interested can gain access to the report online through the links provided at www.media.ford.com.

26. *Aktiengesellschaft* denotes a joint-stock company.

27. Ford-Werke Records, File: Minutes of Board Meetings, No. 6 of the Notarial Register for 1925 and Articles of Ford Motor Company Aktiengesellschaft, 5 January 1925 (FW 0004074-0004085; for the English translation, see FW 0004086-0004098).

28. Wilkins and Hill, *American Business Abroad,* 139, 204, 206, and 234.

29. Ford Motor Company (hereafter FMC), AR-75-62-616, Box 57, File: Investments 1951-52, Mellema to Edwards, 25 January 1952 (FMC 0003293-0003306); FMC, AR-75-62-616, Box 23, File: European Countries—Investment Ledger, Ford-Werke AG, no date (FMC 0000346-0000350); Coopers & Lybrand Records, Lybrand, Ross Bros. & Montgomery to Henry Ford II, 19 March 1948 (CL1 0000316-0000318); Wilkins and Hill, *American Business Abroad,* 193–195.

30. United States National Archives (hereafter USNA): RG 56, Acc. 56-68A-209, Box 38, File: TFR-500, Business Holdings in Germany of United States Firms, circa 1943 (USNA 0005992-0006838).

31. FMC, AR-98-213541, Box 131, Palumbo, Survey of German Motor Vehicle Industry, 15 April 1948 (FMC 0000906).

32. Ford Motor Company, *Research Findings About Ford-Werke Under the Nazi Regime,* 22.

33. For an extensive discussion of Ford's relationship with the German state over four decades that supports this contention, see Reich, *The Fruits of Fascism,* 107–146.

34. Ford Motor Company, *Research Findings About Ford-Werke Under the Nazi Regime,* 14–15 and 24–25. For supporting materials see USNA: RG 260, Property Division, External Assets Investigation Section, Box 546, File: Ford Werke AG (Inv), Memo on conversations with Schmidt, 13 June 1945 (USNA 0003559); FMC, AR-98-213541, Box V, Oral History of Erhard Vitger by D.B. Tinnin, April 1987 (FMC 00000573).

35. Ford-Werke Records, Resolution of the Superior Court—Cologne, 15 May 1942 (FW 0008375). For the English translation, see FMC, AR 75-63-430, Box 207, File: Germany AG Minutes of Meetings 1929–1952 (FMC 0003361).

36. USNA: RG 407, Entry 368B, Box 1032, Schneider Report, Exhibit 146A, Meeting Minutes, 20 April 1938 (USNA 0000368-0000369).

37. FMC, AR-65-1500, Box 6, File: Germany 1939–1945 (Sorensen), Albert to Sorensen, 27 November 1939 (FMC 00003161-00003163).

38. See, for example, FMC, AR-65-1500, Box 6, File: Germany 1939–1945 (Sorensen), Tallberg to Gnau, 6 July 1940 (FMC 0003139-0003140); HFM, Acc. 6, Box 321, File: 1940 Correspondence, Albert to Edsel Ford, 11 July 1940 (HFM 0001475-0001477), Albert to Edsel Ford, 18 September 1940 (HFM 0001470-0001471); HFM, Acc. 6, Box 329, File: 1941 Ford-Werke, Schmidt to Edsel Ford, 19 September 1940 (HFM 0000553-0000555).

39. FMC, AR-65-1500, Box 6, File: Germany 1939–1945 (Sorensen), Albert to Sorensen, 18 September 1940 (FMC 0003144-0003145).

40. Ford-Werke Records, Wibel to Schmidt, 28 November 1941 (FW 0001820). An internal Ford Motor Company Patent Department memo in 1944 indicated that there had been no communications with Ford-Werke since 1941: "Since the war, we have had no contact whatever with the German Ford company and no information has been transmitted by us to the German Ford company or persons acting for them." See USNA: RG 60, Entry 285B, Box 67, File: Ford—Yokohama, McRae to Roberge, 20 May 1944 (USNA 0003873). After the war, Schmidt wrote to Lord Perry, confirming that contact by cable and letter was made with Edsel

Ford and Charles Sorensen only until the "outbreak of war with the USA prevented further negotiations." See USNA: RG 407, Entry 368B, Box 1032, Schneider Report, Exhibit 204, Schmidt to Perry, 28 May 1945 (USNA 0000481-0000482). In an interview with U.S. military authorities, Oscar Bornheim, a former employee of Ford-Werke, claimed that Erhard Vitger was a confidant of Henry Ford and had "been in communication via radio-telephone with [Ford Motor Company] subsequent to 1942." Bornheim stated further that Vitger had informed him that Ford of Hungary had also been in contact with Ford Motor Company. However, there is no direct evidence of this, and U.S. Department of Justice officials concluded that no further investigation was warranted. See USNA: RG 60, Entry 114, Classification 146-39, Box 4, File: 146-39-24, Hoover to Clark, 16 December 1944 (USNA 0003163) and Clark to Hoover, 22 January 1945 (USNA 0003165).

41. USNA: RG 226, Microfilm M1499, Reel 263, Department of Justice, Report on Ford-Werke AG, 10 May 1943 (USNA 0004262).

42. Ford Motor Company, *Research Findings About Ford-Werke Under the Nazi Regime,* 109–113.

43. Forced laborers are classified here as mandatory foreign workers and POWs, while slave laborers are classified as unpaid concentration camp inhabitants.

44. Ibid., iv.

45. Ibid.

46. For detailed figures, see ibid., 136–145.

47. Ibid.

48. The latest statement regarding these issues can be read in Neil Baldwin, *Henry Ford and the Jews: The Mass Production of Hate* (Boulder: Westview Press, 2001).

49. Simon Reich, "Commentary on the Ford Report," in *Research Findings About Ford-Werke Under the Nazi Regime,* 6.

50. Edwin Black, *IBM and the Holocaust: The Strategic Alliance Between Nazi Germany and America's Most Powerful Corporation* (New York: Crown Publishers, 2001).

Chapter Six

WRITING THE HISTORY OF BUSINESS IN THE THIRD REICH

Past Achievements and Future Directions

———— ⋙⋘ ————

Volker R. Berghahn

THIS CONCLUDING ESSAY is designed to take up some of the key problems relating to the role of business in the Third Reich that the other contributors to this volume have raised. It will attempt to contextualize them historiographically as well as historically. In addition to looking back in time, it will suggest a few directions in which future research may fruitfully go.

One of the key issues with which the preceding contributions have been grappling is the political responsibility of German businessmen under Nazism (i.e., how far they had a hand in the rise and consolidation of Hitler's power), on the one hand, and their moral and criminal culpability (i.e., how far they were involved in the regime's crimes as defined by international law and Nuremberg Tribunal codes), on the other, and whether in this context they were, as Gerald D. Feldman puts it, "reluctant or willing collaborators."[1] The question of business responsibility was first debated among Marxist and non-Marxist social scientists during the 1930s as they set out to explain the rise and stabilization of the Hitler regime.[2] It was only during World War II that Western and Soviet analysts fully turned their attention to the question of business culpability, as the world became increasingly aware of the massive crimes committed by Germany after 1938. By 1944–1945, the concepts of political responsibility and moral culpability had become completely intertwined. At war's end, preoccupation with criminal culpability had pushed the question of political responsibility into the background. Later, in the 1950s, there was a reversal of this imbalance, with the issue of political responsibility once again overshadowing that of culpability. Much of the more recent scholarship, it seems, has been concerned with delineating the two concepts more sharply in an attempt to pinpoint where in the period 1933–1945 we can, and indeed must, speak of political responsibility to be borne by a strategic elite group such as businessmen, and where we can and must speak of criminal culpability.

The two concepts had merged during World War II and the early postwar years in the West in part because they were linked to two related and frequently conflated problems: whether or not the Germans were collectively or individually guilty; and whether they should therefore be punished collectively or individually. The notion of collective guilt was, of course, at variance with a deeply ingrained principle of justice, i.e., that guilt is individual and that a perpetrator's deeds have to be scrutinized and assessed individually in a trial that observes the axioms of due process.

Looking at the evolution of this latter debate and its eventual resolution among the Allies during World War II, two factors are of direct relevance. First, the pressure to assign collective guilt did not initially stem from the mass of the population. Not until very late in the conflict did average Americans blame the Germans collectively for the war and the awful truths that were slowly emerging.[3] Instead, the ideas of collective guilt and large-scale summary punishment were conceived among key decision-makers in London and Washington. British Prime Minister Winston Churchill, but also U.S. Treasury Secretary Henry Morgenthau, even went so far as to advocate the execution of thousands of captured Nazis on the spot.[4] No less significant, Morgenthau developed the most comprehensive program for the collective punishment of the Germans by envisioning the postwar demolition of major parts of the country's industrial infrastructure, particularly the heavy industries of the Ruhr region.[5]

Fearing with good reason that Morgenthau's plan would lead to massive starvation, further dislocation, and the threat of rebellion by millions of desperate Germans, the War and State Departments tried to scuttle this program. In this they were not completely successful, for elements of collective guilt and punishment continued to appear in Allied documents, most notably in the Joint Chiefs of Staff directive JCS 1067, issued in early 1945. This is probably also where the pressures of public opinion began to differ in comparison to previous years.

With reports and newsreel footage of the horrific conditions in the camps and the mass murder of Europe's Jews reaching ordinary Americans, opinion hardened considerably and thus strengthened the hand of Morgenthau and his supporters in Washington and London.[6]

The shift in public attitudes was reinforced by the growing popularity of a reinterpretation of the basic character of Nazism. If the Hitler regime had hitherto been seen as a tyranny that had imposed itself from above upon a paralyzed German people, the Third Reich now appeared as a system that had successfully mobilized the masses, who became willing participants in Hitler's wars of aggression and crimes against humanity. It is interesting to compare this development on the Western side with Stalin's interpretations of fascism and his policies during World War II. As far as culpability was concerned, he insisted from the start of inter-Allied cooperation and negotiation that guilt could only be individual, and that massive collective punishment of the kind proposed by Morgenthau was unacceptable.[7]

This position was of course related to the Stalinist understanding of the fascist phenomenon more generally. In this view, Hitler and his entourage had established a criminal regime for which they were to be tried individually. By contrast, the mass of the population, and the German working class in particular, had been terrorized by the political leadership, but never truly won over by Nazi ideology. At the same time, the actual wire-pullers behind the rise and the consolidation of the Hitler dictatorship had, in Stalin's eyes, been a small band of "monopoly capitalists."[8] Insofar as these men could be found and tried for individual crimes, for example, as employers of slave labor, their guilt or innocence was to be weighed by the courts. Meanwhile, their political responsibility as Germany's "ruling class" was to be assessed by the postwar Soviet occupation authorities, resulting in the expropriation of their property and hence the destruction of their economic and political power base. A new socialist economy and society was then to be built on the ruins of German capitalism and the fascist puppet regime it had created.

There is not space here to examine how the Stalinist position revealed itself in the Soviet zone of occupation after 1945.[9] As is well-known, with the beginning of the Cold War and division of Germany, the occupying powers began to pursue their separate policies in their respective spheres of influence in Central Europe. We are here concerned only with the Western zones, where the balance of opinion and power increasingly tilted toward a modification, if not a rejection, of the notion of collective guilt. One manifestation of this was the adoption of specific denazification procedures.[10] Fundamentally, the system of tribunals before which adult Germans had to appear established the principle of a search for individual culpability or innocence. The same principle also undergirded the Nuremberg trials of the major war criminals, as well as the subsequent prosecutions of individual physicians, lawyers, officers, bureaucrats, businessmen, and other members of elite groups. Vestiges of collective guilt appeared merely in the practice of summarily declaring certain Nazi organizations, such as the SS, to have been criminal, resulting in an automatic presumption of culpability for former members of these organizations.[11]

However, the triumph of the notion that guilt is individual and can only be shown through careful judicial examination created opportunities for the defendants, opportunities that the assumption of collective guilt followed by mass executions of the kind that Churchill had advocated, would never have offered. To avoid a guilty verdict and punishment, the accused individual (and in the end it was hundreds of thousands of them) deployed the full panoply of traditional techniques and arguments to prove his or her innocence. These techniques included submitting *Persilscheine* (evidence of lack of involvement in Nazi crimes), offering incomplete or false testimony, arguing about insufficient evidence, or taking advantage of the postwar chaos. Moreover, the inability of the courts and tribunals to deal with the huge caseloads deliberately and equitably led to a relaxation in the search for the individual culpability of millions of Germans. Many of them successfully defended themselves and were classified as mere "followers."[12] Others fell under various amnesties even before reaching the trial stage. The East-West conflict made it seem more urgent to finish the whole process and to obtain the cooperation of the West Germans in the building of a parliamentary-democratic and anti-communist political system and in the physical reconstruction of the country's industries and infrastructure. Both were preconditions for the integration of the emergent Federal Republic into the Atlantic economic and anti-Soviet defense community.[13]

The reversal from the days when Morgenthau had been a major voice in Washington was certainly striking, and some now argued that, as a consequence of these developments, the endeavor to establish the guilt even of individuals who had been directly involved in the Nazi dictatorship and its crimes had failed. But there were many others who felt that, after the major war criminals tried at Nuremberg had either been sentenced to death or had been given longer prison sentences, as much had been done as could be expected. In their view, it was now more important to "re-orient" the Germans toward a parliamentary constitutional order and political culture.[14] This, they added, was a goal that could not be achieved overnight, and that required patient persuasion and education of the next generation, untainted by the Nazi experience. The West Germans were to be led toward political democracy and then, slowly, to be allowed to practice it themselves without foreign tutelage. With this, the guilt question began to fade into the background.

It is not difficult to see that the country's elite groups greatly benefited from these shifts of emphasis from collective to individual culpability and, later, from the question of criminal guilt toward political responsibility. True, the searchlight was turned back on the older question of political failure during the rise and consolidation of the Nazi regime. But it could also be claimed that the lessons had been learned and that the political irresponsibility of the past would not be repeated. This is particularly true of the business community. The owners and managers had experienced the shifts in Allied policies directly. Accused of having been involved in the heinous crimes of the Hitler dictatorship, they were first arrested and interned as a group.[15] Subsequently, many of them were released and underwent denazification proceedings. At the same time, the most prominent among them, but also many others, were tried as war criminals. If found guilty, they were imprisoned or punished by loss of their jobs, their civil rights, or their property. Again, quite a few among them defended themselves successfully and had the charges dropped or reduced. What is more, through systematic and repeated counter-offensives the business community, which by 1948–1949 had reconstituted and organized itself into influential associations, most notably the Bundesverband der Deutschen Industrie, had also undermined and deflected the notion of its collective guilt.

Jonathan Wiesen has shown how many Americans, whose nation had now become the hegemonic power of the West, came to accept the German business community's self-justifications.[16] Looking for business opportunities and having met their potential West German partners, American entrepreneurs in particular were inclined to accept that Hitler had terrorized German businessmen even more than the rest of the population. If businessmen had collaborated with rather than resisted the regime, they had done so because they wanted to secure the survival of their enterprises in difficult times because of a primary duty they felt toward their investors and workers. In addition to this argument, businessmen professed (probably sincerely) that this time they were ready to assume a new co-responsibility for the material reconstruction of the West German economy, the social wellbeing of their workforces, and the fostering of political democracy.

The shift from a defensive posture that attempted to counter the negative images of businessmen found guilty of involvement in Nazi crimes to a more assertive portrayal of their positive role in the reconstruction of the Federal Republic is reflected in the various publications on business in the Third Reich and business in postwar West Germany that appeared in the late 1940s and early 1950s. An older generation of business historians made a significant contribution to this effort.[17] The drawback was that this trend, while playing down the question of guilt, revived an older question first raised in the 1930s: what was the political responsibility of German business for the rise and stabilization of the Nazi dictatorship? It was a question that historians and social scientists made the subject of renewed and vigorous research.

This research was characterized by two peculiarities. First, it was not the very small band of business historians in West Germany who began to work on the political role of business before and during the Nazi dictatorship. While business history was on the rise in the United States and in Britain, the genre in the Federal Republic was little more than an appendix to economic history, and West German economic historians found the twentieth century difficult soil to till. Instead, they devoted themselves, for example, to the study of the origins of the industrial revolution in Central Europe in the nineteenth century and the impressive successes of some regions in the process of industrialization before and after the founding of Bismarck's empire.[18] If these economic historians were at all interested in individual entrepreneurs, they tended to write in a Schumpeterian mode, highlighting the achievements of famous captains of industry such as Siemens, Krupp, or Rathenau. Those who did not confine themselves to analyzing macroeconomic trends in the nineteenth century, and who ventured into the interwar period, tended to de-emphasize the significance of individual entrepreneurs' agency, thereby buttressing the earlier argument that German business had been no more than a victim or plaything of a brutal Nazi dictatorship.

As a result, the business history of the Third Reich that was produced in the early Federal Republic, wittingly or unwittingly, assumed an apologetic tone. This led some to suspect that the scholars around

Wilhelm Treue's journal, which bore the programmatic title *Tradition,* acted as the historiographical arm of West Germany's conservative industrial associations and as defenders of business's role in the Third Reich.[19] Of course, the picture was complex, and this leads us to the second peculiarity of the scholarship of the 1950s. On the one hand, there was the steady stream of books and articles coming out of East Germany, the vast majority of which were stunningly simplistic about "capitalism's" responsibility for Nazism, and which must be viewed as the opposites of the defensive writings of West German business historians.[20]

Some of the most influential interpretations of Nazism had been put forward in the 1930s by refugee social scientists, many of whom wrote in a structuralist *Marxisant* vein.[21] At the same time, there were those structuralists who wrote within a more Weberian framework, seeing the Third Reich (and often also Stalinist Russia) as manifestations of the growing bureaucratization of the industrialized world.[22] It was a world of charismatic totalitarian leaders and faceless administrators who had finally succeeded in putting the helpless liberal individual into the "iron cage of serfdom" that Max Weber had gloomily written about long before the 1930s. It was a world of anonymous political machines that were relentlessly chewing up the human beings that appeared in their way.

These perspectives were taken up in West Germany, to which some of the refugees had returned, either as visiting professors or as permanent holders of chairs. Ernst Fraenkel became one of the most influential of these scholars at West Berlin's Free University, where he was mentor to Karl Dietrich Bracher and a group of historical social scientists from the younger generation.[23] By the late 1950s, the work of this group appeared in a number of bulky structural analyses of the collapse of the Weimar Republic and the consolidation of the Nazi dictatorship. Businessmen made an appearance in these books next to politicians, agrarians, and professionals, but did so not so much as individuals, but as members of collectives and power cartels. They were seen as having maneuvered in a force field defined by the gradual dissolution of Weimar's power structure and the creation of a power vacuum. That vacuum was finally filled in 1933 when the Nazis seized power.[24]

These interpretations proved immensely fruitful to an understanding of the larger forces underlying the Nazi seizure and consolidation of power, and they spawned many important studies that analyzed the institutional and organizational history of the Weimar Republic. These studies challenged early postwar notions, promoted by an older generation of historians with Gerhard Ritter most prominent among them, that Hitler had been an "accident" of German history, and that there was hence no continuity between the Third Reich and Weimar.[25] If Bracher had effectively undermined that notion, Fritz Fischer subsequently traced the lines of continuity even further back in time, linking the rise of Hitler to the developments and failures of the Hohenzollern monarchy.[26]

For the next thirty years, these structuralist approaches to modern German history complemented the structuralism of the economic historians. In the 1960s and 1970s, they received a fresh boost by the neo-Marxist interpretations of fascism and the more Weberian visions of the past developed at the University of Bielefeld and elsewhere.[27] Even the studies that were inspired by Hans Mommsen at Bochum University basically adhered to a structuralist perspective, although the Nazi dictatorship was assumed to have been propelled by the dynamics of a Social Darwinist struggle among a welter of Nazi party and state-bureaucratic agencies that resulted in the chaos of the Nazi decision-making process.[28]

Within this larger picture of the Third Reich that historians and social scientists were drawing in the 1970s, business was one such factor in this cutthroat competition for power and influence. Yet, the alternative view never disappeared from scholarly debate during the heyday of structuralism. It was a view that started from the question of agency, and found that industry and finance had demonstrated much less of it than the Marxists and those who had charged business with a criminal culpability had assumed. This argument is perhaps most powerfully presented in Henry A. Turner's books and articles which, at least in part, had their origins in a desire to disprove the orthodox Marxist hypothesis that Hitler had been in the pay of German big business.[29] Turner certainly demonstrated, through a meticulous evaluation of the sources, that it was indeed not "the monopoly capitalists," but the mass of faithful party members and small businessmen in the provinces who had provided the funding for Hitler's movement and propaganda campaigns.

If his *Big Business and the Rise of Hitler* proves that particular point, many reviewers of the book subsequently criticized Turner for his all too narrow conception of political responsibility and of what constituted the forces behind Hitler's rise and eventual seizure of power.[30] Although big business did not pay Hitler, it still bears a heavy political share in the fall of the Weimar Republic and in the dictatorship that came thereafter. It was their lack of support for, and indeed their active undermining of, the republican constitutional order (so the counterargument went) that had made industry and finance co-responsible. Not only did they fail to lift a finger in Weimar's defense, but they also promoted those on the right who wanted to destroy it for good.

That structuralist interpretations continued side-by-side into the 1980s, with studies written in a more Turnerian vein, is evidenced in Gerhard Mollin's *Montankonzerne und "Drittes Reich,"* on the one hand, and Peter Hayes's *Industry and Ideology,* a history of the IG Farben chemicals trust, on the other.[31] While the former is heavily structuralist and ultimately *menschenleer* (devoid of human agency), the latter begins his book with the following words: "The problem in history is to explain, not why bad men do evil, but why good men do."[32] In Hayes's view, "the leaders of IG Farben, Europe's largest private corporation between 1925 and 1945, were conventionally good men," who "brought the world a succession of beneficial inventions and who helped during the 1920s to attenuate the antagonisms between labor and management within Germany and between the country and its former enemies." No less important, "nearly all of them sensed the dangers Nazism posed and shunned the movement before 1933," and during Hitler's rule, "most of them futilely dissented from his worst excesses: aryanization, autarky, aggression, and forced labor." Hayes acknowledges that they were not "small men"; nor were they "greedy, union-bashing, revanchist wire-pullers who, according to vulgar Marxist caricatures, hired Hitler's party to serve their rapacious interests."[33] But he also sees them as men who "presided over the firm most widely credited, then and since, with carving out a lucrative and murderous place for itself. Farben's products became ubiquitous and essential. It made not only the synthetic rubber on which most Nazi vehicles rode and the fuel-from-coal that powered many of them, but also the gas that murdered more than a million people at Auschwitz.... Nearly 50 percent of IG Farben's 330,000-person workforce had come to consist of conscript or slave laborers, among whom were some of the perhaps 30,000 inmates of Auschwitz who eventually died in the company's new factory and mines near the camp."[34]

At first glance, Hayes seems to continue along the path that West German business historians had cleared in the 1950s and that Turner had extended in the 1960s and 1970s, supporting a trend that attempted to explain the behavior of reluctant businessmen who tried to do their best for their companies in increasingly difficult circumstances. However, as the last quotation indicates, Hayes also stands at the beginning of yet another shift in the research on the role of business in the

Third Reich, for he is moving the debate away from the question of political responsibility and back toward that of criminal culpability. True, Hayes stresses "the studied neutrality of my account,"[35] and wants to "enter into the subject at hand and stand back from it, attempting, in a sense, the impossible task of being in two places at one time." In the end, however, he does not shy away from making value judgments and from rejecting "the amoral pragmatism and profession-alism" of IG Farben's executives. Indeed, their drives

> ... make Farben an instructive case study in the plasticity of private interests and the consequences of permitting any single-minded doctrine to grasp the levers of the state. Lest that point be lost and readers distance themselves too far and easily from Farben's behavior, I have emphasized here the specious rationality of the concern's deeds and largely let the self-evident wickedness of some of them speak for itself.

However, what became, in the 1990s, another shift away from structure toward agency, and away from political responsibility toward criminal culpability, cannot be fully understood outside the context of larger changes that had affected the writing of history, changes that were slowly also reaching business history as one of its sub-disciplines. The beginnings of the change have several roots, but may perhaps be found most tangibly in social and labor history, as illustrated by the impact of E. P. Thompson's *The Making of the English Working Class*.[36] Although he approached his topic from a Marxist perspective, Thompson's book represents a rebellion against the orthodoxies of the interpretations of human history and class conflict produced by Marxism-Leninism. Although class remained a key category of analysis, he did not see it as something fixed and structural, nor as something predetermined. For Thompson, class is something that is "made" by human beings as they experience major socio-economic change. In the case of the working class, this change was the industrial revolution. In other words, class formation did not take place as the result of an iron law of scientific Marxism, but occurred through the agency and the active involvement of people in the historical process.

If the origins of this approach can be found already in the writings of Marx himself, the impact of Thompson's book on social and labor history in England and the United States can hardly be overestimated. It moved the whole field away from its erstwhile focus on organizations and institutions toward the analysis of collective and ultimately even individual experience and actors. The turn toward sociocultural questions in

British and American labor history was complemented in France at this time by the metamorphosis of the once decidedly structuralist Annales School, of which Fernand Braudel had become the most influential representative by the 1950s and 1960s, toward a culturalist approach of the kind to be found in the books of Alain Corbin.[37] The later *Annalistes* were less interested in Braudel's *structures et conjonctures* than in people's mentalities and perceptions of reality.

These developments, whether Thompson's preoccupation with experience or the *Annalistes'* interest in *mentalité,* spilled over into business history much more slowly than into other genres of historical writing. To some extent, this may have been because business historians had taken many of their tools of analysis from economics and economic history, both of which remained firmly wedded to the idea of being rigorously "scientific." Accordingly, both disciplines continued to support their basic structuralism with mathematical equations and statistical materials. Just as economic historians had been working with "hard" data on macroeconomic change, business historians focused on the hard evidence of profit and loss, of production and sales figures of individual firms in a supposedly free market, peopled by coolly calculating economic actors.

Again, we cannot go into the details of the evolution of economic and business history during the postwar period. With the emergence of business schools as separate entities in the American university system, the case method of studying organizational behavior and performance of companies within a competitive market began to dominate the field. This did not leave much room for questions that could not easily be quantified, that were shaped by subjective reactions to a particular economic or political milieu, or that might even be connected to strongly held political ideologies or the cultural conditioning of supposedly rational entrepreneurial and managerial actors.

In West Germany, the culturalist turn was delayed further by the institutional peculiarities of the historical profession. Still compromised by their work during the Third Reich, the early postwar generation of economic and business historians turned, as we have seen, toward the nineteenth century and the industrial revolution, in many cases even to the preceding history of agriculture and preindustrial societies. Under these circumstances, it took longer than in the U.S. or in Britain for a younger generation of scholars to assert itself, one that was ready to apply the newer methods that had been developed across the Atlantic. After this relatively late acceptance of modern economic and business history in the Federal Republic, fallout from the above-mentioned shift of the 1980s further delayed the study of experience, perception, mentality, and ideology.[38]

All this means that work in the Federal Republic of Germany on the role of business in the Third Reich had begun to change well before the collapse of communism. Despite their separation from history departments in many universities, business historians began to exchange the new ideas about experience, perception, and mentality across departmental boundaries. What probably gave the greatest boost to these developments in the field of Nazi history more generally was the veritable explosion of work on the Holocaust. It would be too easy to explain this upsurge purely in terms of Hollywood's discovery of the Jewish catastrophe with its focus on the victims, their lives, their agency, and their humanity.[39] But film and visual images, whether fictionalized or based on newsreel material, certainly had something to do with the shift away from the focus on totalitarian structures and all-consuming faceless bureaucracies. With major World War II anniversaries in the offing, commemoration became a preoccupation of sorts, and in its wake, the study of memory also became something like a historiographical growth industry.

This trend was accelerated by the fall of the Berlin Wall and the collapse of communism, a process that discredited much of East German historical writing on modern German economic and business history. It brought into the public arena the memories of millions of people whose voices had been subordinated to the official communist party line on the history of fascism. Although their numbers had shrunk during more than forty years of conflict between East and West, there were still enough victims of the Third Reich in the territories once occupied by the Wehrmacht to move the system of forced and slave labor into the public view, and with it, the question that Peter Hayes had raised in his book, i.e., the question of culpability, and not merely that of large anonymous organizations, but the culpability of individual companies and their leaders.

This volume contains much information on the wave of litigations against major industrial firms and banks following the collapse of communism, and on the legal settlements that were reached. The preceding essays also make clear that although problems of organization and structure have not disappeared from the historian's agenda, questions of agency have again moved into the foreground. With regard to German business history, it is not so much the experience of the victims that is at the center of attention, as they tried to escape and resist mass murder or being worked to death, but that of the perpetrators. At first, scholars put the organizers of the Holocaust in the higher and middle echelons of the German bureaucracy, the SS, and the Wehrmacht under the microscope.[40] Then it was the turn of "ordinary Germans," the German people and their role as "bystanders" in the persecution and destruction of the Jews of Europe.[41] In this larger context of a reexamination of the Third Reich, Germany's business elites, financial institutions, industries, and corporations also received increased scrutiny, leading to a fresh harvest of major studies.[42]

We are thus left with identifying areas where more work needs to be done, work that considers not only business responsibility for the Nazi rise to and consolidation of power, but also the question of culpability, of reluctant or willing collaboration in Nazi crimes. As a point of principle, it might be said that the job of the business historian of the Nazi period will not be done until all larger enterprises and all branches of industry and finance have been analyzed. The major questions to be asked in these studies are well illuminated by the preceding essays. Others will no doubt be added in due course by a younger generation of business historians interested in both structure and mentality, economic rationality and ideology.

With this agenda in mind, two phases in the evolution of the relationship between business and the Nazis would seem to warrant particularly close attention, namely, 1936–1939 and 1940–1942. To understand the dynamics of the first phase and the role of business within it, it is important to remember that Hitler's view of Germany's future revolved around certain dogmas. Fundamental to his thinking and that of his top aides was their racism and social Darwinism. History, in this view, was exclusively determined by the struggles between "races," in the course of which the allegedly superior "race" would conquer the inferior ones with the aim of ruthlessly exploiting them and their territories. Hence the constant talk about the need to acquire "living space," whereby Hitler's eyes were initially directed toward the East, though ultimately his vision encompassed the entire globe.

A reading of *Mein Kampf*, in which the fundamentals of Hitler's Weltanschauung may be found, reveals that his economic ideas revolve around the problem of the provision of food and the establishment of a territorial empire in the East, secure against any enemy blockade and built on the ruins of the "Jewish-Bolshevik" Soviet Union.[43] While these ideas were partly rooted in the traumatic memory of World War I, which, in Hitler's view and that of many other Germans, had been lost because the country lacked a sufficiently large land base, the Führer was never an agrarian ideologue like the Nazi Minister of Agriculture, R. Walther Darré. He knew that he needed industry and an advanced technological foundation not only to succeed with his conquests and empire-building, but also to create a prosperous mass consumption society of contented Aryans who would be resettled in larger towns in the newly acquired "living space," and surrounded by an exploited and carefully controlled helot society of "inferior races."[44]

However deeply ingrained these visions of Germany's future were in Hitler's mind, there is another fundamental point to be considered: once in power, if not in the years just before January 1933, he began to prioritize strictly his plans and to divulge only as many details as were necessary to formulate and implement policy in the years immediately ahead. This meant that he first began his program of rearming the land forces as an indispensable prerequisite of his projected conquest of living space in the East. For this he obtained the support of both the officer corps and business soon after his seizure of power, whereby the latter saw rearmament as a way of moving the economy out of the severe slump with the help of what has been called "military Keynesianism."[45]

With this aim in mind, business also accepted the nationalist and autarkic implications of the Nazi economic program. For heavy industry, which was primarily oriented toward the domestic market, this was a relatively easy course to follow. It was more difficult for enterprises whose production was geared toward the world market and which had traditionally been internationalist. Yet, with the international economy in a state of collapse there was, at least for the moment, a strong incentive for the export-oriented industries as well as banking to fall into line.[46]

However, by 1935, the compromise between the Nazi regime and business had come under growing strain. At this point, and with the national economy clearly emerging from its depression, it was a matter of either abandoning or at least sharply scaling back the rearmament program of the previous years and returning to civilian production as well as exports, or of increasing the pace of rearmament, thereby accepting a further growth of the already enormous Reich debt. The only justification for pursuing this latter course was to use the military hardware in due course in a victorious war, after which Germany would recoup its previous military expenditures through the exploitation of the conquered territories in a German-dominated Europe.[47]

As is well known, Hitler adopted the latter strategy by promulgating the infamous Four Year Plan in 1936, with its secret appendix decreeing that Germany be ready for war in four years' time.[48] Earlier studies that focused on this crucial period of 1935–1936 have unearthed enough evidence to show that not only Reichsbank president and Minister of Economics Hjalmar Schacht, but also top managers, especially in the Ruhr industries, appreciated the significance of the Four Year Plan as a turning point. Nevertheless, it is worthwhile for future research to revisit this period and to examine the behavior of all larger and smaller enterprises and financial institutions, and to do so also from a sociological perspective. What do I mean by this? Much valuable recent work has concentrated on aryanization and the exclusion of Jews from the Nazi economy.[49] But 1935–1936 was also a period in which an older generation of non-Jewish entrepreneurs and senior managers went either into retirement or into "inner emigration," often after "promotion" to their company's supervisory board. They were either opposed to, or fatalistic about, the Nazi regime that, they realized, was now launched on a course of violent expansionism to implement its Social Darwinist and racist aims, and to stave off national financial bankruptcy.

They were replaced by men whose dynamism and energy, as Lutz Schwerin von Krosigk has put it, "degenerated into brutality, and who would not be impressed by anything."[50] These were the men who, while perhaps not favoring a war of aggression, certainly shared the view that Germany needed to extend its economic domination of Eastern Europe. Only when a more self-sufficient position had been reached on the European continent would some of them contemplate the rebuilding of the country's former ties with the international economy. Like the Nazi elite, many of them envisioned the economic future of the world in terms of large blocs or empires, like that of Britain, like the economic dominion that the Japanese had begun to construct by force on the East Asian mainland, or like the U.S.-dominated "American Hemisphere."[51] After 1936, the members of this generation had three years to consolidate their positions within their enterprises, and to demonstrate their collaboration, more willing than reluctant, with the political leadership, the ministerial bureaucracy, and the officer corps charged with the implementation of the Four-Year Plan. This is when they nazified themselves. In a speech of November 1937, Hitler had outlined the next stage of conflict and expansionism, arguing that Germany had to be prepared from about 1944–1945 onward for a confrontation with the sea powers. Shortly thereafter, the aircraft industry began to lay its plans for stepped-up production, and by January 1939 the navy discussed the "Z-Plan" and the buildup of a *Weltmachtflotte*, a fleet commensurate with the status of a world power.[52]

The years 1936–1939 form the background to the second crucial period that warrants further investigation: the years 1940–1942. A close reading of the contributions to this volume will reveal how each of the authors emphasizes this period. But these were not just the years when the Nazi regime initiated its program of resettlement and mass murder in which, as Michael Thad Allen demonstrates, German industry and finance became deeply and criminally involved; these are also the years of the "splendid victories" of the Wehrmacht when, especially in the summer of 1941, most Germans assumed victory over Stalin to be just around the corner. This expectation not only generated the decisions to murder the Jews of Europe, but also led to hectic activity among the now firmly entrenched generation of managers. They scoured the conquered territories in the hope of grabbing industrial and commercial assets. To be sure, not all of them were so brutal as to turn up in the boardroom of a French or Czech company to announce a wholesale takeover. There were also those who offered cooperation and participation within the "new economic order."[53]

Again, though much good work has already been done, we need a more detailed picture of the behavior and mentalities of businessmen in this period of apparent boundless optimism and far-reaching self-nazification. What precisely were the attitudes and perceptions of those years of seemingly impending victory, and not only with respect to forced and slave labor, but also to foreign commercial property? The point is that in this period of triumph, blueprints were no longer just vague plans. Just as the regime put into practice its racist doctrines, the Ministry of Economics and other agencies, together with business, began to realize their aims of economic domination.[54] There was no doubt that the national economies of the conquered nations would have to serve the perceived needs of the German hegemon.

Another question that scholars such as Ludolf Herbst have been asking, but that requires further exploration, concerns the balance of power between the regime and business, and the kind of an economic system that would have emerged had the Third Reich not faced defeat from 1943 onward.[55] It is worth hypothesizing about the future structure and organization of a Nazi new economic order, also as a way of trying to understand the dynamics of National Socialism. As far as Hitler himself is concerned, this apparently remained one of the issues on which he did not clearly show his hand, even in the hour of what was regarded as likely military victory in 1941. There are a few casual remarks in his *Table Talk* that revolve primarily around his ideas of resettlement in the East.[56] He also spoke about how to cover the Reich's enormous debt. We also know that planning for an administration of overseas colonies that had been set up in 1940 continued in 1941–1942. Finally, it is relevant that Albert Speer eagerly built scale models for an array of building projects in Germany's major cities, and work on the reconstruction of the Nuremberg rally grounds, for example, continued as late as 1943.[57] Meanwhile, Hermann Göring and other leading Nazis occasionally dropped hints that the relationship between the business community and the state would be fundamentally reshaped once the war was over. How did the many industrialists and bankers react to these hints?

What we need, therefore, is a picture of this state-business relationship that is both more comprehensive and nuanced than what we have at present. We also have to integrate into this picture the contributions that various institutes and researchers working on *Grossraumwirtschaft* (closed space economy) made to the debate that raged at this time in the higher echelons of business and bureaucracy.[58] At this point it may not be too far-fetched to predict that once this work has been done, the question not only of political responsibility but also of criminal culpability among businessmen may well appear in a more glaring light. The managers of the early 1940s were not merely anxious to secure the survival of their enterprises; they had been taken in by the imperialist and racist ideology of Nazism, some of them perhaps still reluctantly, but many more willingly. It is not a pretty picture, and Hayes is correct in holding up the record of these men as warning examples of the total bankruptcy to which political irresponsibility, moral corruption, and collusion in crime must inevitably lead.

Notes

1. See this volume, 15.
2. For summaries of these debates, see, for example, John Hiden and John Farquharson, *Explaining Hitler's Germany: Historians and the Third Reich* (Totawa, N.J.: Barnes & Noble, 1983).
3. Thus, a poll by the National Opinion Research Center of the end of 1944 showed that relatively few Americans held feelings of animosity toward ordinary Germans. See Telford Taylor, *The Anatomy of the Nuremberg Trials: A Personal Memoir* (Boston: Little Brown, 1992), 39.
4. See, for example, Michael Marrus, *The Nuremberg War Crimes Trial, 1945–1946: A Documentary History* (Boston: Bedford Books, 1997), esp. 25.
5. See, for example, Bernd Greiner, *Die Morgenthau-Legende. Zur Geschichte eines umstrittenen Plans* (Hamburg: Hamburger Edition, 1995).
6. See, for example, Ariel J. Kochavi, *Prelude to Nuremberg: Allied War Crimes Policy and the Question of Punishment* (Chapel Hill: University of North Carolina Press, 1998).
7. See, for example, Taylor, *Anatomy of the Nuremberg Trials*, esp. 34, though the Soviet position seems to have wavered over time.
8. See, for example, Reinhard Kühnl, ed., *Texte zur Faschismusdiskussion. Positionen und Kontroversen* (Reinbek: Rowohlt, 1974), 14ff.
9. On this theme, see Norman Naimark, *The Russians in Germany: A History of the Soviet Zone of Occupation* (Cambridge: Harvard University Press, 1995).
10. On Western denazification, see, for example, Constantine Fitzgibbon, *Denazification* (London: Joseph, 1969); Edward N. Peterson, *The American Occupation of Germany* (Detroit: Wayne State University Press, 1977); Nicholas Pronay and Keith Wilson, eds., *The Political Re-education of Germany and Her Allies after World War II* (Totawa: Barnes & Noble, 1985).
11. See Articles 9 and 10 of the Charter of the International Military Tribunal. See also Bradley Smith, *The Road to Nuremberg* (New York: Basic Books, 1981), 185.
12. See, for example, Justus Fürstenberg, *Entnazifizierung: ein Kapitel deutscher Nachkriegspolitik* (Neuwied: Luchterhand, 1969).
13. See, for example, John Gimbel, *The American Occupation of Germany: Politics and the Military* (Stanford: Stanford University Press, 1968).
14. See, for example, James F. Tent, *Mission on the Rhine: Reeducation and Denazification in American-Occupied Germany* (Chicago: University of Chicago Press, 1983).
15. See, for example, Volker R. Berghahn, *The Americanization of West German Industry, 1945–1973* (New York: Cambridge University Press, 1986), 40ff.
16. See, for example, Jonathan Wiesen, *West German Industry and the Challenge of the Nazi Past, 1945–1955* (Chapel Hill: University of North Carolina Press, 2001), 52ff.
17. Ibid., 94ff.
18. See Volker R. Berghahn, "Foreign Influences on German Social and Economic History," in *Vierteljahrschrift für Sozial- und Wirtschaftsgeschichte*, Sonderband (2003), in press.
19. Ibid.
20. See, for example, Andreas Dorpalen, *German History in Marxist Perspective: The East German Approach* (Detroit: Wayne State University Press, 1985).

21. See, for example, Franz Neumann, *Behemoth: The Structure and Practice of National Socialism, 1933–1944* (New York: Oxford University Press, 1944).

22. See, for example, Abbott Gleason, *Totalitarianism: The Inner History of the Cold War* (New York: Oxford University Press, 1995), 31ff.

23. See, for example, Arno Mohr, "Politikwissenschaft als Alternative" (Ph.D. diss., Universität Heidelberg, 1985).

24. Karl Dietrich Bracher, *Die Auflösung der Weimarer Republik. Eine Studie zum Problem des Machtverfalls in der Demokratie,* 3rd ed. (Villingen: Ring-Verlag, 1960).

25. See, for example, Winfried Schulze, *Deutsche Geschichtswissenschaft nach 1945* (Munich: Oldenbourg, 1989).

26. Fritz Fischer, *Krieg der Illusionen* (Düsseldorf: Droste Verlag, 1969).

27. For a summary of these debates, see Ian Kershaw, *The Nazi Dictatorship: Problems and Perspectives of Interpretation,* 3rd ed. (London: E. Arnold, 1993), 17ff.

28. Ibid., 59ff.

29. Henry A. Turner, *German Big Business and the Rise of Hitler* (New York: Oxford University Press, 1985).

30. See, for example, Dick Geary, "The Industrial Elite and the Nazis in the Weimar Republic," in *The Nazi Machtergreifung,* ed. Peter D. Stachura (London: Allen & Unwin, 1983), 85–100.

31. Gerhard Mollin, *Montankonzerne und "Drittes Reich": der Gegensatz zwischen Monopolindustrie und Befehlswirtschaft in der deutschen Rüstung und Expansion 1936–1944* (Göttingen: Vandenhoeck und Ruprecht, 1988); Peter Hayes, *Industry and Ideology. IG Farben in the Nazi Era* (New York: Cambridge University Press, 1987).

32. Hayes, *Industry and Ideology,* xi.

33. Ibid.

34. Ibid., xii.

35. Ibid., xv.

36. See, for example, Harvey Kaye and Keith McClelland, eds., *E.P. Thompson: Critical Perspectives* (Philadelphia: Temple University Press, 1990).

37. See, for example, Peter Burke, *The French Historical Revolution: The Annales School, 1929–1989* (Stanford: Stanford University Press, 1990).

38. Volker R. Berghahn, "Unternehmer in der frühen Bundesrepublik. Selbstverständnis und politischer Einfluss in der Marktwirtschaft," in *Unternehmerwirtschaft zwischen Markt und Lenkung,* ed. Thomas Grossbölting und Rüdiger Schmidt (Munich: Oldenbourg, 2002), 283–300, esp. 296ff.

39. See, for example, Saul Friedländer, *Mass Murder and German Society in the Third Reich: Interpretations and Dilemmas* (London: Royal Holloway, University of London, 2001), 7–25.

40. See Michael Wildt, *Generation der Unbedingten: Das Führungskorps des Reichssicherheitshauptamtes* (Hamburg: Hamburger Edition, 2002).

41. See, for example, Daniel Goldhagen, *Hitler's Willing Executioners: Ordinary Germans and the Holocaust* (New York: Knopf, 1996); Christopher Browning, *Ordinary Men: Reserve Police Battalion 101 and the Final Solution* (New York: HarperCollins, 1992).

42. See, for example, the recent publications of Gerald Feldman, Harold James, Peter Hayes, and Lothar Gall. See also Christopher Kobrak, *National Cultures and*

International Competition: The Experience of Schering AG, 1851–1950 (New York: Cambridge University Press, 2002).

43. See, for example, Eberhard Jaeckel, *Hitler's Weltanschauung: A Blueprint for Power* (Middletown: Wesleyan University Press, 1972).

44. See, for example, Volker R. Berghahn, *Europa im Zeitalter der Weltkriege* (Frankfurt am Main: Fischer Verlag, 2002), 148ff.

45. See, for example, Klaus Hildebrand, *The Foreign Policy of the Third Reich* (Berkeley: University of California Press, 1973); Karl Dietrich Bracher et al., *Die nationalsozialistische Machtergreifung. Studien zur Errichtung des totalitären Herrschaftssystems in Deutschland 1933–34* (Opladen: Westdeutscher Verlag, 1960), 785ff.

46. See, for example, Hayes, *Industry and Ideology,* 69ff, n. 31.

47. See, for example, Dieter Petzina, *Autarkiepolitik im Dritten Reich. Der nationalsozialistische Vierjahresplan* (Stuttgart: Deutsche Verlags-Anstalt, 1968); Volker R. Berghahn, ed., *Quest for Economic Empire: European Strategies of German Big Business in the Twentieth Century* (Oxford: Berghahn Books, 1996), esp. 17ff.

48. See Petzina, *Autarkiepolitik.*

49. See, for example, Frank Bajohr, *"Aryanization" in Hamburg: The Economic Exclusion of the Jews and the Confiscation of Their Property in Nazi Germany* (New York: Berghahn Books, 2002).

50. Lutz Schwerin von Krosigk, *Die grosse Zeit des Feuers,* vol. 3 (Tübingen: Wunderlich, 1959), 560.

51. On Japan, see Joyce Lebra-Chapman, *Japan's Greater East Asia Co-prosperity Sphere in World War II* (Oxford: Oxford University Press, 1975).

52. Klaus Hildebrand, *Vom Reich zum Weltreich: Hitler, NSDAP und Kolonialfrage 1919–1945* (Munich: Wilhelm Fink Verlag, 1969).

53. See, for example, Volker R. Berghahn and Paul J. Friedrich, *Otto A. Friedrich, ein politischer Unternehmer: sein Leben und seine Zeit, 1902–1975* (Frankfurt am Main: Campus Verlag, 1993), 19ff.

54. See, for example, Reinhard Opitz, ed., *Europastrategien des deutschen Kapitals 1900–1945* (Cologne: Pahl-Rugenstein, 1977).

55. Ludolf Herbst, *Der totale Krieg und die Ordnung der Wirtschaft. Die Kriegswirtschaft im Spannungsfeld von Politik, Ideologie und Propaganda, 1939–1945* (Stuttgart: Deutsche Verlags-Anstalt, 1982). Herbst was among the first to raise these questions.

56. See Henry Picker, ed., *Hitlers Tischgespräche im Führerhauptquartier* (Stuttgart: Seewald Verlag, 1965), 143.

57. See Albert Speer, *Inside the Third Reich* (New York: Macmillan, 1970); Jochen Thies, *Architekt der Weltherrschaft. Die Endziele Hitlers* (Düsseldorf: Droste Verlag, 1976).

58. Eckart Teichert, *Autarkie und Grossraumwirtschaft in Deutschland 1930–1939: Aussenwirtschaftspolitische Konzeptionen zwischen Wirtschaftskrise und Zweiten Weltkrieg* (Munich: Oldenbourg, 1984).

Appendix A

Law for the Restoration of the Professional Civil Service, 7 April 1933

The Reich Government has enacted the following Law, promulgated herewith:

§ 1

1) To restore a national professional civil service and to simplify administration, civil servants may be dismissed from office in accordance with the following regulations, even where there would be no grounds for such action under the prevailing Law.

2) For the purposes of this Law the following are to be considered civil servants: direct and indirect officials of the Reich, direct and indirect officials of the *Länder,* officials of Local Councils, and of Federations of Local Councils, officials of Public Corporations as well as of Institutions and Enterprises of equivalent status... The provisions will apply also to officials of Social Insurance organizations having the status of civil servants...

§ 2

1) Civil servants who have entered the service since November 9, 1918, without possessing the required or customary educational background or other qualifications are to be dismissed from the service. Their previous salaries will continue to be paid for a period of three months following their dismissal.

2) They will have no claim to temporary pensions, full pensions or survivors' benefits, nor to retain designation of rank or titles, or to wear uniforms or emblems...

§ 3

1) Civil Servants who are not of Aryan descent are to be retired (§ 8 ff.); if they are honorary officials, they are to be dismissed from their official status.

2) Section 1 does not apply to civil servants in office from August 1, 1914, who fought at the Front for the German Reich or its Allies in the World War, or whose fathers or sons fell in the World War. Other exceptions may be permitted by the Reich Minister of the Interior in coordination with the Minister concerned or with the highest authorities with respect to civil servants working abroad.

§ 4

1) Civil servants whose previous political activities afford no assurance that they will at all times give their fullest support to the national State, can be dismissed from the service…

> Reich Chancellor
> Adolf Hitler
> Reich Minister of Interior
> Frick
> Reich Minister of Finance
> Graf Schwerin von Krosigk

Source: Yitzhak Arad, Israel Gutman, and Abraham Margaliot, eds., *Documents on the Holocaust* (Lincoln: University of Nebraska Press, 1999).

APPENDIX B

The Leadership of the German Government on the Effect
on the Economy of German Policy toward the Jews,
August 1935

At the … meeting of senior officials called on August 20, 1935, President of the Reichsbank Dr. Schacht first of all described the worrying effects that German policy with regards to the Jews was having on the economic situation by quoting specific examples. His account was climaxed by the observation that he was forced to entertain serious doubts whether in view of the increasingly radical trend in the policy on the Jews it would be possible to achieve the economic targets set by the Führer, finding work for the unemployed and reconstruction of the Wehrmacht (and obtaining raw materials from abroad) … Schacht rejected any suggestion that he might be called pro-Jewish. All he was doing was to point out the results for his field of operations of irresponsible incitement against the Jews. Schacht was most sharply critical of the independent operations of certain Party agencies, the Labor Front, the National Socialist Trade and Crafts Association (NS-Hago), as well as the activities of *Gauleiter* Streicher.

Reich Minister of the Interior Frick supported Mr. Schacht's criticism in general and had a memorandum read, which was directed at the Governments of the German Länder, which, in a sharp tone, demanded determined intervention by the police against individual operations directed against Jews. Frick added the explanation that the police would remain absolutely passive if Party Organizations themselves carried out anti-Semitic operations. In that case, however, the responsibility would remain exclusively that of the Party.

Minister of State Wagner, as Representative of the Party, declared that the Party also disapproved of individual operations. But nevertheless the State must take the anti-Semitic mood of the population into account, and proceed with the gradual elimination of the Jews from the economy by means of legislation. This would reduce the unrest that now existed within the population.

Secretary of State von Bülow pointed out the importance of the Jewish Question in foreign affairs. Foreign affairs suffered considerably from the backlash following excesses against the Jews by irresponsible organizations. In view of the approaching Olympics, whose importance for foreign relations could not be overestimated, some arrangement must be made to prevent incidents such as that on the Kurfürstendamm, in consideration of the expected influx of foreigners.

It emerged from the discussion that, generally speaking, the Party's Jewish Program should be retained as to substance, but the methods applied be subjected to criticism. There would be legal measures to put a stop to the limitless growth of anti-Semitic activities on the part of irresponsible organizations and private individuals in every possible area of life. But at the same time there would be special legislation to control Jewry in certain areas, particularly in all economic matters; as for the rest, they were on principle to retain their freedom of movement.

No general and unified aim of German policy with respect to the Jews was produced by the debate. The arguments of Ministers responsible for various departments merely revealed that the Jewish Question made their political task more difficult. The observation made by Mr. Schacht that he would not be able to accept responsibility for the completion of the program of Reconstruction unless something were done about anti-Semitic excesses, sounded, in its various forms, like an ultimatum. But Mr. Schacht did not draw the conclusion that he must demand a radical change in the Party's Jewish Program, or even the methods by which it was carried out, for example, a ban on the *Stürmer*. On the contrary, he maintained the fiction of the 100-percent execution of the Jewish Program.

Both Mr. Schacht and the Party Representative pointed out during the debate that in this question there was a divergence in the basic attitudes of the Party and State, which was significant in principle beyond the concrete question under discussion. The representatives of the departments in most cases pointed out practical disadvantages which developed in their areas, while the Party based the need for radical steps against the Jews on political-emotional and abstract-philosophical grounds.

Source: Yitzhak Arad, Israel Gutman, and Abraham Margaliot, eds., *Documents on the Holocaust* (Lincoln: University of Nebraska Press, 1999).

Appendix C

The Launching of the Four-Year Plan,
August to September 1936

This memorandum was given to me personally by A.H. in 1944 with the following statement:

The lack of understanding of the Reich Ministry for Economics and the opposition of German business to all large-scale plans induced him to compose this memorandum at Obersalzberg.

He decided at that time to carry out a Four-Year Plan and to put Göring in charge of it. On the occasion of Göring's appointment as the official in charge of the Four-Year Plan he gave him this memorandum. There are only three copies, one of which he gave to me.

[signed] ALBERT SPEER

The Political Situation

Politics are the conduct and the course of the historical struggle of nations for life. The aim of these struggles is survival. Even ideological struggles have their ultimate cause and are most deeply motivated by nationally determined purposes and aims of life. But religions and ideologies are always able to impart particular bitterness to such struggles, and therefore also to give them great historical impressiveness. They leave their imprint on centuries of history. Nations and States living within the sphere of such ideological or religious conflicts cannot opt out of or dissociate themselves from these events. Christianity and the barbarian invasions determined the course of history for centuries. Mohammedanism convulsed the Orient as well as the Western world for half a millennium. The consequences of the Reformation have affected the whole of central Europe. Nor were individual countries—either by skill or by deliberate non-participation———able to steer clear of events. Since the outbreak of the French Revolution the world has been moving with ever-increasing speed towards a new conflict, the most extreme solution of which is Bolshevism; and the essence and goal of Bolshevism is the elimination of those strata of mankind which have hitherto provided the leadership and their replacement by world-wide Jewry.

No nation will be able to avoid or abstain from this historical conflict. *Since Marxism, through its victory in Russia, has established one of the greatest empires as a forward base for its future operations, this question has become a menacing one. Against a democratic world which is ideologically split stands a unified aggressive will, based on an authoritarian ideology.*

The military resources of this aggressive will are in the meantime rapidly increasing from year to year. One has only to compare the Red Army as it actually exists today with the assumptions of military men of ten or fifteen years ago to realize the menacing extent of this development. Only consider the results of a further development over ten, fifteen or twenty years and think what conditions will be like then.

Germany

Germany will as always have to be regarded as the focus of the Western world against the attacks of Bolshevism. I do not regard this as an agreeable mission but as a serious handicap and burden for our national life, regrettably resulting from our disadvantageous position in Europe. We cannot, however, escape this destiny. Our political position results from the following:

At the moment there are only two countries in Europe which can be regarded as standing firm against Bolshevism—Germany and Italy. The other nations are either corrupted by their democratic way of life, infected by Marxism and therefore likely to collapse in the foreseeable future, or ruled by authoritarian Governments, whose sole strength lies in their military resources; this means, however, that being obliged to protect their leadership against their own peoples by the armed hand of the Executive, they are unable to use this armed hand for the protection of their countries against external enemies. None of these countries would ever be capable of waging war against Soviet Russia with any prospects of success. In fact, apart from Germany and Italy, only Japan can be considered as a Power standing firm in the face of the world peril.

It is not the aim of this memorandum to prophesy the moment when the untenable situation in Europe will reach the stage of an open crisis. I only want, in these lines, to express my conviction that this crisis cannot and will not fail to occur, and that Germany has the duty of securing her existence by every means in the face of this catastrophe, and to protect herself against it, and that this obligation has a number of implications involving the most important tasks that our people have ever been set. *For a victory of Bolshevism over Germany would lead not to a Versailles Treaty but to the final destruction, indeed to the annihilation, of the German people.*

The extent of such a catastrophe cannot be estimated. How, indeed, would the whole of densely populated Western Europe (including Germany) after a collapse into Bolshevism, live through probably the most gruesome catastrophe which has been visited on mankind since the downfall of the states of antiquity. *In face of the necessity of warding off this danger, all other considerations must recede into the background as completely irrelevant.*

Germany's Defensive Capacity

Germany's defensive capacity is based upon several factors. I would give pride of place to the intrinsic value of the German people *per se*. The German nation with an impeccable political leadership, a firm ideology, a thorough military organization, certainly constitutes the most valuable factor of resistance in the world today. Political leadership is ensured by the National Socialist Party; ideological solidarity has, since the victory of National Socialism, been introduced to a degree that has never previously been attained. It must be constantly deepened and strengthened on the basis of this concept. This is the aim of the National Socialist education of our people.

The development of our military capacity is to be effected through the new Army. *The extent of the military development of our resources cannot be too large, nor its pace too swift.* It is a major error to believe that there can be any argument on these points or any comparison with other vital necessities. However well-balanced the general pattern of a nation's life ought to be there must at particular times be certain disturbances of the balance at the expense of other less vital tasks. *If we do not succeed in bringing the German Army as rapidly as possible to the rank of premier army in the world so far as its training, raising of units, armaments, and, above all, its spiritual education also is concerned, then Germany will be lost!* In this the basic principle applies that omissions during the months of peace cannot be made good in centuries.

Hence all other desires without exception must come second to this task. For this task involves life and the preservation of life, and all other desires—however understandable at other junctures—are unimportant or even mortally dangerous and are therefore to be rejected. Posterity will ask us one day, not what were the means, the reasons or the convictions by which we thought fit today to achieve the salvation of the nation, but *whether* in fact we achieved it. And on that day it will be no excuse for our downfall for us to describe the means which were infallible, but, alas, brought about our ruin.

Germany's Economic Situation

Just as the political movement among our people knows only one goal, the preservation of our existence, that is to say, the securing of all the spiritual and other prerequisites for the self-assertion of our nation, so neither has the economy any other goal than this. The nation does not live for the economy, for economic leaders, or for economic or financial theories; on the contrary, it is finance and the economy, economic leaders and theories, which all owe unqualified service in this struggle for the self-assertion of our nation. Germany's economic situation is, however, in the briefest outline as follows:

1. We are overpopulated and cannot feed ourselves from our own resources.
2. When our nation has six or seven million unemployed, the food situation improves because these people lack purchasing power. It naturally makes a difference whether six million people have 40 marks a month to spend, or 100 marks. It should not be overlooked that a third of all who earn their living is involved, that is to say that, taken as a proportion of the total population, through the National Socialist economic policy about 28 million people have been afforded an increase in their standard of living of, an average, from at least 50 marks a month to at most 100—120 marks. This means an increased and understandable run on the foodstuffs market.
3. But if this rise in employment fails to take place, the effect of undernourishment will be that a higher percentage of the population must

gradually be deducted from the body of our nation, so far as its effective contribution is concerned. Thus, despite the difficult food situation, the most important task of our economic policy is to see to it that all Germans are incorporated into the economic process, and so the prerequisites for normal consumption are created.

4. In so far as this consumption concerns articles of general use, it can be satisfied to a *large* extent by an increase in production. In so far as this consumption falls upon the foodstuffs market, it cannot be satisfied from the domestic German economy. For, although the output of numerous products can be increased without difficulty, the yield of our agricultural production can undergo no further substantial increase. It is equally impossible for us at present to manufacture artificially certain raw materials which we lack in Germany or to find other substitutes for them.

5. There is, however, no point in endless repetition of the fact that we lack foodstuffs and raw materials; what matters is the taking of those measures which can bring about a *final* solution for the *future* and a *temporary* easing of conditions during the *transition* period.

6. The final solution lies in extending our living space, that is to say, extending the sources of raw materials and foodstuffs of our people. It is the task of the political leadership one day to solve this problem.

7. The temporary easing of conditions can be achieved only within the framework of our present economy. In this connexion, the following must be noted:

   (a) Since the German people will be increasingly dependent on imports for their food and must similarly, whatever happens, import a proportion at least of certain raw materials from abroad, every effort must be made to facilitate these imports.

   (b) An increase in our own exports is possible in theory but in practice hardly likely. Germany does not export to a political or economic vacuum, but to areas where competition is very intense. Compared with the general international economic depression, our exports have fallen, not only *not more,* but in fact *less* than those of other nations and states. But since imports of food on the whole cannot be substantially reduced and are more likely to increase, an adjustment must be found in some other way.

   (c) It is, however, impossible to use foreign exchange allocated for the purchase of raw materials to import foodstuffs without inflicting a heavy and perhaps even fatal blow on the rest.

> *But above all it is absolutely impossible to do this at the expense of national rearmament.* I must at this point sharply reject the view that by restricting national rearmament, that is to say, the manufacture of arms and ammunition, we could bring about an 'enrichment' in raw materials which might then benefit Germany in the event of war. Such a view is based on a complete misconception, to put it mildly, of the tasks and military requirements that lie before us. For even a successful saving of raw materials by reducing, for instance, the production of munitions would merely mean that we should stockpile these raw materials in time of peace so as to manufacture them only in the event of war, that is to say, we should be depriving ourselves during the most critical months of munitions in exchange for raw copper, lead, or possibly iron. But in that case it would nonetheless be better for the nation to enter the war without a single kilogram of copper in stock but with full munition depots rather than with empty munition depots but so-called 'enriched' stock of raw material.

War makes possible the mobilization of even the last remaining supplies of metal. For it then becomes not an *economic problem,* but solely a *question of will.* And the National Socialist leadership of the country will have not only the will but also the resolution and the toughness necessary to solve these problems in the event of war. But it is much more important to prepare for war in time of peace. Moreover, in this respect the following must be stated:

There can be no building up of a reserve of *raw materials* for the event of war, just as there can be no building up of foreign exchange reserves. The attempt is sometimes made today so to represent matters as if Germany went to war in 1914 with well-prepared stocks of raw material. That is a lie. No country can assemble in advance the quantities of raw materials necessary for war lasting longer than, say, one year. But if any nation were really in a position to assemble those quantities of raw material needed for a year, then its political, military and economic leaders would deserve to be hanged. For they would in fact be setting aside the available copper and iron in preparation for the conduct of a war instead of manufacturing shells. But Germany went into the world war without any reserves whatsoever. What was available at that time in Germany in the way of apparent peacetime reserves was counterbalanced and rendered valueless by the miserable war stocks of ammunition. *Moreover, the quantities of war materials that are needed for a war are so large that there has* NEVER *in the history of the world been a real stockpiling for a period of any length!* and as regards preparations in the form of piling up foreign exchange it is quite clear that:

1. War is capable of devaluing foreign exchange at any time, unless it is held in gold.
2. There is not the least guarantee that gold itself can be converted in time of war into raw materials. During the world war Germany still possessed very large assets in foreign exchange in a great many countries. It was not, however, possible for our cunning economic policy-makers to bring to Germany, in exchange for them fuel rubber, copper or tin in any sufficient quantity. To assert the contrary is ridiculous nonsense. For this reason, and in order to secure the food supplies of our people, the following task presents itself as imperative:

It is not sufficient merely to establish from time to time raw material or foreign exchange balances, or to talk about the preparation of a war economy in time of peace; on the contrary, it is essential to ensure all the food supplies required in peacetime and, above all, those means for the conduct of a war which can be secured by human energy and activity. I therefore draw up the following programme for a final provision of our vital needs:

I. Parallel with the military and political rearmament and mobilization of our nation must go its economic rearmament and mobilization, and this must be effected in the same tempo, with the same determination, and if need be with the same ruthlessness as well. In future the interests of individual gentlemen can no longer play any part in these matters. There is only one interest, the interest of the nation; only one view, the bringing of Germany to the point of political and economic self-sufficiency.

II. For this purpose, foreign exchange must be saved in all those areas where our needs can be satisfied by German production, in order that it may be used for those requirements which can under no circumstances be fulfilled except by import:

III. Accordingly, German fuel production must now be stepped up with the utmost speed and brought to final completion within eighteen months. This task must be attacked and carried out with the same determination as the waging of a war, since it is on the discharge of this task, not upon the laying in of stocks of petroleum, that the conduct of the future war depends.

IV. The mass production of synthetic rubber must also be organized and achieved with the same urgency. From now on there must be no talk of processes not being fully determined and other such excuses. It is not a matter of discussing whether we are to wait any longer; otherwise time will be lost, and the hour of peril will take us all by surprise. Above all, it is not the job of the economic institutions of Government to rack their brains over methods of production. This has nothing whatever to do with the Ministry of Economics. Either we possess today a private industry, in which case its job is to rack its brains about methods of production; or we believe that it is the Government's job to determine methods of production, and in that case we have no further need of private industry.

V. The question of the cost of producing these raw materials is also quite irrelevant, since it is in any case better for us to produce expensive tyres in Germany which we can use, than to sell theoretically cheap tyres, but tyres for which the Minister of Economics cannot allocate any foreign exchange, and which therefore cannot be produced for lack of raw materials and consequently cannot be used at all. If we really are obliged to build up our domestic economy on autarkic lines, which we are—for lamenting and harping on our foreign exchange plight will certainly not solve the problem—then the price of raw materials individually considered no longer plays a decisive part.

It is further necessary to increase German iron production to the utmost limits. The objection that with German ore, which has a 26 per cent ferrous content, we cannot produce pig iron as cheaply as with the 45 per cent Swedish ores, etc., is irrelevant; we are not faced with the question of what [we] would *rather* do, but what we *can* do. The objection, moreover, that in that event all the German blast-furnaces would have to be converted is equally irrelevant, and, what is more, this is no concern of the Ministry of Economics. The job of the Ministry of Economics is simply to set the national economic tasks; private industry has to fulfil them. But if private industry thinks itself incapable of doing this, then the National Socialist State will know how to resolve the problem on its own. In any case, for a thousand years Germany had no foreign iron ores. Even before the war, more German iron ores were being processed than during the period of our worst decline. *Nevertheless, if there is still the possibility of our importing cheaper ores, well and good. But the future of the national economy and, above all, of the conduct of war, must not depend on this.*

Moreover, the distillation of potatoes into alcohol must be prohibited forthwith. Fuel must be obtained from the ground, not from potatoes. Instead it is our duty to use any arable land that may become available either for human or animal foodstuffs or for the cultivation of fibrous materials.

It is further necessary for us to make our supplies of *industrial* fats independent of imports as quickly as possible. This can be done by using our coal. This problem has been solved by chemical means and the technique is actually crying out to be put into practice. Either German industry will grasp the new economic tasks or else it will show itself incapable of surviving any longer in this modern age in which a Soviet State is setting up a gigantic plan. *But in that case it will not be Germany that will go under, but at most a few industrialists.* Moreover, the extraction of other ores must be increased, *regardless of cost,* and, in particular, the production of light metals must be increased to the utmost limits, in order to produce a substitute for certain other metals.

Finally, it is also necessary for the rearmament programme to make use even now whenever possible of those materials which must and will replace high-grade metals in time of war. *It is better to consider and resolve these problems in time of peace than to wait for the next war and only then, in the midst of a multitude of tasks, to try to undertake these economic researches and experiments with methods.*

In short, I consider it necessary that now, with iron determination, a 100 per cent self-sufficiency should be attained in every sphere where it is feasible, and that not only should the national requirements in these most essential raw materials be made independent of other countries, but we should also thus save the foreign exchange which in peacetime we need for our imports of foodstuffs. *In this connexion, I want to emphasize that in these tasks I see the only true economic mobilization and not in the throttling of armament industries in peacetime in order to save and stockpile raw materials for war.*

But I further consider it necessary to make an immediate investigation of the outstanding debts in foreign exchange owed to German business abroad. There is no doubt that the outstanding claims of German business abroad are quite enormous. Nor is there any doubt that behind this in some cases there lies concealed the contemptible desire to possess, whatever happens, certain reserves abroad which are thus withheld from the grasp of the domestic economy. I regard this as deliberate sabotage of our national self-assertion, that is to say, of the defence of the Reich, and I therefore consider it necessary for the Reichstag to pass the following two laws:

1. A law providing the death penalty for economic sabotage, and
2. A law making the whole of Jewry liable for all damage inflicted by individual specimens of this community of criminals upon the German economy, and thus upon the German people.

Only the fulfilment of these tasks, in the form of a Several Years Plan for rendering our national economy independent of foreign countries, will make it possible for the first time to demand sacrifices from the German people in the economic sphere and in that of foodstuffs. For then the nation will have a right to demand of their leaders whom they blindly acknowledge, that they should not only talk about the problems in this field but tackle them with unparalleled and determined energy, not only point them out but solve them.

Nearly four precious years have now gone by. There is no doubt that by now we could have been completely independent of foreign countries in the spheres of fuel supplies, rubber supplies, and partly also iron ore supplies. Just as we are now producing 700,000 or 800,000 tons of petroleum, we could be producing 3 million tons. Just as we are today manufacturing a few thousand tons of rubber, we could already be producing 70,000 or 80,000 tons per annum. Just as we have stepped up the production of iron ore from 2.5 million tons to 7 million tons, we could process 20 or 25 million tons of German iron ore and even 30 millions if necessary. There has been time enough in four years to find out what we cannot do. Now we have to carry out what we can do.

I thus set the following tasks;

I. The German armed forces must be operational within four years.
II. The German economy must be fit for war within four years.

Source: J. Noakes and G. Pridham, eds., *Nazism 1919–1945: A Documentary Reader,* vol. 2 (Exeter: University of Exeter, 1988).

APPENDIX D

The Structure of Business Organization

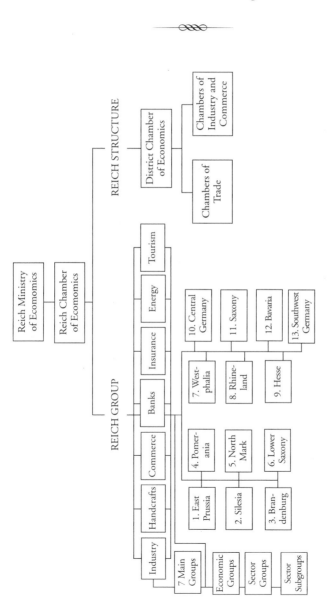

Source: J. Noakes and G. Pridham, eds., *Nazism 1919–1945: A Documentary Reader*, vol. 2 (Exeter: University of Exeter, 1988).

APPENDIX E

Regulation for the Elimination of the Jews
from the Economic Life of Germany,
12 November 1938

On the basis of the regulation for the implementation of the Four-Year Plan of October 18, 1936 (*Reichsgesetzblatt*, I, p. 887), the following is decreed:

§ 1

1) From January 1, 1939, Jews (§ 5 of the First Regulation to the Reich Citizenship Law of November 14, 1935, *Reichsgesetzblatt,* I, p. 1333) are forbidden to operate retail stores, mail-order houses, or sales agencies, or to carry on a trade [craft] independently.

2) They are further forbidden, from the same day on, to offer for sale goods or services, to advertise these, or to accept orders at markets of all sorts, fairs or exhibitions.

3) Jewish trade enterprises (Third Regulation to the Reich Citizenship Law of June 14, 1938, *Reichsgesetzblatt*, I, p. 627) which violate this decree will be closed by police.

§ 2

1) From January 1, 1939, a Jew can no longer be at the head of an enterprise within the meaning of the Law of January 20, 1934, for the Regulation of National Work (*Reichsgesetzblatt*, I, p. 45).

2) Where a Jew is employed in an executive position in a commercial enterprise he may be given notice to leave in six weeks. At the expiration of the term of the notice all claims of the employee based on his

contract, especially those concerning pension and compensation rights, become invalid.

§ 3

1) A Jew cannot be a member of a cooperative.

2) The membership of Jews in cooperatives expires on December 31, 1938. No special notice is required.

§ 4

The Reich Minister of the Economy, in coordination with the Ministers concerned, is empowered to publish regulations for the implementation of this decree. He may permit exceptions under the Law if these are required as a result of the transfer of a Jewish enterprise to non-Jewish ownership, for the liquidation of a Jewish enterprise or, in special cases, to ensure essential supplies.

Berlin, November 12, 1938

Plenipotentiary for the Four-Year Plan
Göring
Field Marshal General

Reichsgesetzblatt, I, 1938, p. 1580.

Source: Yitzhak Arad, Israel Gutman, and Abraham Margaliot, eds., *Documents on the Holocaust* (Lincoln: University of Nebraska Press, 1999).

APPENDIX F

An "Aryanization" Contract

⊸⊷⊸

For the original, 10,000 Reichsmark have been paid as deed tax.
Frankfurt a.M. 27th December 1938
Notary (signature by Wirth)
No. 1162 Year 1938 in the deed roll Negotiated
Frankfurt am Main, December 17, 1938.

Appearing today before the undersigned, Kurt Wirth, resident notary in Frankfurt am Main in the district of the Main Provincial Court, Frankfurt am Main, were

1. The merchant Lothar Adler, Frankfurt a. M. Schwindt Street 23
2. The merchant Friedrich, known as Fritz Adler, Frankfurt a. M. Beethoven Street 43 both acting on their own behalf as well as partners personally liable for the firm J. & C. A. Schneider, Frankfurt a. M.,
3. The director Bruno Seletzky currently resident in Zurich, Tal Street 1. The party mentioned in 1. is known to the officiating notary personally, the parties in 2. and 3. are not but were introduced to him by the [party] Provincial Economic Adviser Karl Eckardt, Frankfurt a. M. whom he knows and who was present. Thereby the officiating notary obtained certainty about the identity of the parties 2. and 3. The parties allowed the following contract to be witnessed:

§1. *Sold Enterprise. Right of Firm.*

(1) Messrs. Lothar and Fritz Adler are selling the above-mentioned firm known until now as J. & C. A. Schneider, which produces and sells shoes, especially slippers, together with all that pertains thereto, to Mr. Bruno Seletzky.

(2) The sellers expressly agree herewith that the buyer continue (sic) to use the firm name "J. & C. A. Schneider" with or without an addendum indicating the successor relationship. The buyer is not obligated to continue the use of the firm name and may change it any time for reasons of his own.

§2. *Sold Property.*

(1) Together with the enterprise, all properties (assets and rights) which are possessed by the firm and which were in stock as of May 1, 1938, or which should have been in stock on that date in accordance with standard bookkeeping practice, are hereby sold, provided however that there is no inclusion of any changes which occurred after May 1, 1938 as a consequence of normal business activity.

(2) Amongst sold properties are included under any circumstances the following objects, materials, lots, and rights even if they have not been entered in the books of the firm:

1) The lots, together with buildings and plant installations registered in the deed book of Frankfurt am Main

> District 15 Sheet 312 Kt Sheet 204, parcels 13/8, 4, 5, 6, 7, 12/8
> District 15 Sheet 421 Kt Sheet 206, parcel 4
> District 15 Sheet 832 Kt Sheet 206, parcel 16/12
> District 15 Sheet 857 Kt Sheet 206, parcel 19/2
> District 15 Sheet 1190 Kt Sheet 209, parcels 19/2, 3, 22/1

Use and liabilities are transferred as of May 1, 1938, to the acquirer who from this date assumes also insurance and rental contracts pertaining to the lots and buildings.

> The transfer has already taken place.

> The parties to the contract hereby define the cession: "We are agreed that the properties under (2) 1) should be transferred to the acquirer and consent and request to have the legal changes recorded in the deed book."

> For purposes of calculating taxes and costs, the value of the single units is given as follows:

> Re 15 Leaf 312 noted parcels: RM 154,500
> Re 15 Leaf 421 noted parcels: RM 253,200
> Re 15 Leaf 832 noted parcels: RM 25,400
> Re 15 Leaf 857 noted parcels: RM 17,800
> Re 15 Leaf 1190 noted parcels: RM 247,400

2) All inventory pieces used in the sold enterprise, including vehicles as well as transport and store installations with the exception of the two passenger cars which carry license plates IT 106839 and IT 111652

3) all the machines, tools and plant installations used in the sold enterprise with the exception of any leased machines

4) all the available supplies in the sold enterprise

5) all existing claims against customers, claims arising from exchanges, bank deposits, credits from prepayments and other claims or credits pertaining to the sold enterprise

6) all cash

7) all patents or trademarks of any kind used by the sold enterprise or entered in the name of the firm or its partners

8) the contractual rights vis-à-vis the Württembergische Notenbank in Stuttgart and the Dresdner Bank in Frankfurt am Main for erasing the debts entered with respect to the above-mentioned properties in the deed book in part III.

(3) Except for any express provisions to the contrary the sold properties including the real properties are being sold as they stand, without liability for any defects of any sort. The sellers guarantee, however, that the sold properties are available and not encumbered by rights of third parties with the exception of the following on real properties

a) the Dresdner Bank Reichsmark 600,000
b) the Dresdner Bank Goldmark 100,000
c) the Würtemb. Notenbank Goldmark 200,000
d) the Würtemb. Notenbank Goldmark 400,000

and with the exception of any title reservations customarily exercised by suppliers. The sellers are obligated to remove at their own cost any rights of third parties which may exist in spite of this agreement, especially encumbrances entered in the deed book so far as they do not coincide with the agreement. Excepted therefrom is the entry in Part II of the deed book which provides for cession of property to the city of Frankfurt a. M. for street construction purposes.

So far as the sellers are still indebted under the loans in Part III, they agree to the immediate erasure of these loans.

§3. *Obligations to be Taken Over.*

[Deals with normal business obligations and tax obligations. For taxes due from March 1, 1938, buyer makes himself liable to a maximum of RM 100,000.]

§4. *Contracts to be Taken Over.*

(1) The buyer is entitled and obligated to take over the following contracts to which the sold firm was a party and which were in force on May 1, 1938:

a) all contracts for purchases and deliveries

b) all the contracts for service employment and representation with Aryan persons, which are appropriate to the normal business activity of the firm and which are not to be enforced after December 31, 1939, or which may be dissolved as of that date on the basis of rights existing on May 1, 1938

c) all rental contracts which are appropriate to the normal business of the firm and which expire not later than December 31, 1939 or which may be dissolved as of that date on the basis of rights existing on May 1, 1938

d) insurance contracts listed in appendix I

e) the following construction contracts
    1. for reconstruction of the main entrance on Mainzerland Street 281
    2. for mixing room and installations and
    3. for reconstruction of sanitary facilities

f) other contracts not mentioned, especially forgotten contracts of lesser importance which are appropriate for normal activity of the firm and which should be taken over as matter of full faith and credit.

(2) The following contracts are taken over in deviation from section (1)

1) employment contracts with Aryan persons named in appendix II,

2) employment contracts with non-Aryan persons named in appendix III, provided that the contracts agree with the description in the appendix especially with regard to their expiration or termination. However, there will be no employment of non-Aryan persons from the day of contract termination. They must nevertheless be available to the new management for as long as they are contractually entitled to indemnification,

3) rental contracts contained in appendix IV.

(3) With respect to the non-Aryan persons, whose contracts are to be taken over under article 2, section 2, the sellers are answerable to the buyer for the following:

1. Every contract must unconditionally expire on the date listed in appendix III.
2. Upon their separation, the persons involved must not present any settlement claims against the buyer. Any settlement claims to be granted or paid to these persons for moral or legal reasons must be arranged with final and terminal effect between the sellers and the persons involved and also paid to these persons before the buyer takes over the contractual relationship, so that the buyer is liable only for current wages or other emoluments to the day of their separation, apart from claims which these persons may develop from an employment lasting beyond the time periods listed in appendix III.

(4) The sellers are answerable to the buyer for the fact that the rental contract in respect of Kleyer Street 70 mentioned in appendix IV runs to May 31, 1945.

§5. *Takeover, Utilization, and Liabilities.*

[Provides for considering the enterprise as being run on the account of the buyer as of May 1, 1938.]

§6. *Introduction into the Enterprise.*

(1) The sellers are handing over the management at once to the new entrepreneur and are basically no longer active in the enterprise. However, they will be available to the new management for a minimum of 2 months and a maximum of 6 months, if the latter for any reason, including orientation in business habits, introduction to suppliers and customers, or other reasons, requires their participation.

(2) So long as the buyer does not relinquish the availability of the sellers, he must recompense Mr. Lothar Adler 5000 Reichsmark monthly and Mr. Fritz Adler 4000 Reichsmark.

§7. *Competition Clause.*

The sellers obligate themselves not to set up or operate directly or indirectly a slipper factory in Germany until December 31, 1948 nor participate in such an enterprise directly or indirectly. The sellers obligate themselves especially not to participate or act in such an enterprise within Germany as manager, employee, representative or owner. The term activity includes also general consultations as well as service in a board of directors or service in an office which is equivalent to that of member of the board. The term participation does not include capital participation which is not at the same time competitive activity.

§ 8. *Sales Price.*

(1) The sales price for the enterprise to be delivered under this contract, including properties, objects, lots, rights, and the further obligations assumed by the sellers under this contract (excepting those of §6), is to be paid by the buyer, taking account of the obligations to be assumed by him, to the sellers in the amount of

4,000,000.—Reichsmark.

(2) The sales price is due upon receipt of necessary official approval with annual interest of 4% from May 1, 1938. The sales price of 4,000,000.—Reichsmark will be discharged in Reichsmark in the amount of 1,350,000 Reichsmark, and in Swiss Francs in the amount of 350,000.—(three hundred and fifty thousand Swiss Francs) payable to the sellers abroad.

§9. *Costs.*

[Each party pays own costs of legal and financial counsel.]

§ 10. *Foreign Currency Approval.*

So far as foreign currency approval is required for the fulfillment of particular stipulations in this contract, these stipulations enter into force only after receipt of foreign currency approval. For the rest, any disapproval of foreign currency does not affect the validity of the contract.

The parties obligate themselves to make joint efforts for required approval.

§11.

This contract is concluded as of November 14, 1938, but should receive renewal certification today in notary form.

The sellers are Jews; the buyer is Aryan and a foreigner for foreign currency purposes.

The protocol, together with appendices, was read in the presence of the notary, approved by the parties, and signed by them in person as follows

signed	Bruno Seletzky
signed	Lothar Adler
signed	Fritz Adler
signed	Kurt Wirth, Notary

To §4 Article Section 2

Appendix III to the notary protocol of December 17, 1938, deed roll No. 1162/1938 signed K. Wirth, Notary

Contracts with non-Aryan employees and non-Aryan representatives

1) Contract with Mr. Fritz Ballin, sub-representative for Berlin. The contractual relationship which extended to September 30, 1939, ends in accordance with settlement agreement on June 30, 1939.

2) Contract with Mr. Arthur Bramsen, officer of the firm and principal commercial traveler in Germany and abroad (Belgium and Scandinavia). The contractual relationship which extended to December 31, 1939, ends in accordance with settlement agreement on March 31, 1939.

3) Contract with Mr. Felix Freund, representative for Southern Germany, Rheinpfalz. The contractual relationship, which in accordance with legal requirements is terminable, ends in accordance with settlement agreement on December 31, 1938.

4) Contract with Mr. M. Goldschmidt, commercial traveler for Holland, England, Switzerland, and Morocco. The contractual relationship ends in accordance with agreement on December 31, 1938.

5) Contract with Mr. S. Gromowski, representative for Pomerania, East and West Prussia. The contractual relationship ends in accordance with agreement of September 30, 1938.

6) Contract with Main Provincial Court Judge (retired) Hess. The contractual relationship ends in accordance with agreement on March 31, 1939.

7) Contract with Miss Oppenheim, director of the samples division. The contractual relationship ends in accordance with agreement on March 31, 1939.

8) Contract with Mr. Leon Schmerbach, commercial traveler for Southern Germany. The contractual relationship ends in accordance with agreement on December 31, 1938.

9) Contract with Mr. J. Schoen, commercial traveler for North Germany. The contractual relationship ends in accordance with agreement on September 30, 1938.

10) Contract with Mr. Ludwig Strauss, commercial traveler in the Rhineland. The contractual relationship that extended to September 30, 1939, ends in accordance with settlement agreement on March 31, 1939.

11) Contract with Mrs. Weinberger, director of camel's-hair disposition, camel's-hair removal, and camel's-hair sample division. The contractual relationship ends in accordance with agreement on December 31, 1938.

12) Contract with Mr. A. Apfelbaum, Berlin representative. The contractual relationship ends in accordance with agreement on September 30, 1939.

13) Contract with Mr. Michael Cohn, Copenhagen, representative for Denmark. The contractual relationship ends in accordance with agreement on December 31, 1938.

14) Contract with Mr. Gaston Haas, Casablanca, representative for Morocco. The contractual relationship ends in accordance with agreement on December 31, 1938.

15) Contract with Mr. Achille Kahn, Brussels, representative for Belgium. The contractual relationship ends in accordance with agreement on December 31, 1938.

16) Contracts with all other non-Aryan employees not named under 1) to 15), provided that these contracts were terminated not later than June 30, 1938, or ended by that date.

Source: Raul Hilberg, ed., *Documents of Destruction: Germany and Jewry, 1933–1945* (Chicago: Quadrangle Books, 1971).

Appendix G

German Court Order Declaring Ford-Werke Enemy Property and Placing It under Nazi Custodianship

Copy

OLG. VU 209/42

Resolution

In accordance with the decree of 15 January 1940 (RGBl I. p. 191 ff.) in the version of decree implementation III dated 9 April 1942, and in accordance with the General Order of the Reichsminister of Justice dated 20 June 1940

an administrative unit is hereby commissioned in compliance with the request of the Reichskommissar for the disposition of enemy assets submitted in Berlin on 9 May 1942

for the firm

Ford Werke A.G. in Cologne

which is under the definitive control of the Ford Motor Company in Dearborn (Mass. [*sic*]), USA, a concern under the definitive control of the enemy.

General Director R. H. Schmidt, am Römerhof 5, Junkersdorf near Cologne is hereby named as Administrator.

The Administrator is authorized to deal with all judicial, extra-judicial, and legal matters that stem from normal business transactions. He may act on the following matters only with express prior permission of the Reichskommissar

1) the acquisition, disposal, or encumbrance of property or rights to property
2) the acquisition or disposal of shares in other businesses
3) the incorporation of new businesses or business branches, or the disposal of extant businesses or business branches
4) the establishment or liquidation of branch offices
5) the undertaking of new building projects or renovations and conversions
6) the changing of statutes
7) the disposal, dissolution, or liquidation of the business or of parts of the business

Furthermore, the Administrator is required to obtain, in addition to the approval of the Reichskommissar, confirmation from the Superior Regional Court in all matters pertaining to basic measures that relate to the building up of and continued existence of the firm (e.g. statute changes, disposal or liquidation of the firm). He is required to issue to the board members or deputy board members, whose responsibilities lie within the period of administration, a power of attorney enabling them to carry out their former duties. Changes in such a power of attorney, or the provision of a new power of attorney, as well as changes in the composition of the board require the approval of the Reichskommissar for the Disposal of Enemy Assets in Berlin.

The Administrator is required to submit a report on the business to the Reichskommissar on a regular basis every three months, beginning on 30 June 1942.

Cologne, 15 May 1942.
Superior Regional Court, Third Civil Senate:
Signed: Decking, Dr. Wolf, Dr. Rosell

To: District Court, Department of Trade and Business Registration-Cologne

Re: Section B No. 8855 Drawn up by:
and signed Esser, Judicial Assistant
as office document clerk

Source: Ford Motor Company, *Research Findings About Ford-Werke Under the Nazi Regime* (Dearborn, MI: Ford Motor Company, 2001). Translated from the original German by David Scrase.

APPENDIX H

Research Findings about Ford-Werke
under the Nazi Regime

———— ∞∞∞ ————

REPORT SUMMARY

Introduction/Project Background

This report summarizes information from a 3 1/2 year research project conducted by Ford Motor Company ("Ford") into the World War II activities of its German subsidiary, Ford-Werke AG ("Ford-Werke" [Ford-Works]). The project was launched in January 1998 following an inquiry from the British Broadcasting Corporation (BBC) regarding the use of forced labor at Ford-Werke during World War II. On March 4, 1998, attorneys filed a class action lawsuit against Ford. The suit has since been dismissed.

Ford instituted the research project in an effort to locate documents that would shed new light on the historical facts. More than 45 archivists, historians, researchers and translators were involved in the effort to collect and study documents from three countries and two continents. Research was conducted on records held by the company and on records held by more than 30 public and private repositories in the United States, Germany and Great Britain. The project yielded more than 98,000 pages of source material.

Historical Background of Ford Motor Company and Ford-Werke

Henry Ford founded Ford Motor Company in 1903 and was its president from 1906 to 1919, and 1943 to 1945. Ford-Werke was incorporated as

Ford Motor Company Aktiengesellschaft (AG) [joint-stock company] on January 5, 1925, in Berlin. A plant was built along the Rhine River in Cologne and opened in 1931. Ford's direct and indirect ownership stake fluctuated widely from 1925 through the early postwar period.

At the start of World War II, 250 American firms owned more than $450 million in assets in Germany. Ten of those firms owned 58.5 percent of the total. Ranked 16th by investment holdings, Ford held 1.9 percent of the total American investment. A chart showing the top 59 firms is attached as Appendix A, Investment of U.S. Companies in Germany, 1943.

Although Ford owned a majority interest in Ford-Werke, the Dearborn company's control over Ford-Werke's operations was constrained by Nazi policies aimed at limiting foreign influences in German businesses. The board meeting in April 1938 was the last one attended by an American or British member until after the war. On May 15, 1942, the Nazi government, through a court order, declared Ford-Werke enemy property, appointed a custodian and replaced the board of directors with a board of advisors. Heinrich Albert, a former German diplomat and prominent lawyer whose clients included major U.S. corporations doing business in Germany, was chairman of the board of directors from 1937 through May 15, 1942, when he became chairman of the board of advisors through the end of the war. A list of all board members of Ford-Werke from 1925 through 1953 is attached as Appendix B, Board of Directors – Ford-Werke, 1925–1953.

Henry Ford remained opposed to the war, except in direct defense of the United States, even after World War II began in Europe. However, in 1940, Ford Motor Company accepted a U.S. government contract to build aircraft engines, and Ford engineers assisted with design of the jeep. In March 1941, construction of Ford's Willow Run plant began. By early 1942, Ford was a major contributor to the Allied war effort. And by early 1944, Willow Run was the leading producer of heavy bombers for the U.S. military. See Appendix C, Ford's Contributions to the Allied War Effort, 1939–1945.

Nazi Economic Policies and Controls over the Automotive Industry

In 1933, Adolf Hitler's Nazi government instituted measures to extend its influence throughout German society. The regime promoted German self-sufficiency in raw materials and military production. Economic controls increased, particularly on foreign trade and currency transactions. In 1935, binding regulations required that automotive parts sold in Germany be German-made using German raw materials, and that they be standardized. Government policies regulated the industry, allocating and distributing raw materials based on approved production. Ford-Werke resisted standardization and rationalization, and its production initially fell.

German Industrial Mobilization and Preparations for War, 1936–1939

In 1936, the Nazi government imposed the Four-Year Plan to make the economy self-sufficient. The underlying motive was military buildup. During the implementation of the Four-Year Plan, German firms with foreign connections were used to import raw materials in barter for exports. Ford and Ford-Werke entered an agreement with the German government in 1936, whereby Ford-Werke exported vehicles and parts in exchange for licenses to but [*sic*] crude rubber from Ford subsidiaries. German tire manufacturers got the rubber and the German government got 30 percent of the tires. Under later, broader agreements, Ford shipped other raw materials to Ford-Werke in exchange for parts. Some of the raw materials were distributed throughout Germany under government order. The allocation of raw materials to Ford-Werke was tied to the expansion of exports.

At the German government's urging, and with Ford's approval, Ford-Werke and a supplier produced troop carriers for the German military in Berlin. To meet government demands, Ford-Werke imported partially assembled U.S.-built trucks from Ford for assembly in Cologne in late 1938. The trucks were used in the invasion and occupation of Czechoslovakia.

Ford-Werke in the German Wartime Economy, 1939–1945

After war broke out in September 1939, commercial transactions between the United States and Germany were difficult. Ford and Ford-Werke had problems communicating. In June 1941, the German government froze all U.S. assets in Germany. A postwar U.S. military investigation concluded that American influence over Ford-Werke decreased after the outbreak of war and ceased altogether in December 1941 with U.S. entry into the war.

As part of the wartime economy, Ford-Werke and its operations fell under the control of the German armaments ministry and other government agencies. In April 1941, the German government appointed Robert Schmidt, co-manager of Ford-Werke, to the position of Wehrwirtschaftsführer, one of the economic leaders who coordinated army needs with industry. A German Army Inspection Office was established at the plant.

Soon after the United States entered the war in December 1941, Ford-Werke was directly regulated by the Reich Commissioner for the Treatment of Enemy Property. On May 15, 1942, the Superior Court in Cologne declared Ford-Werke to be under enemy influence and appointed Schmidt, a German who had been a key manager at Ford-Werke since 1926, as custodian. Schmidt was required to submit reports to the Reich Commissioner and to get approval for major business decisions. He was forbidden to have any contact with "enemy stockholders or their intermediaries" without approval from the Reich Commissioner, a Nazi official vested with broad authority over businesses whose controlling interests were based in countries at war with Germany. (The Reich Commissioner named Heinrich Albert as chairman of the board of advisors, the body which by government order replaced the board of directors.)

Military Production at Ford-Werke

At the beginning of the war, Ford-Werke was one of the four largest automotive firms in Germany and manufactured cars, trucks, vans, tractors and other vehicles. During the war, Ford-Werke produced three-ton trucks, a half-track personnel carrier, spare parts and engines, and provided vehicle repair and reconditioning services. From September 1939 through early 1945, Ford-Werke produced between 87,000 and 92,000 vehicles, mostly for the German army, accounting for about one-third of Germany's wartime military truck production. From 1938 to the end of the war, the Nazi government determined the type and number of vehicles to be produced by Ford-Werke and other manufacturers. By 1940, passenger car production was prohibited. Ford-Werke gradually switched to trucks and, after February 1941, produced only military vehicles and parts for Ford subsidiaries in occupied Europe. In March 1943, Schmidt was assigned by the armaments ministry to coordinate military production at Ford subsidiaries in all Axis territories in Europe. Ford-Werke production peaked in 1943. Operations were hampered in late 1944 due to supply shortages, dispersal and war damage.

Ford-Werke had ties to other government military contracts. In late 1939, the German authorities asked Schmidt to establish a new firm to manufacture war matériel. Without Ford's prior approval, he and Albert joined with a supplier to manufacture military equipment in a separate facility using machinery and equipment from Ford-Werke. Schmidt described it as a strategy to permit Ford-Werke to continue manufacturing vehicles rather than war matériel. Also, Ford-Werke sent mechanics and skilled workers to the Eastern frontlines to train soldiers in vehicle repair. Several independent Ford-Werke dealers were involved with their own repair shops set up and run by the army as quasi-military operations near Eastern combat zones. Jewish laborers were employed in at least one of these repair shops.

Foreign and Forced Labor at Ford-Werke

Overview – Germany

From 1939 to 1945, millions of non-Germans were registered to work, usually forcibly, in factories, farms, mines and construction sites throughout the German Reich, as military conscription worsened an existing labor shortage. Most industrial companies in Germany applied for and used foreign workers during this time. The foreign work force comprised several different groups. The overall treatment of the various groups was determined by Nazi ideology and practice that placed foreigners on a scale according to race, nationality and gender. The foreign work force included: laborers recruited from German allies, who were paid and treated better than any other group of foreign workers; prisoners of war (POWs), who received only token wages; forced workers (civilians) taken from occupied territory in Western and Eastern Europe, the latter receiving lower wages and worse treatment than their Western counterparts; Italian Military Internees sent to Germany after Italy's surrender in September 1943; and concentration camp inmates who worked unpaid, as slave laborers.

Large-scale use of foreign workers started almost immediately after the war began in September 1939 and was expanded after Germany occupied Western Europe in the spring of 1940. Extensive recruitment in the occupied territories of the Soviet Union began in early 1942, and evolved into a more coercive system. Forced workers were distributed to industries that requested workers through government labor offices. Eastern workers were subject to additional regulations enforced by guards and the Gestapo, and lived in separate camps surrounded by barbed wire. Their wages were lower than for Western and German workers, and they had to pay extra taxes. Their food rations were poor. Italian POWs sent to Germany after the autumn of 1943 were often treated as poorly as Russian workers. In mid-1943, the SS began to send slave laborers from concentration camps to satellite camps, or sub-camps, at companies throughout Germany in order to support the war economy. At first, concentration camp labor was restricted to construction work, bomb clearance and critical war industries. In August 1944, the automotive industry was permitted to apply for concentration camp labor. The government set the rules for payment, food, housing, clothing, working hours and reporting procedures. The SS guarded the prisoners. Wages were paid by the companies to the government; prisoners received no wages. Companies could deduct expenses for food and housing.

Overview – Ford-Werke

Wartime use of foreign and forced labor at Ford-Werke generally followed the pattern described. Foreigners from Eastern and Western Europe, Italian POWs and men from the Buchenwald concentration camp were put to work at Ford-Werke. Foreign workers lived in barracks adjacent to the plant. The first contingent of POWs – between 100 and 200 men, possibly French – arrived at Ford-Werke in September, 1940. This occurred after Ford-Werke, with an acute labor shortage, was asked by the government to quickly produce a large number of specialized motors for barges. By April 1942, more than 300 Eastern civilians were working there. The total number of forced laborers at Ford-Werke is hard to determine for several reasons: Some records provide general numbers, others provide numbers for selected groups or periods, and records differ in describing workers. The range shown in Ford-Werke's financial records for 1942 through 1944 goes from a low of 314 foreign workers in April 1942 to a high of 1,932 in

August 1944. A chart, Labor Trends at Ford-Werke, shows the makeup of the work force from January 1941 through August 1944. See Section 7.3. of the report. See Appendix D, Numbers of Workers at Ford-Werke, January 1941–December 1944, for month-by-month statistical breakdowns for the period.

Compensation for Foreign and Forced Workers at Ford-Werke

Few records are available regarding compensation. Postwar reports and interrogations of Ford-Werke managers provide some information, as shown in a chart, Ford-Werke Wage Schedule During World War II, in Section 7.5. of the report. French and Italian POWs initially received less than Western civilian workers and had 60 percent of their pay deducted and sent to the POW camp that supplied the prisoners. Both groups eventually were reclassified as civilian laborers and received more pay, with deductions of 25 percent. Western civilian workers were paid about the same as German workers, minus deductions for those who lived on the premises. In keeping with government decrees, Eastern workers at Ford-Werke initially were paid less than all other workers, with women receiving less than men. Deductions for taxes and living expenses amounted to over half the pay for Eastern workers. In the autumn of 1943, Eastern workers' pay was increased and their deductions reduced. Postwar financial records from Ford-Werke include references to monies owed to former foreign workers. As of December 31, 1945, RM (Reichsmarks) 63,419 in unclaimed wages and salaries of foreign workers was in a blocked account at the Deutsche Bank, Cologne, by order of the military government. During 1947, the funds were transferred to a special account at the Deutsche Bank and thereafter do not appear in Ford-Werke's financial records. (In May 1952, the Allied High Commission asked the West German government to accelerate the collection of back pay owed to former POWs and foreign workers. As determined by the London Debt Conference, former workers were entitled to apply for the money that had been placed in financial institutions.)

Conditions for Foreign and Forced Workers at Ford-Werke

The average workweek for all workers at Ford-Werke grew longer as the war continued, from 40 hours a week to 60 hours or more. Most former forced workers interviewed in recent years recalled doing manual labor in production; postwar documents indicate that Germans and foreigners worked together. Some POWs were sent to work at Ford-Werke supplier companies. Foreign and forced workers lived in wooden barracks adjacent to the plant, separated by nationality and supervised by plant guards and the Gestapo. The Eastern workers' camp was surrounded by barbed wire. Western workers lived in an unfenced camp, or offsite. Some Western workers were allowed vacation time. Plant guards administered punishments, including house arrest, and foremen delivered punishments on the plant floor. Some arrests were made by German authorities, and there are indications that male and female forced laborers from Ford-Werke were imprisoned in the Gestapo prison in Cologne.

Food was prepared in kitchens according to nationality. Denazification files indicate that Russian workers and their children received poor food rations. Several foreign workers remembered that food was in short supply. Three physicians, several nurses and a dentist were responsible for medical needs in a medical barracks that included an operating room and separate men's and women's infirmaries. An air raid shelter was available for foreign and forced laborers. The foreign workers' camp sustained air raid damage in October 1944. The names of about 15 foreigners from Ford-Werke appear on surviving portions of Cologne death lists from the war, but without any indication as to the cause of death.

After the war, the chief physician was accused of performing unwanted abortions on Eastern forced laborers. The physician, Dr. Carl Wenzel, estimated there were 10 abortions on Eastern workers. He said the women chose abortion because of their circumstances. He said he initiated improvements in maternity and nursery facilities. Other medical staff corroborated his statements, as did some former Eastern workers who said he gave good care.

Slave Labor from the Buchenwald Concentration Camp

In August 1944, shortly after concentration camp labor was made available to the automotive industry, 50 men from Buchenwald arrived at Ford-Werke. At any given time from August 1944 through February 1945, about 50 or fewer Buchenwald prisoners worked at Ford-Werke. Altogether, at least 65 different men were assigned there at one time or another. Sixteen SS men guarded the prisoners, who lived in separate barracks and performed outside work. Work records indicate the men worked seven days a week, six to 10 hours per day. A former worker recalled 12-hour days in production. Five inmates fled during 1944; one died at Ford-Werke. In February and March 1945, shortly before the American army liberated Cologne, 48 Buchenwald inmates were transferred from the camp, and one fled.

Liberation at End of War

The factory had become a combat zone during the final fighting in Cologne, and production was limited. Equipment and materials had been largely dispersed. American army units found 300 to 500 foreign workers living in the Ford-Werke factory, primarily in a large shelter. Foreign workers were sent to nearby displaced person camps operated by the U.S. Army.

Ford-Werke's Relationship with Other Ford Facilities in Occupied Europe

Several Ford subsidiaries in occupied Europe did business with Ford-Werke during the war. Ford-Werke coordinated production of Ford vehicles throughout occupied Europe. Shortly after the Germans over-ran Belgium, Holland, Luxembourg and France in 1940, the Germans appointed Schmidt commissioner for those properties. After the U.S. entry into the war, these subsidiaries were placed under the control of the Reich Commissioner for the Treatment of Enemy Property, who appointed Ford-Werke personnel as custodians. Ford-Werke had business ties to subsidiaries in other occupied countries and established its own subsidiaries in Austria late in the war. Ford-Werke had some involvement with Ford operations in countries allied with Germany early in the war.

Impact of the War on Communications

With the rise of tensions in Europe in the late 1930s, the U.S. government began examining the economic activities of U.S. firms and their European subsidiaries. Monitoring increased after 1940. The U.S. government investigated correspondence between Ford and Ford of France, but closed the matter in 1943. No action was taken. Ford corresponded periodically with its German subsidiary and with subsidiaries in countries under German occupation until the U.S. entry into the war in 1941. Direct communications did not resume until after the war. The final Ford-Werke board meeting attended by a non-German board member occurred in April 1938. Ford, Ford of Britain and Ford-Werke continued to have contact with subsidiaries in neutral countries. Allied liberation of France in August 1944 opened up some communications with subsidiaries in occupied Europe. A delegation from Ford of Britain visited Ford-Werke in May 1945 and drafted a report on Ford-Werke's activities during the war. The first known direct postwar communication between Ford and Ford-Werke was in November 1946.

End-of-War and Postwar Military Government Supervision

Ford-Werke and other industrial facilities in Cologne were administered by U.S. military authorities from March to June 1945. In July 1945, Cologne became part of the British military occupation zone, and Ford-Werke was placed under British military government control. Erhard Vitger, a key manager at the plant before and during the war and a Dane, was appointed as custodian. Directors and shareholders had no authority, and permission had to be sought to transfer stock ownership and to do repairs. British military officials determined steel supply quotas, regulated production, approved prices and determined who received vehicles produced at the plant. Trade had to be approved by Allied authorities.

Limited operations resumed in March 1945, beginning with servicing and repair of U.S. military vehicles. The plant was authorized to produce new trucks from existing spare parts, and on May 8, 1945, V-E Day, produced its first postwar vehicle, a truck for the U.S. Army. After the British military government took over, Ford-Werke began repairing and producing trucks for the British military. Production in 1945 was limited by scarcity of raw materials and parts, and by war damage. In 1946, Ford-Werke increased production and began reconditioning motors for the British. Production dropped in 1947 because of supply problems, but climbed in 1948 and 1949. A summary is provided in a chart, Overview of Ford-Werke Postwar Production, May 1945–1949, in Section 10.3.

Investigations at Ford-Werke began immediately after the Allies occupied Cologne and continued for months. Military officers reported on conditions and operations, equipment dispersal, suppliers, operational needs and the health of foreign workers and refugees. The U.S. military government undertook an in-depth investigation, completing an overview on June 21, 1945, and a detailed report in September 1945. Military authorities conducted personnel investigations at Ford-Werke in 1945 and 1946 as part of the denazification effort to rid Germany of National Socialism. Approximately 40 employees were arrested by the Allies. Most were released and later re-employed by Ford-Werke. Among them was Schmidt, who was cleared in 1947 and returned to work at Ford-Werke in 1950 as a technical adviser, with the support of Ford executives. He and Vitger served on the management board until 1958. Both served on the board of directors. Military government controls were removed gradually beginning in 1947. On August 8, 1948, Vitger became general manager. In December 1949, German courts formally ended the custody order that had been imposed on Ford-Werke on May 15, 1942, by the Nazi regime.

War Damage to Ford-Werke

Early in the war, most damage was to parts in warehouses and materials in transit. In August 1944, bombs caused some damage. Twice in October 1944, the plant was targeted by bombs that damaged the proving grounds and the labor camps. In early March 1945, as the Allies moved into Cologne, artillery shells destroyed the recreation hall and shed buildings, damaged offices and a garage, and broke many windows in the plant.

Ford-Werke submitted war damage claims of RM 11,929,803 to the German government and received RM 361,181 for damages in 1941 and 1942. A 1942 law kept Ford-Werke from collecting subsequent damages from the German government. War damage claims were filed after the war with the U.S. government. In 1965, Ford submitted a claim for $7,050,052 for losses and damage to Ford-Werke and its subsidiaries in Austria. The claim was based on $12,461,427 in damages (the claim reduced in keeping with Ford's 56.575 percent ownership of Ford-Werke). A settlement commission agreed to award Ford $785,321. An itemized list summarizing the 1965 claim is attached as Appendix E, War Damage Claims.

Financial Overview of Ford-Werke

Brief Financial History

From the time of its incorporation in 1925, Ford-Werke experienced periods of prosperity as well as instability as a result of management decisions and prevailing economic and political environments. In 1933, Ford-Werke completed a major upgrade to permit a new line of smaller cars to meet consumer demand. An earnings deficit forced a reorganization and change in the capital structure in 1934. An aggressive global exporting program began during the 1930s. Economic growth resulted in rising demand. In the late 1930s, Ford-Werke expanded capacity and increased investment in machines and equipment. Sales rose from 1940 through 1943, but fell in 1944 and 1945. Balance sheets and results of operations were affected by taxes, government controls on production and prices, war damages and related costs. Sales and production in 1946 were constrained by shortages of supplies. In the early 1950s, significant investments were made to increase the facility's productive capability and reduce per-vehicle costs.

Balance Sheet Information

Currency reform and devaluation instituted by Allied military authorities in June 1948 is of significance in reviewing balance sheets. German currency changed from Reichsmarks to Deutsche Marks (DM). Companies had to devalue monetary assets and liabilities, but were allowed to revalue inventories, property, plants and equipment. As a result, Ford-Werke's cash balances, accounts receivable from customers and amounts payable to suppliers, all of which had increased significantly during the war, were devalued by 90 percent or more. Most buildings, machinery, equipment and inventory balances were revalued at higher amounts. The net result was a reduction in reserves and other stockholder equity accounts. In 1950, capital investments were made for expansion, modernization, reconstruction and repair from war damage. In 1951 and 1953, additional expansion was undertaken to meet demand for products. Ford-Werke's assets and liabilities, as reported in financial statements at key points during the war and in the postwar period, are presented in Appendix F, Ford-Werke Balance Sheets.

Results of Operations/Net Income

A wide array of taxes and controls imposed by the Nazi regime affected sales, trading income, net income and production levels from 1939 to 1945. Trading income was a prominent performance measurement and was defined as sales less the cost of operations, excluding salaries and wages. Between 1933 and 1935, trading income rose as a result of increased sales and production. After price controls were enacted in 1936, trading income fell. Changes in taxes and controls, combined with other changes, resulted in generally increased trading income after 1939. Net income was flat in the mid-1930s but grew from 1938 until 1943, with losses in 1944 and 1945. Ford-Werke income fluctuation during the years 1933 through 1953 is shown in a chart, Net Income and Trading Income as a Percentage of Sales, Ford-Werke, 1933–1953, in Section 12.3. Additional detail is provided in Appendix G, Ford-Werke Results of Operations, 1933–1953.

Capital Structure and Dividend Analysis

Ford's ownership in Ford-Werke evolved from nearly 100 percent at the outset to varying proportions of direct and/or indirect ownership. In 1943, as permitted by U.S. law, Ford recorded its investment in Ford-Werke as a total loss by establishing a reserve account equal to its investment balance (about $8 million). In 1954, Ford restored its investment in Ford-Werke at about $557,000, the estimated fair value at the time of recovery (August 8, 1948).

Ford-Werke's first shareholder dividends were payable in March 1930. At the time, Luxembourg was the only Ford entity with a direct interest in Ford-Werke. Payments were delayed or incomplete because Ford-Werke had to request permission from the German government. The next dividends were declared in 1938, when Ford controlled, directly and indirectly, 81 percent of Ford-Werke stock. These dividends were held in a blocked account because the German government prohibited distribution outside Germany. Dividends from 1939 through 1943 also were blocked. No further dividends were declared until 1950. In 1951, blocked dividends from 1938 through 1943 were devalued by 90 percent in the conversion from Reichsmarks to Deutsche Marks. Ford used the resulting funds (about $60,000 in 1951 dollars) to under-write part of the cost of acquiring Ford-Werke stock held by I.G. Farbenindustrie AG (I.G. Farben), which was being liquidated.

Disposition of Research Findings

Each of the 98,000 pages of source material collected for this project carries a unique alphanumeric label that specifies the document and page, and identifies the repository where the original document was located. Descriptions of each document have been entered into a searchable database. The database and collection are being donated (except where prohibited by privacy laws or regulations of the original repositories) to Henry Ford Museum & Greenfield Village, an independent, nonprofit educational institution unaffiliated with Ford Motor Company. At the museum, the donated collection and database will be made available to the public at the Benson Ford Research Center. See Appendix H, Glossary of Repository Sources, for a guide to the repository abbreviations used in the document labels. See Appendix I (Bibliography) for a list of relevant published sources.

Ford Motor Company's goal in instituting this research project was to conduct a deep search for additional facts to supplement the historical record. Every effort was made to perform a thorough and comprehensive search. As additional information comes to light, Ford Motor Company will update the document collection and the database at the Benson Ford Research Center, an archival repository. The material collected as a result of this project will provide a significant resource for understanding the history of this period and of Ford-Werke under the Nazi regime.

Source: Ford Motor Company, *Research Findings About Ford-Werke Under the Nazi Regime* (Dearborn, MI: Ford Motor Company, 2001).

CONTRIBUTORS

Michael Thad Allen teaches history at the University of Connecticut. He is the author of *The Business of Genocide: The SS, Slave Labor, and the Concentration Camps* (University of North Carolina Press, 2002).

Volker R. Berghahn is the Seth Low Professor of History at Columbia University. Among his many books on modern German history are *The Americanization of West German Industry, 1945–1973* (Cambridge University Press, 1986), *Modern Germany: Society, Economy, and Politics in the Twentieth Century* (Cambridge University Press, 1987), and *Imperial Germany, 1871–1914: Economy, Society, Culture, and Politics* (Berghahn Books, 1994).

Gerald D. Feldman is Professor of History and Director of the Institute of European Studies at the University of California, Berkeley. Among his many books on German economic and business history are most recently *Hugo Stinnes. Biographie eines Industriellen 1870–1924* (Beck-Verlag, 1998), and *Allianz and the German Insurance Business, 1933–1945* (Cambridge University Press, 2001). He also served as scholarly editor for and contributor to Lothar Gall et al., *The Deutsche Bank, 1870–1995* (Weidenfeld & Nicolson, 1995).

Peter Hayes is Professor of History and the Theodore Z. Weiss Professor of Holocaust Studies at Northwestern University. He is the author of *Industry and Ideology: IG Farben in the Nazi Era* (Cambridge University Press, 1987) and *From Cooperation to Complicity: Degussa in the Third Reich* (Cambridge University Press, forthcoming), and coeditor with Irmtrud Wojak of *"Arisierung" im Nationalsozialismus: Volksgemeinschaft, Raub und Gedächtnis* (Campus Verlag, 2000).

Jonathan Huener is Assistant Professor of History at the University of Vermont. He is the author of *Auschwitz, Poland, and the Politics of Commemoration, 1945–1979* (Ohio University Press, 2003) and coeditor with Francis R. Nicosia of *Medicine and Medical Ethics in Nazi Germany: Origins, Practices, Legacies* (Berghahn Books, 2002).

Harold James is Professor of History at Princeton University. Among his books on the German economy and society are *The German Slump: Politics and Economics, 1924–1936* (Oxford University Press, 1986) and *The Deutsche Bank and the Nazi Economic War Against the Jews* (Cambridge University Press, 2001). He also served as scholarly editor for and contributor to Lothar Gall et al., *The Deutsche Bank, 1870–1995* (Weidenfeld & Nicolson, 1995).

Francis R. Nicosia is Professor of History at Saint Michael's College in Vermont. He is the author of *The Third Reich and the Palestine Question* (Transaction Publishers, 2000), coauthor with Donald Niewyk of *The Columbia Guide to the Holocaust* (Columbia University Press, 2000), and coeditor with Jonathan Huener of *Medicine and Medical Ethics in Nazi Germany: Origins, Practices, Legacies* (Berghahn Books, 2002).

Simon Reich is Professor of Political Science at the University of Pittsburgh. He is the author of *The Fruits of Fascism: Postwar Prosperity in Historical Perspective* (Cornell University Press, 1990), coauthor with Andrei S. Markovits of *The German Predicament: Memory and Power in the New Europe* (Cornell University Press, 1997), and coauthor with William Keller, Louis Pauly, and Paul Doremus of *The Myth of the Global Corporation* (Princeton University Press, 1998).

SELECTED BIBLIOGRAPHY

Economics, Business, and the Jews

Bähr, Johannes. *Der Goldhandel der Dresdner Bank im Zweiten Weltkrieg. Ein Bericht des Hannah-Arendt-Instituts.* Leipzig: Kiepenheuer und Witsch, 1999.

Bajohr, Frank. *"Aryanization" in Hamburg: The Economic Expulsion of the Jews and the Confiscation of Their Property in Nazi Germany.* New York: Berghahn Books, 2002.

Baldwin, Neil. *Henry Ford and the Jews: The Mass Production of Hate.* Boulder: Westview Press, 2001.

Banken, Ralf. "Der Edelmetallsektor und die Verwertung konfiszierten jüdischen Vermögens im 'Dritten Reich.'" *Jahrbuch für Wirtschaftsgeschichte* 39 (1999): 135–162.

Barkai, Avraham. *From Boycott to Annihilation: The Economic Struggle of German Jews, 1933–1943.* Hanover: University Press of New England, 1989.

———. *Nazi Economics: Ideology, Theory, and Policy.* New Haven: Yale University Press, 1990.

———. "German Entrepreneurs and Jewish Policy in the Third Reich." *Yad Vashem Studies* 21 (1991): 122–155.

Barkan, Elazar. *The Guilt of Nations: Restitution and Negotiating Historical Injustices.* New York: Norton, 2000.

Berghahn, Volker R., ed. *Quest for Economic Empire: European Strategies of German Big Business in the Twentieth Century.* Oxford: Berghahn Books, 1996.

Black, Edwin. *IBM and the Holocaust: The Strategic Alliance Between Nazi Germany and America's Most Powerful Corporation.* New York: Crown Publishers, 2001.

Boelcke, Willy. *Die Deutsche Wirtschaft 1930–1945: Interna des Reichswirtschaftsministeriums.* Düsseldorf: Droste, 1983.

Borkin, Joseph. *The Crime and Punishment of IG Farben: The Unholy Alliance of Adolf Hitler and Germany's Great Chemical Combine.* New York: Free Press, 1978.

Botur, André. *Privatversicherung im Dritten Reich. Zur Schadensabwicklung nach der Reichskristallnacht unter dem Einfluss nationalsozialistischer Rassen- und Versicherungspolitik.* Berlin: Verlag A. Spitz, 1995.

Buchheim, Christoph. "Die Wirtschaftsentwicklung im Dritten Reich – mehr Disaster als Wunder. Eine Erwiderung auf Werner Abelshauser." *Vierteljahrshefte für Zeitgeschichte* 49 (2001): 653–664.

Buchheim, Christoph, Harold James, and Michael Hutter, eds. *Zerrissene Zwischen-kriegszeit: Wirtschaftshistorische Beiträge. Knut Borchardt zum 65. Geburtstag.* Baden-Baden: Nomos Verlagsgesellschaft, 1994.

Dobbs, Michael. "Ford and GM Scrutinized for Alleged Nazi Collaboration: Firms Deny Researchers' Claims on Aiding German War Effort." *Washington Post,* 30 November 1998, A1.

Eichholtz, Dietrich, ed. *Krieg und Wirtschaft: Studien zur deutschen Wirtschafts-geschichte 1939–1945.* Berlin: Metropol, 1999.

Erbe, Rene. *Die Nationalsozialistische Wirtschaftspolitik im Lichte der Modernen Theorien.* Zürich: Polygraphischer Verlag, 1958.

Feldenkirchen, Wilfried. *Siemens 1918–1945.* Columbus: Ohio State University Press, 1999.

Feldman, Gerald D. *Allianz and the German Insurance Business, 1933–1945.* New York: Cambridge University Press, 2001.

———. "The German Insurance Business in National Socialist Germany." *Bulletin of the German Historical Institute, Washington, D.C.* 31 (fall 2002): 19–33.

Feldman, Gerald D., and Wolfgang Seibel, eds. *Networks of Persecution: The Holocaust as a Division-of-Labor Based Crime.* New York: Berghahn Books, 2003.

Fischer, Wolfram. *Deutsche Wirtschaftspolitik 1918–1945.* Opladen: C.W. Leske Verlag, 1968.

Ford Motor Company. *Research Findings About Ford-Werke Under the Nazi Regime.* Dearborn: Ford Motor Company, 2001.

Gall, Lothar. "A Man for All Seasons: Hermann Josef Abs im Dritten Reich." *Zeit-schrift für Unternehmensgeschichte* 44 (1998): 123–175.

Gall, Lothar, et al., eds. *A History of the Deutsche Bank, 1870–1995.* London: Weidenfeld & Nicolson, 1995.

Geary, Dick. "The Industrial Elite and the Nazis in the Weimar Republic." In *The Nazi Machtergreifung,* edited by Peter D. Stachura, 85–100. London: Allen & Unwin, 1983.

Genschel, Helmut. *Die Verdrängung der Juden aus der Wirtschaft im Dritten Reich.* Berlin: Musterschmidt-Verlag, 1966.

Georg, Enno. *Die wirtschaftlichen Unternehmungen der SS.* Stuttgart: Deutsche Ver-lags-Anstalt, 1963.

Geyer, Michael. *Deutsche Rustungspolitik, 1860–1980.* Frankfurt am Main: Suhrkamp, 1984.

Gregor, Neil. *Star and Swastika: Daimler Benz in the Third Reich.* New Haven: Yale University Press, 1998.

Hayes, Peter. *Industry and Ideology: IG Farben in the Nazi Era.* 2nd ed. New York: Cambridge University Press, 1987, 2001.

———. "Big Business and 'Aryanization' in Germany, 1933–1939." *Jahrbuch für Antisemitismusforschung* 3 (1994): 254–281.

———. "State Policy and Corporate Involvement in the Holocaust." In *The Holocaust and History: The Known, the Unknown, the Disputed, and the Reexam-ined,* edited by Michael Berenbaum and Abraham Peck, 197–218. Bloomington: Indiana University Press, 1998.

———. "The Deutsche Bank and the Holocaust." In *Lessons and Legacies III: Memory, Memorialization and Denial,* edited by Peter Hayes, 71–98. Evanston: Northwestern University Press, 1999.

———. "The Degussa AG and the Holocaust." In *Lessons and Legacies V: The Holocaust and Justice,* edited by Ronald Smelser, 140–177. Evanston: Northwestern University Press, 2002.

———. *From Cooperation to Complicity: Degussa in the Third Reich.* New York: Cambridge University Press (forthcoming).

Hayes, Peter, and Irmtrud Wojak, eds. *"Arisierung" im Nationalsozialismus: Volks-gemeinschaft, Raub und Gedächnis.* Frankfurt am Main: Campus, 2000.

Hentschel, Volker. "Daimler-Benz im Dritten Reich." *Vierteljahrsschrift für Sozial-und Wirtschaftsgeschichte* 75 (1988): 74–100.

Hepp, Michael. *Deutsche Bank und Dresdner Bank: Gewinne aus Raub, Enteignung und Zwangsarbeit 1933–1944.* Bremen: Stiftung für Sozialgeschichte des 20. Jahrhunderts, 1999.

Herbst, Ludolf. *Der totale Krieg und die Ordnung der Wirtschaft. Die Kriegswirtschaft im Spannungsfeld von Politik, Ideologie und Propaganda 1939–1945.* Stuttgart: Deutsche Verlags-Anstalt, 1982.

Isabel, Vincent. *Hitler's Silent Partners: Swiss Banks, Nazi Gold, and the Pursuit of Justice.* New York: Morrow, 1997.

James, Harold. *The Deutsche Bank and the Nazi Economic War Against the Jews: The Expropriation of Jewish-Owned Property.* New York: Cambridge University Press, 2001.

———. *Verbandspolitik im Nationalsozialismus. Von der Interessenvertretung zur Wirtschaftsgruppe. Der Centralverband des Deutschen Bank- und Bankiergewerbes 1932–1945.* Munich and Zürich: Piper Verlag, 2001.

———. *The German Slump: Politics and Economics 1924–1936.* Oxford: Oxford University Press, 1986.

Janssen, Gregor. *Das Ministerium Speer: Deutschlands Rüstung im Krieg.* Berlin: Verlag Ullstein, 1968.

Kalthoff, Jürgen, and Martin Werner. *Die Händler des Zyklon B. Tesch & Stabenow: Eine Firmengeschichte zwischen Hamburg und Auschwitz.* Hamburg: VSA, 1998.

Kobrak, Christopher. *National Cultures and International Competition: The Experience of Schering AG, 1851–1950.* New York: Cambridge University Press, 2002.

Kopper, Christopher. *Zwischen Marktwirtschaft und Dirigismus. Staat, Banken und Bankenpolitik im "Dritten Reich" von 1933 bis 1939.* Bonn: Bouvier, 1995.

LeBor, Adam. *Hitler's Secret Bankers: The Myth of Swiss Neutrality During the Holocaust.* Secaucus, N.J.: Carol Publishing Group, 1997.

Lorentz, Bernhard. "Die Commerzbank und die 'Arisierung' im Altreich." *Vierteljahrshefte für Zeitgeschichte* 50 (2002): 238–268.

Lurie, Samuel. *Private Investment in a Controlled Economy: Germany 1933–1939.* New York: Columbia University Press, 1947.

Mason, Tim. "The Primacy of Politics: Politics and Economics in National Socialist Germany." In *Nazism and the Third Reich,* edited by Henry A. Turner, 175–200. New York: Quadrangle Books, 1972.

Mayer-Wegelin, Heinz. *Aller Anfang ist Schwer.* Frankfurt am Main: Degussa, 1973.

Mehl, Stefan. *Das Reichsfinanzministerium und die Verfolgung der Deutschen Juden 1933–1943.* Berlin: Zentralinstitut für Sozialwissenschaftliche Forschung, 1990.

Mollin, Gerhard. *Montankonzerne und "Drittes Reich": der Gegensatz zwischen Monopol-industrie und Befehlswirtschaft in der deutschen Rüstung und Expansion 1936–1944.* Göttingen: Vandenhoeck & Ruprecht, 1988.

Mommsen, Hans, and Manfred Grieger. *Das Volkswagenwerk und seiner Arbeiter im Dritten Reich.* Düsseldorf: Econ, 1996.

Mönnich, Horst. *BMW: Eine Deutsche Geschichte.* Vienna and Darmstadt: Paul Zsolnay Verlag, 1989.

Naasner, Walter. *Neue Machtzentren in der deutschen Kriegswirtschaft 1942–1945.* Boppard am Rhein: Harald Boldt Verlag, 1994.

Nevins, Allen, and Frank Ernest Hill. *Ford: Decline and Rebirth, 1933–1962.* New York: Scribners, 1962.

Nolan, Mary. *Visions of Modernity: American Business and the Modernization of Germany.* New York: Oxford University Press, 1994.

Opitz, Reinhard, ed. *Europastrategien des deutschen Kapitals 1900–1945.* Cologne: Pahl-Rugenstein, 1977.

Overy, Richard J. *War and Economy in the Third Reich.* Oxford: Clarendon Press, 1994.

Perrenoud, Marc. *La place financière et les banques suisses à l'époque du national-socialisme.* Zürich: Chronos, 2002.

Petzina, Dieter. *Autarkiepolitik im Dritten Reich. Der Nationalsozialistische Vierjahres-plan.* Stuttgart: Deutsche Verlags-Anstalt, 1968.

Plumpe, Gottfried. *Die I.G. Farbenindustrie AG: Wirtschaft, Technik und Politik 1904–1945.* Berlin: Duncker & Humblot, 1990.

Pohl, Hans. *Die Daimler-Benz AG in den Jahren 1933–1945.* Wiesbaden: Steiner, 1986.

Reich, Simon. *The Fruits of Fascism: Postwar Prosperity in Historical Perspective.* Ithaca: Cornell University Press, 1990.

Roth, Karl Heinz. "Hehler des Holocaust: Degussa und Deutsche Bank." *Zeitschrift für Sozialgeschichte des 20. und 21. Jahrhunderts* 13 (1998): 137–144.

Silverman, Dan. *Hitler's Economy: Nazi Work Creation Programs, 1933–1936.* Cambridge: Harvard University Press, 1998.

Simpson, Christopher, ed. *War Crimes of the Deutsche Bank and the Dresdner Bank. Office of Military Government (U.S.) Reports.* New York: Holmes and Meier, 2001.

Speer, Albert. *Inside the Third Reich.* New York: Macmillan, 1970.

Stahlbaumer, L.M. "Big Business and the Persecution of the Jews: The Flick Concern and the 'Aryanization' of Jewish Property Before the War." *Holocaust and Genocide Studies* 13 (1999): 1–27.

Steinberg, Jonathan. *The Deutsche Bank and Its Gold Transactions during the Second World War.* Munich: Beck Verlag, 1999.

Stiefel, Dieter, ed. *Die Politische Ökonomie des Holocaust. Zur wirtschaftlichen Logik von Verfolgung und 'Wiedergutmachung.'* Vienna: Verlag für Geschichte und Politik, 2001.

Teichert, Eckart. *Autarkie und Grossraum Wirtschaft in Deutschland 1930–1939: Aussenwirtschaftspolitische Konzeptionen zwischen Wirtschaftskrise und Zweiten Weltkrieg.* Munich: Oldenbourg, 1984.

Turner, Henry A. *German Big Business and the Rise of Hitler.* New York: Oxford University Press, 1985.

Wiesen, Jonathan. *West German Industry and the Challenge of the Nazi Past, 1945–1955.* Chapel Hill: University of North Carolina Press, 2001.

Wilkins, Mira, and Frank Ernest Hill. *American Business Abroad: Ford on Six Continents.* Detroit: Wayne State University Press, 1964.

Wixforth, Harald. *Auftakt zur Ostexpansion. Die Dresdner Bank und die Umgestaltung des Bankwesens im Sudetenland 1938/39.* Dresden: Hannah-Arendt-Institut für Totalitarismusforschung, 2001.

Wolf, Mechthild. *Im Zeichen von Sonne und Mond: von der Frankfurter Münzscheiderei zum Weltunternehmen Degussa AG.* Frankfurt am Main: Degussa, 1993.

Ziegler, Dieter. "Die Verdrängung der Juden aus der Dresdner Bank 1933–1938." *Vierteljahrshefte für Zeitgeschichte* 47 (1999): 187–216.

Ziegler, Jean. *The Swiss, the Gold, and the Dead.* New York: Harcourt Brace, 1998.

Forced and Slave Labor

Allen, Michael Thad. *The Business of Genocide: The SS, Slave Labor, and the Concentration Camps.* Chapel Hill: University of North Carolina Press, 2002.

Benz, Wolfgang. *Sklavenarbeit im KZ.* Munich: Deutscher Taschenbuch-Verlag, 1993.

Billstein, Reinhold, Karola Fings, Anita Kugler, and Nicholas Levis. *Working for the Enemy: Ford, General Motors, and Forced Labor in Germany during the Second World War.* New York: Berghahn Books, 2000.

Brüninghaus, Beate, et al. *Zwangsarbeit bei Daimler-Benz.* Stuttgart: Franz Steiner Verlag, 1994.

Eizenstat, Stuart. *Imperfect Justice: Looted Assets, Slave Labor, and the Unfinished Business of World War II.* New York: Public Affairs, 2003.

Gruner, Wolf. *Der geschlossene Arbeitseinsatz deutscher Juden. Zur Zwangsarbeit als Element der Verfolgung 1938–1943.* Berlin: Metropol, 1997.

———. *Zwangsarbeit und Verfolgung: Österreichische Juden im NS-Staat 1938–1945.* Innsbruck: Studienverlag, 2000.

Herbert, Ulrich. *Hitler's Foreign Workers: Enforced Labor in Germany under the Third Reich.* Cambridge: Cambridge University Press, 1997.

Heusler, Andreas. *Ausländereinsatz: Zwangsarbeit für die Münchner Kriegswirtschaft 1939–1945.* Munich: Hugendubel, 1996.

Hoffmann, Katharina, ed. *Nationalsozialismus und Zwangsarbeit in der Region Oldenburg.* Oldenburg: Bibliotheks- und Informationssystem der Universität Oldenburg, 1999.

Jaskot, Paul. *The Architecture of Oppression: The SS, Forced Labor and the Nazi Monumental Building Economy.* New York: Routledge, 2000.

Kaiser, Ernst, and Michael Knorn. *"Wir lebten und schliefen zwischen den Toten": Rüstungsproduktion, Zwangsarbeit und Vernichtung in den Frankfurter Adlerwerken.* Frankfurt am Main: Campus, 1996.

Libonati, Genevieve, ed. *The German Remembrance Fund and the Issue of Forced and Slave Labor.* Washington, D.C.: Friedrich-Ebert-Stiftung, 2001.

Piper, Franciszek. *Auschwitz Prisoner Labor: The Organization and Exploitation of Auschwitz Concentration Camp Prisoners as Laborers.* Oswiecim: Auschwitz-Birkenau State Museum, 2002.

Pohl, Dieter. "Die grossen Zwangsarbeiterlager der SS- und Polizeiführer für Juden im Generalgouvernement 1942–1945." In *Die nationalsozialistischen Konzentrationslager. Entwicklung und Struktur,* edited by Ulrich Herbert et al. 2 vols. Vol. 1, 415–438. Göttingen: Wallstein Verlag, 1998.

Siegfried, Klaus-Jörg. *Rüstungsproduktion und Zwangsarbeit im Volkswagenwerk 1939–1945.* Frankfurt am Main: Campus, 1999.

Wagner, Bernd C. *IG Auschwitz: Zwangsarbeit und Vernichtung von Häftlingen des Lagers Monowitz 1941–1945.* Munich: K.G. Saur, 2000.

Other Professions

Annas, George, and Michael Grodin. *The Nazi Doctors and the Nuremberg Code: Human Rights in Human Experimentation.* New York: Oxford University Press, 1992.

Beyerchen, Alan. *Scientists under Hitler: Politics and the Physics Community in the Third Reich.* New Haven: Yale University Press, 1977.

Burleigh, Michael. *Death and Deliverance: "Euthanasia" in Germany, c. 1900–1945.* Cambridge: Cambridge University Press, 1994.

Caplan, Arthur L., ed. *When Medicine Went Mad: Bioethics and the Holocaust.* Totowa: Humana Press, 1992.

Deichmann, Uta. *Biologists Under Hitler.* Cambridge: Harvard University Press, 1996.

Friedlander, Henry, and Sybil Milton, eds. *The Holocaust: Ideology, Bureaucracy, and Genocide.* New York: Kraus International Publications, 1980.

Friedlander, Henry. *The Origins of Nazi Genocide: From Euthanasia to the Final Solution.* Chapel Hill: University of North Carolina Press, 1995.

———. "Step by Step: The Expansion of Murder, 1939–1941." *German Studies Review* 17 (1994): 495–507.

———. "Die Entwicklung der Mordtechnik: Von der 'Euthanasie' zu den Vernichtungslagern der 'Endlösung'." In *Die nationalsozialistischen Konzentrationslager: Entwicklung und Struktur,* edited by Ulrich Herbert et al. 2 vols. Vol. 1, 493–507. Göttingen: Wallstein Verlag, 1998.

———. "Motive, Formen und Konsequenzen der NS-Euthanasie." In *NS-Euthanasie in Wien,* edited by Eberhard Gabriel and Wolfgang Neugebauer, 47–59. Vienna: Böhlau Verlag, 2000.

Gabriel, Eberhard, and Wolfgang Neugebauer, eds. *NS-Euthanasie in Wien.* Vienna: Böhlau Verlag, 2000.

Gallagher, Hugh. *By Trust Betrayed: Patients, Physicians, and the License to Kill in the Third Reich.* New York: Henry Holt, 1990.

Jarausch, Konrad. *The Unfree Professions: German Lawyers, Teachers, and Engineers, 1900–1950.* New York: Oxford University Press, 1990.

———. "The Conundrum of Complicity: German Professionals and the Final Solution." Joseph and Rebecca Meyerhoff Annual Lecture. Washington, D.C.: United States Holocaust Memorial Museum, 2001.

Kater, Michael. "Dr. Leonardo Conti and His Nemesis: The Failure of Centralized Medicine in the Third Reich." *Central European History* 18 (1985): 299–325.

———. "Hitler's Early Doctors: Nazi Physicians in Pre-Depression Germany." *Journal of Modern History* 59 (1987): 25–52.

———. "Medizin und Mediziner im Dritten Reich: Eine Bestandsaufnahme." *Historische Zeitschrift* 244 (1987): 299–352.

———. *Doctors Under Hitler.* Chapel Hill: University of North Carolina Press, 1989.

————. *The Twisted Muse: Musicians and Their Music in the Third Reich.* New York: Oxford University Press, 1997.

Klee, Ernst. *"Euthanasie" im NS-Staat: Die "Vernichtung lebensunwerten Lebens."* Frankfurt am Main: S. Fischer Verlag, 1983.

————. *Auschwitz, die NS-Medizin und ihre Opfer.* Frankfurt am Main: S. Fischer Verlag, 1997.

Lifton, Robert Jay. *The Nazi Doctors: Medical Killing and the Psychology of Genocide.* New York: Basic Books, 1986.

Lifton, Robert Jay, and Amy Hackett. "Nazi Doctors." In *Anatomy of the Auschwitz Death Camp,* edited by Yisrael Gutman and Michael Berenbaum, 301–316. Bloomington: Indiana University Press, 1998.

Macrakis, Kristie. *Surviving the Swastika: Scientific Research in Nazi Germany.* New York: Oxford University Press, 1993.

————. "The Rockefeller Foundation and German Physics under National Socialism." *Minerva* 27 (1989): 33–57.

McFarland-Icke, Bronwyn Rebekah. *Nurses in Nazi Germany: Moral Choice in History.* Princeton: Princeton University Press, 1999.

Müller-Hill, Benno. *Murderous Science: Elimination by Scientific Selection of Jews, Gypsies and Others, Germany 1933–1945.* New York: Oxford University Press, 1988.

Nicosia, Francis R., and Jonathan Huener, eds. *Medicine and Medical Ethics in Nazi Germany: Origins, Practices, Legacies.* New York: Berghahn Books, 2002.

Petropoulos, Jonathan. *Art as Politics in the Third Reich.* Chapel Hill: University of North Carolina Press, 1999.

————. *The Faustian Bargain: The Art World of Nazi Germany.* New York: Oxford University Press, 2000.

Platen-Hallermund, Alice. *Die Tötung Geisteskranker in Deutschland.* Bonn: Psychiatrie-Verlag, 1998.

Potter, Pamela. *Most German of the Arts: Musicology and Society from the Weimar Republic to the End of Hitler's Reich.* New Haven: Yale University Press, 1998.

Proctor, Robert. *Racial Hygiene: Medicine Under the Nazis.* Cambridge: Harvard University Press, 1988.

————. *The Nazi War on Cancer.* Princeton: Princeton University Press, 1999.

Schmidt, Gerhard. *Selektion in der Heilanstalt, 1939–1945.* 2nd ed. Frankfurt am Main: Edition Suhrkamp, 1983.

Schulze, Winfried, and Otto Oexle, eds. *Deutsche Historiker im Nationalsozialismus.* Frankfurt am Main: Fischer Taschenbuch Verlag, 1999.

Schwarberg, Günther. *Der SS-Arzt und die Kinder: Bericht über den Mord vom Bullenhuser Damm.* Hamburg: Gruner und Jahr, 1979.

Seidelman, William. "Medical Selection: Auschwitz Antecedents and Effluent." *Holocaust and Genocide Studies* 4 (1989): 435–448.

————. "Medicine and Murder in the Third Reich." *Dimensions: A Journal of Holocaust Studies* 13 (1999): 9–13.

————. "Medicine and the Holocaust: Physician Involvement in Genocide." In *Encyclopedia of Genocide,* edited by Israel Charney, 412–415. Santa Barbara: ABC-CLIO, 2000.

Sieman, Hans Ludwig. *Menschen blieben auf der Strecke…: Psychiatrie zwischen Reform und Nationalsozialismus.* Gütersloh: J. van Haddis, 1987.

Steinweis, Alan. *Art, Ideology, and Economics in Nazi Germany: The Reich Chambers of Music, Theater and the Visual Arts.* Chapel Hill: University of North Carolina Press, 1996.

Steppe, Hildegard, ed. *Krankenpflege im Nationalsozialismus.* Frankfurt am Main: Mabuse-Verlag, 1989.

Thom, Achim, and Genadij Ivanovic Caregorodcev, eds. *Medizin unterm Hakenkreuz.* Berlin: Verlag Volk und Geschichte, 1989.

Weale, Adrian. *Science under the Swastika.* London: Channel 4 Books, 2001.

Weinreich, Max. *Hitler's Professors: The Part of Scholarship in Germany's Crimes against the Jewish People.* New Haven: Yale University Press, 1999.

Racism and Anti-Semitism

Arendt, Hanna. *The Origins of Totalitarianism.* Part I: *Antisemitism.* New York: Harcourt Brace Jovanovich, 1973.

Bankier, David, ed. *Probing the Depths of German Antisemitism: German Society and the Persecution of the Jews, 1933–1941.* New York: Berghahn Books, 2000.

Barkan, Elazar. *The Retreat of Scientific Racism: Changing Concepts of Race in Britain and the United States between the World Wars.* Cambridge: Cambridge University Press, 1992.

Efron, John. *Defenders of Race: Jewish Doctors and Race Science in Fin-de-Siècle Europe.* New Haven: Yale University Press, 1994.

Field, Geoffrey. *Evangelist of Race: The Germanic Vision of Houston Stewart Chamberlain.* New York: Columbia University Press, 1981.

Hertzberg, Arthur. *The French Enlightenment and the Jews: The Origins of Modern Antisemitism.* New York: Columbia University Press, 1990.

Massing, Paul. *Rehearsal for Destruction: A Study of Political Antisemitism in Imperial Germany.* New York: Harper, 1949.

Mosse, George. *Toward the Final Solution: A History of European Racism.* New York: Harper & Row, 1978.

———. *The Crisis of German Ideology: Intellectual Origins of the Third Reich.* New York: Schocken, 1981.

Pauley, Bruce. *From Prejudice to Destruction: A History of Austrian Antisemitism.* Chapel Hill: University of North Carolina Press, 1992.

Poliakov, Leon. *The Aryan Myth: A History of Racist and Nationalist Ideas in Europe.* New York: Basic Books, 1971.

Pulzer, Peter. *The Rise of Political Antisemitism in Germany and Austria.* Cambridge: Harvard University Press, 1988.

Rose, Paul Lawrence. *German Question/Jewish Question: Revolutionary Antisemitism from Kant to Wagner.* Princeton: Princeton University Press, 1992.

Stern, Fritz. *The Politics of Cultural Despair: A Study of the Rise of Germanic Ideology.* Berkeley: University of California Press, 1961.

Zimmermann, Moshe. *Wilhelm Marr: The Patriarch of Antisemitism.* New York: Oxford University Press, 1986.

Holocaust, Final Solution, the German People

Aly, Götz. *"Final Solution": Nazi Population Policy and the Murder of the European Jews.* New York: Arnold, 1999.

Arendt, Hannah. *Eichmann in Jerusalem: A Report on the Banality of Evil.* New York: Penguin, 1994.

Bankier, David. *The Germans and the Final Solution: Public Opinion under Nazism.* Oxford: Basil Blackwell, 1992.

Bartov, Omer. *Hitler's Army: Soldiers, Nazis and War in the Third Reich.* New York: Oxford University Press, 1991.

———. *Murder in Our Midst: The Holocaust, Industrial Killing, and Representation.* New York: Oxford University Press, 1996.

———, ed. *The Holocaust: Origins, Implementation, Aftermath.* New York: Routledge, 2000.

Browder, George. *Hitler's Enforcers: The Gestapo and the SS Security Service in the Nazi Revolution.* New York: Oxford University Press, 1996.

Browning, Christopher. *Fateful Months: Essays on the Emergence of the Final Solution.* New York: Holmes & Meier, 1985.

———. *Ordinary Men: Reserve Police Battalion 101 and the Final Solution in Poland.* New York: HarperCollins, 1992.

———. *The Path to Genocide: Essays on Launching the Final Solution.* New York: Cambridge University Press, 1992.

———. *Nazi Policy, Jewish Workers, German Killers.* New York: Cambridge University Press, 2000.

Burleigh, Michael, and Wolfgang Wippermann. *The Racial State: Germany 1933–1945.* New York: Cambridge University Press, 1991.

Burleigh, Michael, ed. *Confronting the Nazi Past: New Debates on Modern German History.* New York: St. Martin's Press, 1996.

———. *Ethics and Extermination: Reflections on Nazi Genocide.* Cambridge: Cambridge University Press, 1997.

Cesarani, David, ed. *The Final Solution: Origins and Implementation.* London and New York: Routledge, 1994.

Dwork, Deborah, and Robert Jan van Pelt. *Holocaust: A History.* New York: W.W. Norton, 2002.

Friedländer, Saul. *Nazi Germany and the Jews: The Years of Persecution, 1933–1939.* New York: HarperCollins, 1997.

Gellately, Robert. *The Gestapo and German Society: Enforcing Racial Policy, 1933–1945.* Oxford: Oxford University Press, 1990.

———. *Backing Hitler: Consent and Coercion in Nazi Germany.* New York: Oxford University Press, 2001.

Goldhagen, Daniel. *Hitler's Willing Executioners: Ordinary Germans and the Holocaust.* New York: Alfred A. Knopf, 1996.

Gordon, Sarah. *Hitler, Germans and the Jewish Question.* Princeton: Princeton University Press, 1984.

Hamburg Institute for Social Research, ed. *The German Army and Genocide: Crimes against War Prisoners, Jews, and Other Civilians in the East, 1939–1944.* New York: New Press, 1999.

Hilberg, Raul. *The Destruction of the European Jews.* 3 vols. New York: Holmes and Meier, 1985.

———. *Perpetrators Victims Bystanders: The Jewish Catastrophe, 1933–1945.* New York: HarperCollins, 1992.

Höhne, Heinz. *The Order of the Death's Head: The Story of Hitler's SS.* London: Penguin, 1969.

Kershaw, Ian. *Popular Opinion and Political Dissent in the Third Reich: Bavaria.* Oxford: Clarendon Press, 1984.

Langbein, Hermann. *Menschen in Auschwitz.* Vienna and Munich: Europa Verlag, 1995.

Lewy, Guenther. *The Nazi Persecution of the Gypsies.* New York: Oxford University Press, 2000.

Peukert, Detlev. *Inside Nazi Germany: Conformity, Opposition, and Racism in Everyday Life.* New Haven: Yale University Press, 1987.

Reitlinger, Gerald. *The Final Solution: The Attempt to Exterminate the Jews of Europe, 1939–1945.* New York: A.S. Barnes, 1961.

Rückerl, Adalbert. *NS-Vernichturgslager im Spiegel deutscher Strafprozesse: Belzec, Sobibor, Treblinka, Chelmno.* Munich: DTV, 1977.

Steinert, Marlis. *Hitler's War and the Germans: Public Mood and Attitude during the Second World War.* Athens: Ohio University Press, 1977.

Yahil, Leni. *The Holocaust: The Fate of European Jewry.* New York: Oxford University Press, 1990.

INDEX

Note: Page references with an *f* or a *t* indicate a figure or table on the designated page.

Monographs in German History, Volume 11

RECASTING WEST GERMAN ELITES
Higher Civil Servants, Business Leaders, and Physicians in Hesse between Nazism and Democracy, 1945-1955

Michael R. Hayse

The rapid shift of German elite groups' political loyalties away from Nazism and toward support of the fledgling democracy of the Federal Republic, in spite of the continuity of personnel and professional structures, has surprised many scholars of postwar Germany. The key, Hayse argues, lies in the peculiar and paradoxical legacy of these groups' evasive selective memory, by which they cast themselves as victims of the Third Reich rather than its erstwhile supporters. The avoidance of responsibility for the crimes and excesses of the Third Reich created a need to demonstrate democratic behavior in the post-war public sphere. Ultimately, this self-imposed pressure, while based on a falsified, selective group memory of the recent past, was more important in the long term than the Allies' stringent social change policies.

Michael R. Hayse is Assistant Professor of History at the Richard Stockton College of New Jersey.

2003. 304 pages, bibliog. index
ISBN 1-57181-271-7 hardback
Monographs in German History, Vol. 11

orders@berghahnbooks.com ⏳ www.berghahnbooks.com

Berghahn Books

FLIGHT OF FANTASY
New Perspectives on Inner Emigration in German Literature 1933-1945

Edited by **Neil H. Donahue** and **Doris Kirchner**

During the Nazi era many German writers chose, or were forced into, exile. Many others stayed and, after the end of this period, claimed to have retreated into "Inner Emigration." The nature of this kind of emigration and the underlying motives of these writers have been hotly debated to this day. Though the reception of Inner Emigration has often been confounded by disputes over the term

itself, the issue is ultimately not a matter of nomenclature, but of more far-reaching issues of literary evaluation, moral discernment and the writing of history. This volume presents, for the first time, to an English-speaking readership the complexity of Inner Emigration through the analysis of problematic individual cases of writers who, under constant pressure from a watchful dictatorship to conform and to collaborate, were caught between conscience and compromise.

Neil H. Donahue is Professor of German and Comparative Literature at Hofstra University. **Doris Kirchner** is Associate Professor of German at the University of Rhode Island.

2003. 336 pages, bibliog. index
ISBN 1-57181-001-3 hardback

Monographs in German History, Volume 9

THE AMBIVALENT ALLIANCE

Konrad Adenauer, the CDU/CSU,
and the West 1949-1966

Ronald J. Granieri,
University of Pennsylvania

Whenever asked to name his most significant accomplishment as West Germany's first Chancellor, Konrad Adenauer would invariably reply: *"The alliance with the free West."* Scholars have echoed his assessment, citing the Federal Republic of Germany's successful integration into the American-led West (Westbindung) as the key to its postwar economic and political recovery. Behind this simple success story, however, lies a much more complicated history: Adenauer and the CDU/CSU remained ambivalent about the ultimate relationship between Europe, Germany, and the U.S. within the West, torn between visions of Continental European integration based on Franco-German reconciliation and of an Atlantic community linking Europe and the "Anglo-Saxons."

Drawing from recently opened personal and party archives this book re-examines existing conventional wisdom about the period and traces the roles of Adenauer and the CDU/ CSU in shaping the Westbindung. Adenauer emerges as a skilled and resourceful (if also mistrustful and devious) politician, and as a distinctly German statesman, maneuvering between allies and adversaries to shape both the Western community and the German role in it, leaving a legacy that still influences contemporary German-American and European-American relations.

2002. 288 pages, bibliog., index
ISBN 1-57181-272-5 hardback
Monographs in German History, Vol. 9

Berghahn Books

orders@berghahnbooks.com　～　www.berghahnbooks.com

REMEMBERING & FORGETTING NAZISM
Education, National Identity, and the Victim Myth in Postwar Austria

Peter Utgaard

The myth of Austrian victimization at the hands of both Nazi Germany and the Allies became a unifying theme of Austrian official memory and a key component of national identity as a new Austria emerged from the ruins. In the 1980s, Austria's myth of victimization came under intense scrutiny in the wake of the Waldheim scandal that marked the beginning of its erosion. The fiftieth anniversary of 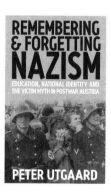 the Anschluß in 1988 accelerated this process and resulted in a collective shift away from the victim myth. Important themes examined include the rebirth of Austria, the Anschluß, the war and the Holocaust, the Austrian resistance, and the Allied occupation. The fragmentation of Austrian official memory since the late 1980s coincided with the dismantling of the Conservative and Social Democratic coalition, which had defined Austrian politics in the postwar period. Through the eyes of the Austrian school system, this book examines how postwar Austria came to terms with the Second World War.

Peter Utgaard currently serves as Chair of History and Social Sciences at Cuyamaca College in San Diego where he was awarded the college's Excellence in Teaching Award.

2003. 256 pages, bibliog. index
ISBN 1-57181-187-7 hardback

orders@berghahnbooks.com ∽ www.berghahnbooks.com

Berghahn Books

UNITED AND DIVIDED

Germany since 1990

Edited by **Mike Dennis** and **Eva Kolinsky**

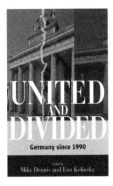

The system transformation after German unification in 1990 constituted an experiment on an unprecedented scale. At no point in history had one state attempted to redesign another without conquest, bloodshed or coercion but by treaties, public policy and bureaucratic processes. Unification was achieved by erasing the eastern political and economic model. However, in the meantime it has become clear that the same cannot be said about social transformation. On the contrary, social and cultural attitudes and differentiation have continued and resulted in deep divisions between West and East Germany. After unification, the injustices of politics seemed to have been replaced, in the eyes of most former GDR citizens, by unexpected injustices in the personal spheres of ordinary people who lost their jobs and faced unknown realities of deprivation and social exclusion.

These are the main concerns of the contributors to this volume. Incorporating new research findings and published data, they focus on key aspects of economic, political, and social transformation in eastern Germany and compare, through case studies, each area with developments in the west.

Mike Dennis is Professor of German History at the University of Wolverhampton and author several books and essays on political and social developments in the GDR. **Eve Kolinsky** is Professor Emerita of German Studies at Keele University and Professorial Research Fellow in German History at the University of Wolverhampton.

Winter 2003/2004
216 pages, bibliog. index
ISBN 1-57181-513-9 hardback

orders@berghahnbooks.com ~ www.berghahnbooks.com

THE GERMAN ECONOMY DURING THE NINETEENTH CENTURY

Toni Pierenkemper and Richard Tilly

" *The data ...collected is so impressive, and the economic history so difficult to master, that most [scholars] will need this book on their shelves.*"

— **Eric Dorn Brose, Drexel University**

In the nineteenth century, economic growth was accompanied by large-scale structural change, known as industrialization, which fundamentally affected western societies. Even though industrialization is on the wane in some advanced economies and we are experiencing substantial structural changes again, the causes and consequences of these changes are inextricably linked with earlier industrialization. This means that understanding nineteenth century industrialization helps us understand problems of contemporary economic growth. There is no recent study on economic developments in nineteenth century Germany. So this concise volume, written specifically with students of German and economic history in mind, will prove to be most valuable, not least because of its wealth of statistical data.

Toni Pierenkemper is Professor of Economic and Social History at University of Cologne. **Richard Tilly** is Emeritus Professor of Economic and Social History at the University of Münster.

2004. 192 pages, bibliog. index
ISBN 1-57181-063-3 hardback

orders@berghahnbooks.com ~ www.berghahnbooks.com